The
All-American
cookie book

The All-American Cookie Book

Nancy Baggett

PHOTOGRAPHS BY ALAN RICHARDSON

HOUGHTON MIFFLIN COMPANY
BOSTON NEW YORK

Visit our Web site: www.houghtonmifflinbooks.com.

Library of Congress Cataloging-in-Publication Data

Baggett, Nancy, date.
    The All-American cookie book / Nancy Baggett.
        p. cm.
    Includes index.
    ISBN 0-395-91537-6
    1. Cookies.   2. Cookery, American.   I. Title.

    TX772 .B25 2001
    641.8'654—dc21   2001033667

Book design by Anne Chalmers
Typeface: Eidetic Neo Family © Emigré
Cover photograph: Chocolate Hearts (page 101), New York Black and
        Whites (page 21), Fantastic Fudgewiches (page 112), Not Neiman
        Marcus's Chocolate Chip Cookies (page 62)
First page photograph: Joe Froggers (page 307)
Title page photograph: Raisin Pockets (page 223)
Food styling by Anne Disrude
Prop styling by Betty Alfenito

Printed in the United States of America

DOW 10 9 8 7 6 5 4 3

aCknowLedgments

Many people had a hand in creating this book and enthusiastically supported my effort. I am grateful to the following:

My editor, Rux Martin, gave me just the right blend of editorial guidance and artistic freedom.

My agent, Linda Hayes, supported the project every step of the way and, as always, attended to key details.

Photographer Alan Richardson, food stylist Anne Disrude, and prop stylist Betty Alfenito captured the spirit of my text and recipes and created the many wonderful photographs in the book.

My kitchen assistants worked cheerfully and diligently throughout. Dollene Targan helped test and retest many recipes, offered suggestions, and gave editorial support. Sandy Giangrande also tested extensively and offered helpful advice. Thanks, too, to La Atwater, Debra Smith, and Brenda Gratton, who assisted with testing.

Binnie Syril Braunstein helped research several subjects and provided editorial support.

Judy Gardner-Flint generously shared examples from her vintage collection of promotional cookbooks.

Drusilla Jones lent several copies of *Godey's Lady's Book,* as well as cookbooks from her private collection and her Baltimore antiquarian bookshop, Drusilla's Books.

Wesley Wilson, Head of Business, Science, and Technology, Enoch Pratt Free Library, Baltimore, Maryland, provided assistance and access to the library's non-circulating historical cookbooks collection.

Nancy Magnuson, College Librarian, and Sydney Robey, Special Collections Librarian, at the Julia Rogers Library, Goucher College, Towson, Maryland, offered guidance and access to the library's rare book collection. Ms. Robey was also very generous with her time.

Rus Johanson, owner of Ravenna Rare Books, Seattle, Washington, generously offered his expertise and time, as well as access to his antique cookbook collection.

Cookbook author Ronni Lundy provided both information and a number of regional American cookbooks.

Beverly Price, of Apple Basket, Pottstown, Pennsylvania, lent me her entire personal collection of vintage cookbooks.

A number of culinary historians offered encouragement and provided information that helped me fill in important blanks: Jan Longone, The Wine and Food Library, Ann Arbor, Michigan; Sandra Oliver, editor of the newsletter *Food History News*; Linda Campbell Franklin, author of *300 Years of Kitchen Collectibles;* Bonnie Slotnick, of Bonnie Slotnick Cookbooks, New York City; Peter G. Rose, author of *Foods of the Hudson;* and Jacqueline B. Williams, author of *The Way We Ate.* Ms. Williams also gave me access to her collection of early Northwest cookbooks and materials.

acknowledgments

contents

introduction

FOR THE LAST SEVERAL YEARS, I've been on an amazing culinary journey. I've traveled throughout the Northwest, Southwest, Midwest, Northeast, and South—all in search of cookies. I visited small-town sweet shops, farmers' markets and county fairs, country inns and bed-and-breakfasts, and chic urban cookie boutiques. I wheedled recipes out of home cooks, chefs, innkeepers, and bakers, rummaged through file boxes, and leafed through handwritten notebooks. I pored over community cookbooks and combed through vintage cookbooks in rare book rooms and private collections. Along the way, I baked between 25,000 and 30,000 cookies to come up with the best versions of our national favorites.

This is a wholly American repertoire. It includes more than 150 recipes gathered during my journey: little-known regional gems, decadent modern creations, homespun classics, rediscovered heirlooms, and some of my own favorite cookie inventions. There are brownies and blondies, dozens of different chocolate chip and sugar cookies, peanut and oatmeal cookies, monster and miniature cookies, drop cookies and rolled cookies, icebox and sandwich cookies, cookies full of fruit, cookies full of nuts, cookies full of candy—and more.

I've collected cookies from many corners of the nation: brandy-and-cinnamon-scented anise cookies from New Mexico, whoopie pies from Pennsylvania, bourbon-spiked fruitcake cookies from Kentucky, and Italian fig cookies from New Orleans. I've managed to duplicate the hazelnut-chocolate sandwich cookies that were the closely guarded secret of a hostess in Oregon's hazelnut country and recreated a fabulous old-fashioned gingerbread cookie from an 1880s notebook. This collection also includes family favorites from the farmhouse kitchen in rural Maryland where I grew up, like my grandmother's spicy, chewy, soft date "rocks." (Today, just the heady cinnamon and clove fragrance of these cookies takes me back to the pleasure of baking at my grandmother's side.) Reflecting the current lively interest in cookies as craft, I've devoted one chapter to decorated cookies and cookie projects, including plans and instructions for making a gingerbread house.

Besides the best-of-the-best cookies, this book also incorporates reminiscences, bits of history, background information, and colorful lore. These give a sense of the cooks and the stories behind the recipes as well as the evolution, art, and simple pleasures of cookie baking in America.

Nearly every person who heard about my American cookie search immediately told me about a memorable baking experience or a favorite recipe from childhood. The mother of a nursery school playmate of my son wistfully described the rolled nutmeg and buttermilk "nutmeggins" her Arkansas grandmother dispensed from a stoneware cookie jar. A former coworker who spent part of her childhood in Pennsylvania Dutch country reminisced about the big, soft "sugar cakes" baked by several older ladies in her neighborhood. Several acquaintances described the Christmas cookies that they iced, decorated, and hung on the holiday tree.

If viewed from the right perspective, cookies not only stir warm memories but also provide insight into our national baking traditions and the skill and resourcefulness of home bakers over several centuries. They tell us a good deal about how everyday life in America used to be and how it has changed. And they say a lot about how we started with a transplanted, mainly European recipe repertoire and then blazed our own thoroughly American culinary trail.

AS American as chocoLate chip cookies

An examination of the cookies baked in this country over the last three centuries reveals one important fact: the maddening conventional wisdom that America borrows its baking traditions from Europe and thus hasn't any of its own is wrong, wrong, wrong!

Yes, most formally trained American pastry chefs do still learn to bake European cookies—like tuiles, sables, florentines, and madeleines. But the repertoire American home cooks usually prepare is purely, unequivocally American to the core. Based largely on American ingredients and catering to homegrown American tastes, our modern-day favorites have been created by generations of pragmatic, busy, yet inventive home cooks who wanted their cookies to taste wonderful, but—like the growing nation—had little time for fussiness or affectation. The result is a collection of exquisitely simple and incredibly good recipes that rely on mostly accessible (but brilliantly paired) ingredients and easy techniques. Typically, these recipes seem too spare or plain at first glance but inevitably turn out to be much more than the sum of their parts.

American cooks came up with so many delectable cookies during the twentieth century that I suspect culinary historians may someday look back on the period as the golden age of American cookie baking. Seventeenth- and eighteenth-century cookies were limited to almond and coconut macaroons, jumbles, rolled gingerbreads, various currant and dried fruit "cakes" and tartlets, and assorted sugar and tea "cakes" that we would call sugar cookies today. (There were no varieties actually called "cookies" until the latter part of the eighteenth century, when Americans began using the Dutch word for little cake, *koekje*.) Early popular "receipts," as recipes were commonly called, were most often flavored with molasses, rose water, caraway seed, lemon, spices, almonds, and coconut. Vanilla, now the most widely used flavoring, was rarely included until the mid-nineteenth century, and not in common use until the early twentieth.

In fact, *none* of the cookie varieties we now love best—chocolate chip, oatmeal, and peanut butter cookies and brownies—even existed until invented here in the late nineteenth or early twentieth century. Changing tastes explain some of the differences between the cookies of the two centuries—Americans today tend to find the flavor of rosewater and caraway cookies odd—but they have as much to do with when various ingredients became available and, equally important, when somebody suddenly realized those ingredients were appropriate for cookies.

The "chocoLafication" of America

Peanuts and oats were around for quite a while before cooks learned to take advantage of them. Until the mid-nineteenth century, both ingredients were generally considered animal feed—oats for horses and peanuts for hogs. Hungry Civil War soldiers were among the first to see the merits of peanuts, and oats gradually gained favor in the 1860s and 1870s when an immigrant miller named Ferdinand Schumacher began promoting them as a breakfast cereal. (Later, Schumacher cofounded the company that eventually became Quaker Oats.) Oatmeal cookies appeared around 1880, possibly inspired by the oatcakes of Scottish immigrants. Peanut butter cookies came on the scene near the end of the century, before commercial peanut butter was even on the market. (Several cookbooks of the time advised households to grind and use their own peanut butter, because it was known to be nourishing.)

Our best-loved modern ingredient, chocolate, was also long overlooked by cookie bakers. The country's first chocolate company, now called Baker's, had manufactured unsweetened chocolate in Massachusetts by 1780, but chocolate was originally used only as a healthful, restorative drink ingredient. (The company was named for one of its owners, a Dr. Baker, not because its product was aimed at bakers.) American homemakers didn't begin to use chocolate in sweets like ice creams and puddings until the early 1800s. And it was rarely added to baked goods until the late nineteenth century, though a few cookbooks did contain chocolate cookie and confection recipes prior to that time.

No one knows who thought of using unsweetened chocolate to create the rich bars called brownies, but they first turned up in Boston cookbooks in 1906 and 1907. The idea of putting small bits of sweetened chocolate into cookie dough also came from Massachusetts, but not until 1930, when the proprietor of the Toll House Inn, Mrs. Ruth Wakefield, tried substituting some chopped chocolate for nuts in a recipe. This delicious serendipity created such a cookie-baking sensation around the country that the

Nestlé company began selling prescored chocolate bars that could easily be broken into bits. Then, in 1939, Nestlé started producing its now ubiquitous chocolate chips. So many cookies containing chocolate have emerged since Mrs. Wakefield's Toll House cookies and chocolate brownies were introduced that our whole repertoire has undergone a noticeable "chocolafication" over the past 50 years.

Early cooks were also constrained by not having the handy chemical leaveners, baking soda and baking powder, to lighten their cookies. Until a forerunner of baking soda called pearlash became available in America in the late 1700s, doughs could only be leavened with yeast or beaten egg whites. Completely unleavened doughs like gingerbreads and early sugar "cakes" were dense, sometimes even leaden, but there was nothing cooks could do about it. This may explain why puffy, egg white-based cookies like macaroons were more popular then than they are today.

Unlike numerous other ingredients, baking soda, which became available in the early 1800s, and baking powder, which appeared in the 1860s, were quickly embraced by home bakers. By the end of the century, many previously unleavened cookie doughs had been reworked to include a little baking soda or powder, a step that went far toward improving the palatability of the genre as a whole. To put the importance of the introduction of chemical leaveners in perspective, it's interesting to note that, except for some brownies, nearly all of today's most popular cookies depend on one or the other of these ingredients for appealing texture.

A Labor of Love

Poring over old American cookbooks, unpublished manuscripts, and handed-down receipt boxes has afforded me a wonderful opportunity to step back in time and make acquaintance with American home bakers at work in their own long-ago kitchens. By paying close attention to their techniques, ingredients, suggestions, and comments, I've learned a little about these women and a lot about the practical details of their lives. Perhaps the most obvious piece of information is that baking was once far more labor-intensive and difficult than it is today. This typical advice on readying ingredients in Sarah Josepha Hale's 1841 *The Good Housekeeper* make the time demands of baking abundantly clear:

> . . . the flour should be dried before the fire, sifted and weighed; currants washed and dried; raisins stoned; sugar pounded, and rolled fine and sifted; and all spices after being well dried at the fire, pounded and sifted.
>
> Almonds should be blanched, which is done by pouring hot water over them, and after standing some minutes taking off the skins then throwing

. Makes 30 to 35
. cookies, depending on
. the cutters used.

The First American "cookey"

"Another Christmas Cookey," in Amelia Simmons's groundbreaking 1796 work, *American Cookery*, marked the first time the word "cookey" appeared in a cookbook written in America. This cookie was notably innovative in one key respect: it called for called pearlash (potassium carbonate), an early alkaline chemical leavener refined from potash. Though the cookie is a bit plain and not really "Christmasy" by contemporary standards, it has a quiet charm and is very pleasant tasting, thanks to the addition of a spice the author apparently liked a lot—ground coriander.

In my adaptation of this landmark recipe, I've substituted baking soda for pearlash, cut down the recipe to a third of the original, reduced the coriander, and rolled out the dough thinner.

3 cups all-purpose white flour	1¼ cups sugar
3–4 tablespoons ground coriander seed, or to taste	¾ teaspoon baking soda
¾ cup cold unsalted butter, cut into chunks	About ⅓ cup whole or low-fat milk

Preheat the oven to 325 degrees F. Grease several baking sheets or coat with nonstick spray.

In a large bowl, thoroughly stir together the flour and coriander. Using forks, a pastry blender, or your fingertips, mix the butter and sugar into the flour until the mixture is the consistency of coarse meal. In a small cup, thoroughly stir the baking soda into ⅓ cup milk. Stir the milk mixture into the dough, then, working in the bowl, knead in enough additional milk to yield a smooth but still stiff dough.

Divide the dough in half. Roll out each portion ⅓ to ½ inch thick on a lightly floured work surface. Amelia Simmons's directions said, "Cut or stamp into any size you please," but I like to use 2¼-to-2½-inch assorted cutters.

Using a spatula, transfer the cookies to the baking sheets, spacing about 1 inch apart. Reroll any dough scraps. Continue cutting out the cookies until all the dough is used.

Bake the cookies, one sheet at a time, for 18 to 23 minutes, or until just lightly browned at the edges. Reverse the sheet from front to back about halfway through baking to ensure even browning. Using a spatula, transfer the cookies to wire racks. Let stand until completely cooled.

Store the cookies in an airtight container for up to 2 weeks or freeze for up to 2 months.

them in cold water. When not pounded, they should be cut lengthwise into thin bits. Lemon and orange-peel must be pared very thin, and pounded with a little sugar.

Butter, after being weighed, should be laid in cold water or washed in rose water; if salt[y], wash it well in several waters.

Except for sultanas, all raisin varieties of the time were extremely seedy and had to be stoned. Mrs. Hale didn't need to remind her readers that someone had to shell the nuts and churn the butter. Nor did she have to explain that because sugar came in large, solid loaves, pieces of it had to be cut off with shears called "nippers" and pounded to a powder before it could be used for baking.

Another difficulty most pre-twentieth-century American homemakers constantly confronted was the baking process itself. Initially in colonial America, baking was done on the hearth, first by putting the baked good (usually bread) directly into the coals, then, as advances occurred, by placing it in a Dutch oven or spider (a Dutch oven with legs) set in or over the fire. By the 1700s, the introduction of a "roasting kitchen" (a reflector oven that sat in front of the hearth and reflected heat from the fire back onto the food) first made it possible to "bake" in the same general manner we do today—with the baked goods in the open and using dry heat rather than coals and flames.

Although more advances in hearth baking soon followed, it was the advent of cookstoves with ovens in the 1800s that made baking large, flat pans of items such as cookies feasible. Even so, early ranges were hardly the boon to the home cook that they might seem today. They had to be constantly refueled with wood or coal and frequently cleaned and maintained. Here are just some of the stove operation and maintenance instructions in Sarah Tyson Rorer's 1886 *Mrs. Rorer's Philadelphia Cook Book*:

> Study the draughts of your range . . . Close the dampers and this will throw the heat around the oven . . . "Fix" your fire as soon as breakfast is over. Open the draughts and dust damper, rake the fire well, until free from every particle of ashes; then open the top and brush the soot and the small pieces of coal . . . into the fire. See that the corners are free from ashes, and fill the fire-box even full with coal. . . . If you add more coal than this you cut off the upper draught, and, of course, lose much heat. Now clean out the ashes and carry them away. Dust the range of the stove and polish it while cool; a paintbrush makes a very nice brush for putting on the polish.

Moreover, even routine baking in a kitchen range was daunting. When President Millard Fillmore installed a range in the White House in 1850, the cooks refused to use it until an expert from the Patent Office came and trained them to work the dampers and manage the heat.

Estelle Woods Wilcox pinpointed a key source of the difficulty in the 1880 edition of *Buckeye Cookery and Practical Housekeeping:*

> The attention of stove-makers seems never to have been directed to the fact that there is no accurate means of testing the heat of ovens, but it is hoped that in the near future some simple device may be found which will render unnecessary such inaccurate and untrustworthy tests as must now be used, and thus reduce baking to a science.

To compensate for this critical stove deficiency, cooking experts devised and promoted a variety of somewhat idiosyncratic "untrustworthy tests." Advised Mrs. Wilcox: "Place a teaspoon of flour on an old piece of crockery (to secure an even heat), and set in the middle of the oven; if it browns in one minute the heat is right. An oven in which the bare hand and arm can not be held longer than to count twenty moderately, is hot enough." Belle DeGraf propounded another method in her eponymous 1922 cookbook: "To test the oven without a thermometer, take a piece of white paper. Place in the oven after it has been heated 10 minutes. . . . If the paper burns black in 5 minutes, the oven is very hot; if it burns a deep brown, it is hot. For the medium oven, the paper should be golden brown in 5 minutes. For a slow oven it should barely turn the most delicate brown in 5 minutes."

Baking remained a very tricky business until the early twentieth century, when more and more home cooks began to have kitchen ranges with temperature gauges and heat regulators. This may help answer the question of why cookies were less popular in early America than they are today. While homemakers were doubtless preoccupied with preparing more necessary baked goods like bread, they may also have been mindful that small, thin sweets like cookies were far more likely to burn in their primitive ovens than sturdier baked goods. I don't think it's a coincidence that American cookie baking really began to take off about the same time as the technology for modern electric and gas ranges did.

perfecting the best of the past

Whenever I stir together butter, eggs, and sugar to make the same cookies as an eighteenth- or nineteenth-century homemaker before me, I feel the bond of our shared heritage as American women taking pleasure in baking "a little something nice" for our families. Somehow, the simple acts of mixing, rolling, and baking cookies bridge the barriers of time.

In the case of the vintage recipes included in *The All-American Cookie Book,* I've tried to update them to ensure success by twenty-first-century cooks yet still remain true to the originals. Almost invariably, I've had to elaborate on cursory instructions and add baking times and temperatures. Since old receipts usually specified ingredient amounts by weight, I've also had to convert to measuring with cups and spoons. I've routinely modernized old recipes to take advantage of improved techniques and labor-saving electrical appliances. However, I've generally left the original ingredients as is and have pointed out any minor substitutions or additions in the recipe notes. The one exception is that I call for unsalted butter—which I prefer for its clean, fresh taste—and then add a little salt separately. Because salt was the only readily available preservative of butter, early cooks almost always used fairly salty butter and thus rarely called for salt.

As we embark on a new century, the challenging and time-consuming tasks of home baking—like washing butter, grinding sugar, and controlling temperamental ovens—are behind us. Now, ingenious bakers across the land are free to concentrate on incorporating new ingredients (or rediscovering old ones), devising fresh flavor combinations, and adding still more extraordinary cookies to the already remarkable American repertoire. If cooks of this century are even half as productive as those of the last one, American cookie jars will be overflowing with wonderful goodies indeed.

How to Make
Great cookies
Every single time

MOST COOKIE-MAKING TECHNIQUES are basic and easily mastered, even by novice cooks and bakers. Here's what you need to know:

Measure, Don't Guess

It's possible to cook many dishes without measuring carefully, but in baking, accuracy really counts. Most cookies (and other baked goods, too) depend on a certain ratio of flour, sugar, fat, egg, and liquid. When these are even slightly out of balance, consistencies can change, sometimes with unwanted results.

FOR MEASURING LIQUIDS, USE TRANSPARENT 1- OR 2-CUP MARKED MEASURING CUPS. Set the cup on a flat surface. After filling to the desired mark, check at eye level to see if the amount is right.

FOR MEASURING DRY INGREDIENTS LIKE SUGAR AND FLOUR, ALWAYS USE GRADUATED MEASURING SETS. They should include at least ¼-, ⅓-, ½- and 1-cup measures. If you bake often, it's worth searching out sets that also include ⅔- and ¾-cup measures; these eliminate a few measuring steps, as well as any chance of getting the math wrong. Graduated cups make it easy to obtain the exact amount needed by leveling off with the sweep of a long-bladed spatula or knife, rather than just judging by sight.

WHEN MEASURING FOR THE RECIPES IN THIS BOOK, BE SURE TO USE THE DIP AND SWEEP METHOD, ESPECIALLY FOR FLOUR. Fill graduated measures by scooping down into the canister or bag, *not* by shaking or spooning the flour into the cups. Dipping up the flour keeps it relatively compact, while spooning fluffs it up and throws off the volume measurement.

MEASURE SMALL AMOUNTS SUCH AS VANILLA, BAKING POWDER, OR SALT USING A GRADUATED SET OF MEASURING SPOONS. It's most convenient to have a deluxe set with not only ⅛-, ¼-, ½-, and 1-teaspoon and 1-tablespoon measures, but ½-tablespoon and 2-tablespoon measures as well. For accuracy, level off dry ingredients flush with the top of the spoon using a small knife.

Read (and Follow!) Directions

My recipes have been tested at least three times, and the directions are carefully written to guide you successfully through the mixing and baking process. Keep in mind the following suggestions:

1. PREPARE THE RECIPE EXACTLY AS IT'S WRITTEN AT LEAST ONCE BEFORE MAKING ANY CHANGES.

2. PAY PARTICULAR ATTENTION TO WHAT TEMPERATURE INGREDIENTS SHOULD BE, because this can have a major effect on baking success: Butter that is too cold or too warm and soft won't fluff up properly. Overly soft butter also melts too quickly in the oven, so dough runs and cookies are too thin. Melted chocolate that is too cool may set into fine, hard bits instead of blending in when added to a dough. Eggs may curdle if overheated or combined with very hot ingredients.

3. FOLLOW THE INSTRUCTIONS ON MIXING PROCEDURES AND THE ORDER FOR ADDING INGREDIENTS. Meringue cookies can deflate if sugar is added too late or if fatty ingredients like nuts and chocolate are added too early. Butter doughs will toughen if liquids and eggs are added to the dry ingredients before fats and sugar. And some doughs will toughen if overbeaten.

4. NOTE THE IMPORTANT BAKING FACTORS: how large cookies should be and how far apart they should be spaced on the baking sheets, where the baking sheets should be placed in the oven, and the ways to tell when the cookies are done. If you decide to make your cookies larger or smaller than specified, keep in mind that baking times as well as yields will change.

Use Fresh, Good-Quality Ingredients

Second-rate ingredients can't produce first-rate flavor. This doesn't mean you have to purchase the most expensive brands of everything (though I wouldn't recommend buying the cheapest, either). But it does mean ingredients should be fresh tasting and in good condition. Be choosy about the following:

BUTTER can become rancid and develop off-flavors if improperly stored. Even in the refrigerator, it begins to stale in just several weeks. However, wrapped airtight and frozen, butter will keep well for up to a year. If possible, choose unsalted butter for baking. You can easily determine if it's fresh just by tasting it, and you can control exactly how much salt goes into a recipe.

SUGAR, especially brown sugar, should be dry and free of lumps, since even long beating may not always smooth them. Manufacturers sometimes suggest heating brown sugar to soften hard lumps, but this isn't a good idea when you're baking. Combining warm sugar with butter can melt the butter and cause the dough to spread excessively. Instead, reserve hard, lumpy sugar for nonbaking recipes, and open a fresh box.

SPICES lose their distinctive flavors and pungent aromas if stored for more than a year or so. If your spices smell musty or flat, replace them; otherwise, your cookies are likely to taste flat, too. For the absolute best flavor, buy whole nutmegs and grate them as needed. Whole spices like cloves and coriander seed are also most intensely flavored when freshly ground. You'll need a spice grinder or coffee grinder reserved for that purpose. (Grinding your own spices is entirely optional.)

NUTS AND PEANUTS have a high fat content and become stale and rancid rapidly. Buy nuts from a source with a high turnover and use them promptly. Or buy ahead and freeze the nuts in an airtight container until needed. Whole nuts, which have less exposed surface area than chopped, keep best.

RAISINS, CRANBERRIES, AND OTHER DRIED FRUIT should be slightly moist and succulent, not hard or dry. Stale dried fruit is not only tough and tasteless, but it also draws out too much moisture from the dough, making the cookies crumbly.

Beware of substitutions

After failure to follow directions, inappropriate substitutions probably account for the largest share of baking difficulties. Perhaps the most common substitution problem is one a friend recently encountered when she tried one of my peanut butter cookie recipes. Not having any butter on hand, she substituted "light" tub-style margarine. This altered the chemistry and balance of ingredients significantly, causing the cookies to run together on the sheets and the recipe to fail. The reason: "light" and "diet" margarines have more water and air and less fat than either butter or stick margarine. In addition, the fat in all soft, or tub-style, margarines remains soft when chilled, which allows rolled doughs to thin out too much during baking and makes them more difficult to handle and shape.

Admittedly, situations arise when a substitution is acceptable. For example, one type of nut can often successfully stand in for another (though cookie flavor and appearance will change). Here is a quick rundown of other substitutions you might be tempted to try, along with insights on the potential problems they pose:

- Semisweet chocolate blocks and semisweet chocolate morsels *are often not* interchangeable, though semisweet chocolate blocks and bittersweet chocolate blocks *usually are* interchangeable.

   Semisweet chocolate blocks and semisweet morsels may yield very different results because they were designed for different purposes. Manufacturers intend semisweet chocolate blocks to be used melted, so these generally melt smoothly and are fairly fluid. Chocolate chips, on the other hand, are designed to hold their shape when heated and so are usually stiff when melted and difficult to drizzle or spread. To ensure that your dough is the right consistency, don't try to use one of these products in place of the other unless a recipe gives you this option.

   Although premium brands of bittersweet chocolate sometimes contain more fat than semisweet chocolate, either will yield good results in the recipes in this book. However, you may find that cookies prepared with bittersweet—which is in fact a sweetened chocolate—taste a bit richer and spread a bit more. (Don't confuse *bittersweet* with *unsweetened* chocolate; unsweetened is very bitter tasting and is not interchangeable with semisweet or bittersweet chocolate in these recipes.)

- Semisweet morsels and milk chocolate morsels *are usually not* interchangeable unless a recipe so indicates. Swapping milk chocolate for semisweet may result in cookies that taste too sweet and lack chocolate flavor, since milk chocolate has a milder flavor than semisweet.

- Plain (nonalkalized) unsweetened American-style cocoa powder and unsweetened Dutch-process cocoa powder *are usually not* interchangeable.

   The basic difference between American-style and Dutch-process cocoa is that the American-style still contains its natural acidity and the Dutch-process has been treated with an alkali to remove its acid. The alkalizing process turns the cocoa darker and changes its flavor, so the two products do not look or taste alike. Equally important, since the amount of baking soda in a recipe depends on the level of acidity, in many cases switching from one type of cocoa to another will upset the chemical balance.

   Unfortunately, not all cocoa manufacturers clearly indicate whether their products are alkalized. Assume that American brands are not alkalized unless the label says otherwise and that European brands are treated with alkali unless the label says otherwise.

- Butter and regular stick margarine *are sometimes* interchangeable; butter and tub-style, light, or diet margarine *are never* interchangeable.

In most cases, you can successfully substitute regular stick margarine for up to half of the butter in a cookie recipe, although the buttery taste will, of course, be diminished. Keep in mind that chilled doughs made with margarine will be softer, which may make cutting out and handling rolled cookies a little trickier than if they were prepared with all butter.

As I've already mentioned, tub-style and light margarines or spreads are not suitable for baking and should not be substituted for butter or stick margarine.

- Baking soda and baking powder *are not* interchangeable, although baking soda can be used in place of baking powder if a recipe adjustment is made.

    Both baking soda and baking powder contain the baking alkali bicarbonate of soda, but only baking powder also contains an acid that activates the alkali and produces aerating gas bubbles. When a recipe calls for baking soda, the necessary acid comes from some other ingredient, often buttermilk, lemon juice, sour cream, or naturally acidic American-style cocoa powder. If you are out of baking powder, you can try approximating it using baking soda along with a little lemon juice. However, as with all experiments, there are no guarantees of results. (There is no easy way to substitute for baking soda if it is needed to neutralize the excess acid in a recipe.)

- Old-fashioned rolled oats and quick-cooking oats *may be* interchangeable; old-fashioned rolled oats and instant oats *are not* interchangeable.

    Quick-cooking oats are simply rolled oats that have been chopped up a bit, so other than producing a less nubby texture, they yield similar results. You can even make your own quick-cooking oats by briefing chopping old-fashioned oats in a food processor.

    Instant oats are another matter. Designed to yield instant breakfast oatmeal, these are very fine and partially cooked; they are not suitable substitutes for either old-fashioned or quick-cooking oats.

- Granulated sugar and brown sugar *are rarely* interchangeable.

    Obviously, granulated sugar and brown sugar will impart entirely different colors and flavors, but this is not the only problem with substituting one for the other. Brown sugar is moister, heavier, and coarser than granulated sugar, so it will also change the cookie texture. In general, switching from one product to the other will yield entirely different cookies.

- Light and dark molasses *are usually* interchangeable; blackstrap molasses *is not* interchangeable with either light or dark.

Some brands of molasses are labeled as light or dark, which suggests not only the color but whether the flavor is mild and light or a bit bold and slightly less sweet. In a pinch, light and dark molasses can be used in place of one other, though the intensity of flavor will change and your cookies may be a lighter or darker shade. Less refined than either light or dark molasses, blackstrap is dark, very viscous, and bitter, and it cannot be substituted for the other two.

ready, set, mix

After reading a recipe all the way through, measure out all the ingredients before mixing.

ALLOW BUTTER, FLOUR, EGGS, NUTS, AND OTHER INGREDIENTS THAT HAVE BEEN STORED IN A COLD SPOT OR REFRIGERATED TO WARM ALMOST TO ROOM TEMPERATURE BEFORE MIXING THEM. This ensures that the dough will be warm enough to come together properly and that the cookies will bake in the time specified.

MANY RECIPES CALL FOR "SLIGHTLY SOFTENED" BUTTER: it should give just slightly when pressed with a finger, and an indentation should remain. Very cold butter will be too stiff to fluff up or "cream" properly; soft or melted butter won't have enough body to fluff at all.

A QUICK WAY TO WARM COLD BUTTER is to put it in a microwave-safe bowl and *briefly* microwave on *low power*. Stir every 20 seconds and watch carefully, as butter can rapidly change from hard to oversoft. Or put the butter in a metal bowl set inside a larger, shallow bowl of warm water and stir frequently.

The majority of the recipes in this book call for mixing using an electric mixer. A hand-held model, regular stand model, or heavy-duty mixer such as a KitchenAid can be used. The latter may mix ingredients a little more quickly, due to its more powerful motor.

NOTE THAT IN ALL RECIPES THAT CALL FOR WHIPPING INGREDIENTS, if you are using a KitchenAid mixer, perform this step using the wire whip and not the paddle.

shaping and rolling

Relying on just a few simple techniques and tips can help you make better cookies and also enable you to turn out rolled and shaped cookies more easily.

RESIST THE TEMPTATION TO ADD EXTRA FLOUR TO TAME OVERLY SOFT, UNMANAGEABLE DOUGH. Overflouring makes dough tough. A far better approach is to firm up dough by chilling it. Whenever it begins to warm and soften again, a short stint in the refrigerator or freezer can bring it back under control without compromising texture. Remember, too, that a just-mixed dough may not need either chilling or extra flour; it will stiffen quite a bit if simply allowed to stand for a few minutes so the flour already added can fully absorb the excess moisture.

To avoid overflouring, roll out dough between sheets of wax paper instead of on a floured work surface. First, sandwich the dough between two long wax paper sheets and pat it flat. Then roll it out to the desired thickness with a rolling pin. Since the wax paper sometimes wrinkles on the underside during this process, occasionally turn over the dough and smooth or roll out the underside as well. (To keep the paper from sliding around during rolling, I either tape it to the countertop using masking tape or simply drape one end of the paper over the counter edge and lean against it.)

Stack the rolled-out dough portions on a tray or baking sheet, still sandwiched between the sheets of paper, then place in the refrigerator or freezer until chilled and firm. Just before cutting out the cookies, peel off one sheet of wax paper, then lightly pat it back into place. (This step loosens the dough from the paper so the cookies can be readily lifted off later.) Finally, flip the dough so the loosened sheet is on the bottom, peel off and discard the second wax paper sheet, cut out the cookies, and transfer them to the baking sheets.

Besides eliminating the need for extra flour, a great advantage of this rolling method is that if the dough becomes soft while cookies are being cut out, it can be returned to the tray (still on the wax paper) and refrigerated until firm again. (In the case of a very tender, soft dough, it's a good idea to chill an extra tray or baking sheet and lay the paper and dough on it when cutting out the cookies.) The end result is that the cookies can always be firmed up before they are transferred to baking sheets, thus guaranteeing a tidy shape. Another obvious advantage is easy kitchen cleanup.

The Business of Baking

NEARLY EVERY RECIPE CALLS FOR PREHEATING THE OVEN. TURN ON THE OVEN TO THE DESIRED SETTING AT LEAST 15 MINUTES BEFORE BAKING.

IF POSSIBLE, BAKE USING MEDIUM- OR HEAVY-GAUGE METAL BAKING SHEETS SPECIFICALLY DESIGNED FOR COOKIES. These are rimless on all or several sides so the cookies can slide off onto a wire rack. Any rims should be very narrow so the heat can circulate readily and brown the cookie tops. Either nonstick or regular shiny or dull gray aluminum cookie sheets work well, but very dark colored sheets may cause overbrowning. Flimsy sheets may not distribute heat evenly, resulting in burning on the bottom, and can warp and cause cookies to be misshapen. Any number of baking sheet sizes is available, but for most standard-sized ovens, sheets that are in the 14-by-17-inch range and that will comfortably hold 12 to 16 medium-sized cookies are a good choice.

WHEN PREPARING THE BAR COOKIES, PAY ATTENTION TO THE PAN SIZE SPECIFIED. That's important to ensure the bars bake through properly and come out the right thickness. Only a few standard-sized pans are called for throughout the book: 8- and 9-inch square and 9-by-13-inch rectangular pans. The 8- and 9-inch are not interchangeable, as their volumes are quite different. If necessary, you can substitute rectangular pans with slightly different dimensions than the standard 9-by-13-inch pan, as long as they hold about the same amount. Although metal and glass pans yield slightly different results— the edges bake a little faster in glass pans—either can be used in these recipes.

IF COOKIES FREQUENTLY BURN IN YOUR OVEN, IT MAY BE THAT THE OVEN THERMOSTAT IS OFF. An oven thermometer can verify that the oven is actually heating to the temperature selected. If the setting is accurate, try baking with one sheet stacked right on top of another to shield the cookies from excess heat. Or try baking with very heavy gauge pans or ones with an air-cushion inset.

Most of the recipes in this book call for preparing baking sheets by greasing or coating with nonstick spray, though if you prefer, you can use parchment paper instead. Cookies with a lot of fat and no eggs (for example, shortbreads) can be baked on ungreased sheets. Cookies with lots of egg whites and little or no fat (for example, meringues) will stick unless baked on parchment, foil, or heavily greased-and-floured pans.

IF YOU CARE ABOUT UNIFORMITY, BAKE ALL THE COOKIES ON THE SAME KIND OF SHEETS. Different sheets cause surprisingly different amounts of spreading, browning, and crisping. Also, try to keep all the cookies on a single sheet about the same size and thickness. Adjust for any differences by placing slightly thicker/larger cookies around the perimeter and thinner/smaller ones in the interior, as exposure to the heat is slightly greater at the edges.

IN STANDARD-SIZED OVENS, IT'S USUALLY BEST TO BAKE ONLY ONE SHEET OF COOKIES AT A TIME. (Meringue cookies are sometimes an exception.) Leave at least 2 inches all around so the heat can circulate. Also, follow any instructions about placing the sheet in the upper, middle, or lower third of the oven, or rotating the sheet halfway through baking to ensure even browning.

SINCE COOKIES CAN OVERBAKE QUICKLY, SET A KITCHEN TIMER AS EACH SHEET GOES INTO THE OVEN. For the first sheet, you may want to set the timer to a minute less than the minimum baking time specified in the recipe. Even though the times suggested have all been determined through testing, factors like an unusually hot oven or very warm dough can cause more rapid baking than expected. A timer can be reset, and the cookies baked longer if necessary, but burned cookies can't be repaired.

When the cookies are done, immediately transfer the sheet to a wire rack. Let the cookies stand on the sheet until firm enough to be lifted off without breaking; every recipe gives an indication of how long this will be. Remove them with a wide, thin-bladed spatula and place them flat on wire racks until thoroughly cooled.

decorating

Decorations need to be in keeping with a cookie's character. For example, chunky chopped nuts and fruit or chocolate chips are wonderful toppings for big, bold-flavored cookies, but fine piping, tiny nonpareils, crystal sugar, or dainty dabs of jam are better suited to delicate wafers and crisps. To keep nonpareils and other toppings in place on cookies, press or pat them into the dough before baking. Another possibility is to brush the cookies lightly with an egg-white wash and then sprinkle on the decorations.

Some of the most effective decorations suggest a cookie's flavor: a blanched almond half to signal an almond taste, a sprinkling of chocolate jimmies to indicate a chocolate filling inside, or a drizzle of yellow-tinted icing to hint at a lemony taste. Cookies can also be painted, stenciled, piped, glazed, or decorated with faux etching; see details on these and other techniques in the decorating chapter.

keeping and carrying

Cookies are better keepers than other baked goods, but, having made and sampled many thousands of them, I'm convinced that most are truly at their best when fresh. (This may help explain the success of shopping-mall cookie kiosks, where the goodies are literally minutes old.) Even dark, spicy honey, molasses, and fruitcake cookies that need a few days of mellowing begin to lose their bold flavors after just a few weeks. And cookies containing lots of nuts, butter, or other fats may even develop an off-taste if stored very long. The good news is that many kinds of cookies freeze well, and when frozen, they will stay in nearly peak condition for several months. (If freezing bar cookies, pack them uncut, then cut into servings when partially thawed.)

There are several simple rules to follow in storing cookies:

- Be certain the cookies are completely cool before packing them. Warm cookies produce steam, which, when trapped in a container, can cause the entire batch to soften or even spoil. Also, let iced or painted cookies set up and dry completely before storing them.

- Pack each variety of cookie in a separate container. Otherwise, the flavors of all the various types will mingle and become muddled, and the moisture in the soft, chewy cookies will cause the crisp ones to become limp.

- Pack cookies in airtight containers. Depending on the sturdiness of the cookies, suitable containers may include plastic boxes, metal tins, glass or ceramic canisters, cookie jars, or heavy-duty plastic bags. In every case, the container should provide some protection against breakage and prevent exposure to the air.

Relatively speaking, cookies not only keep well but carry and ship well. Of course, very sturdy cookies are the most likely to be portable. Those at least ¼ to ⅜ inch thick and firm in consistency are good choices. Most bar cookies also carry and ship well, especially if individually wrapped in strong plastic wrap and placed in airtight containers. (Bars and cookies with a sticky filling or icing or with a soft topping are an exception.)

If carefully packed in tins or hard plastic boxes and cushioned with crumpled wax paper, cookies that are on the *slightly* tender side can be transported or shipped. However, to avoid disappointing both the giver and the receiver, don't try to ship extremely thin or brittle varieties, crumbly fragile ones, or gooey-soft cookies; the result is never pretty!

Containers of cookies should be packed in larger boxes filled with Styrofoam bits, plastic bubbles, popcorn, or another airy filler to protect the goodies inside from random bumps and thumps.

cookies as gifts

Cookies make great gifts, especially when presented in attractive baskets, ceramic or clear canisters, wooden boxes, tins, or cookie jars that can be kept after the sweet treats are gone. For a more economical presentation, use recycled cardboard boxes covered with seasonal wrapping paper or nonstretchy fabrics such as cotton. (Fix fabrics in place with nontoxic craft glue.) Dress up the containers with coordinating ribbon, colored yarn, rickrack, or even fine braid or lace trim. As an extra touch, provide a neatly printed copy of the recipe or a cookie cutter with your gift.

If you sew, another presentation possibility is to stitch your own colorful fabric cookie sacks. These should be lined with a plastic bag (cut down to fit, if necessary) and tied up with a ribbon to keep them airtight. Small sacks—sized for special individual cookies and fitted with drawstrings—are particularly nice to give to children.

Regardless of the container and packaging, don't pack different varieties together, as cookies can pick up one another's flavors. To give an assortment, place individual kinds of cookies in a set of small boxes or in separate plastic or cellophane bags within a larger container.

2

Sugar Cookies and Shortbreads

Best-Ever snickerdoodles

Snickerdoodles are one of my favorite sugar cookies, and this is my favorite snickerdoodle recipe. The cookies are large, lightly spiced, and have a pleasantly mild, homey flavor. What makes them truly remarkable, however, is their wonderful texture. Take a bite at the edge of a cookie, and it's mostly crispy. Move closer to the middle, and it's crispy-chewy. Finally, right in the center, it's nearly all chewy. And the best part is that these snickerdoodles don't dry out or lose their munchability during storage.

Snickerdoodles probably originated in New England in the mid- to late 1800s, gradually becoming popular throughout the country. One great fan of the cookies was James Whitcomb Riley, the nineteenth-century creator of "The Frost Is on the Punkin" and the Little Orphan Annie character. To celebrate Riley's October 7 birthday, snickerdoodles have sometimes been served to visitors at his preserved Victorian house in Indianapolis.

Both the German and Dutch languages have words that sound a bit like "snickerdoodle," but there isn't any evidence linking them to the cookie name. More likely, it's just a made-up nonsense word created in the same spirit as doodly-squat or the repeating phrase from the early American song "Yankee Doodle Dandy."

The following recipe is adapted from one in a 1902 Estherville, Iowa, community cookbook. The original recipe didn't contain corn syrup or vanilla, but I think the syrup makes the cookies a little chewier, and the vanilla brings out the flavor.

2²/₃ cups all-purpose white flour	1³/₄ cups sugar
2 teaspoons cream of tartar	1¹/₂ tablespoons light corn syrup
1 teaspoon baking soda	2 large eggs
¹/₂ teaspoon salt	2¹/₂ teaspoons vanilla extract
¹/₄ teaspoon ground nutmeg (optional)	
1 cup (2 sticks) unsalted butter, slightly softened	¹/₄ cup sugar, combined with 1¹/₂ teaspoons ground cinnamon, for topping

Preheat the oven to 375 degrees F. Grease several baking sheets or coat with nonstick spray.

In a large bowl, thoroughly stir together the flour, cream of tartar, baking soda, salt, and nutmeg, if using; set aside. In another large bowl, with an electric mixer on medium speed, beat together the butter, sugar, and corn syrup until well blended and fluffy, about 2 minutes. Add the eggs and vanilla and beat until well blended and smooth. Beat in half of the flour mixture until evenly incorporated. Stir in the remaining flour mixture until evenly incorporated. Let the dough stand for 5 to 10 minutes, or until firmed up slightly. Put the cinnamon-sugar in a shallow bowl.

Roll portions of the dough into generous 1½-inch balls with lightly greased hands (the dough will be soft). Roll each ball in the cinnamon-sugar. Place on the baking sheets, spacing about 2¾ inches apart. Using your hand, slightly pat down the tops of the balls.

Bake the cookies, one sheet at a time, in the upper third of the oven for 8 to 11 minutes, or until just light golden brown at the edges. Reverse the sheet from front to back halfway through baking to ensure even browning. Transfer the sheet to a wire rack and let stand until the cookies firm up slightly, 1 to 2 minutes. Using a spatula, transfer the cookies to wire racks. Let stand until completely cooled. Let the baking sheets cool between batches to keep the cookies from spreading too much.

Store in an airtight container for up to 10 days or freeze for up to 2 months.

words of kitchen wisdom
"The success of these recipes . . . in which soda and cream of tartar are used, will depend on the purity of these ingredients. Always buy the pure English bicarbonate of soda, and the pure cream of tartar. They are higher priced, but cheaper in the end, and are free from injurious substances. When not found at the grocer's, they may generally be had at the druggist's."

—Estelle Woods Wilcox (ed.), *Buckeye Cookery and Practical Housekeeping,* 1880

nineteenth-century sugar cookies

I discovered this simple yet very good nineteenth-century sugar cookie while leafing through an unpublished, handwritten manuscript, *Book of Cookery and Other Receipts* (Syracuse, New York, 1834), in the rare book collection at the National Agricultural Library near Washington, D.C. The unsigned work offers insights into the domestic life of one American homemaker in the postcolonial period. For example, tucked among the expected recipes are instructions on how to skin an eel!

Unlike many cooks in this era, the author apparently had a well-stocked kitchen. She called for currants, rose water, spices, almonds, and brandy, as well as for basics like butter, flour, sugar, and eggs. However, none of her recipes used baking powder—it didn't come on the market until the 1860s.

As is often the case with old recipes, this one included only snippets of instructions, though the author did include precise decorating details: "Do them over with the white of an egg. Then sprinkle sugar over top." The resulting "tea cakes"—which we would call delicate sugar cookies—are rich, mild, and have a sandy-crisp texture. Straightforward, pleasing, and oh, yes, very nice with tea.

2¾ cups all-purpose white flour

¼ teaspoon salt

1 cup (2 sticks) cold unsalted butter, cut into chunks

Scant 1 cup sugar

1 large egg plus 1 large egg yolk

1½ teaspoons good-quality brandy

¾ teaspoon finely grated lemon zest (colored part of the skin)

⅛ teaspoon ground cinnamon, mace, or nutmeg

1 large egg white, for topping

About 3 tablespoons sugar or crystal sugar, for topping

In a large bowl, thoroughly stir together the flour and salt. Using forks, a pastry blender, or your fingertips, cut the butter into the flour mixture until the mixture is the consistency of coarse meal. In a small bowl, beat together the sugar, egg and egg yolk, brandy, lemon zest, and cinnamon, mace, or nutmeg until well blended and smooth. Stir, then knead, the sugar mixture into the flour mixture until evenly incorporated.

Divide the dough in half. Place each portion between large sheets of wax paper. Roll out each portion a scant ¼ inch thick; check the underside of the dough and smooth out any wrinkles that form. Stack the rolled portions (paper still attached) on a baking sheet. Refrigerate for about 30 minutes, or until cold and firm, or freeze for about 15 minutes to speed chilling.

Preheat the oven to 350 degrees F. Grease several baking sheets or coat with nonstick spray.

Working with one portion at a time and keeping the remaining dough chilled, gently peel away, then pat one sheet of wax paper back into place. Flip the dough over, then peel off and discard the second sheet. Using a 2½-inch fluted round cutter or other desired shape, cut out the cookies. (If at any point the dough softens too much to handle easily, transfer the paper and cookies to a baking sheet and refrigerate until firm again.) Using a spatula, carefully transfer the cookies to the baking sheets, spacing about 1¼ inches apart. Reroll any dough scraps. Continue cutting out the cookies until all the dough is used.

In a small bowl, beat the egg white and 1 teaspoon water until frothy. Using a pastry brush (or if necessary, a paper towel), lightly brush the cookie tops with the egg-white mixture. Generously sprinkle the cookies with the sugar or crystal sugar.

Bake the cookies, one sheet at a time, in the upper third of the oven for 6 to 9 minutes, or until just lightly browned at the edges. Reverse the sheet from front to back halfway through baking to ensure even browning. Using a spatula, immediately transfer the cookies to wire racks. Let stand until completely cooled.

Store in an airtight container for up to 2 weeks or freeze for up to 2 months.

pennsylvania Dutch
soft sugar
cookies

Makes 20 to 24
(4-inch) cookies.

Right in character with most Pennsylvania Dutch fare, these are plain and almost saucer sized. They are also mild and puffy-soft, with a slight crunch of sugar on top—a good example of country comfort food. Although the cookies don't contain raisins, it's traditional to decorate them with granulated sugar and a single plump raisin in the center. Locally, they are called simply "sugar cakes."

3¹/₃ cups all-purpose white flour	2 large eggs
¹/₂ teaspoon baking soda	2¹/₂ teaspoons vanilla extract
¹/₂ teaspoon cream of tartar	1 cup sour cream
¹/₂ teaspoon salt	
1¹/₄ cups (2¹/₂ sticks) unsalted butter, slightly softened	3–4 tablespoons sugar, for topping
1²/₃ cups sugar	Raisins, for topping
1¹/₂ teaspoons finely grated lemon zest (colored part of the skin)	

In a large bowl, sift together the flour, baking soda, cream of tartar, and salt; set aside. In another large bowl, with an electric mixer on medium speed, beat together the butter, sugar, and lemon zest until light and well blended. Add the eggs and vanilla and beat until very smooth and fluffy. Beat in the sour cream, then the dry ingredients, until evenly incorporated. It's all right if the dough seems too sticky; it will firm up when chilled. Freeze the dough until thoroughly chilled and firm, at least 3 hours or overnight. (If necessary, allow the dough to warm up slightly before using, but it is easier to work with when very cold.)

Preheat the oven to 375 degrees F. Grease several baking sheets or coat with nonstick spray.

Working with about a third of the dough at a time and keeping the remaining dough chilled, divide into 7 or 8 equal portions. With well-greased hands, shape and roll the portions into balls. Transfer the balls to baking sheets, spacing about 3 to 3¼ inches apart. Let the balls stand to soften just slightly. Grease the bottom of a large, flat, wide-bottomed glass with vegetable oil. Dip the glass bottom into a shallow saucer containing the sugar, shaking off the excess. One at a time, press down on the balls with the glass until they are about 3 inches in diameter, dipping into the sugar before flattening each cookie. (If necessary, wipe any

buildup from the glass bottom, oil again, dip into the sugar, and continue.) Press a raisin into the center of each cookie. Repeat the cookie-shaping process until all the dough is used.

Bake the cookies, one sheet at a time, in the upper third of the oven for 8 to 11 minutes, until just tinged with brown at the edges and barely firm in the centers; for very moist cookies, be careful not to overbake. Reverse the sheet from front to back halfway through baking to ensure even browning. Transfer the sheet to a wire rack and let stand until the cookies firm up slightly, 1 to 2 minutes. Using a spatula, transfer the cookies to wire racks. Let stand until completely cooled.

Store in an airtight container for up to 1 week or freeze for up to 1 month.

New York
Black and whites

These huge, dramatic-looking chocolate- and vanilla-iced cookies have enticed New Yorkers (as well as some northern New Jersey natives) for the past 40 years or so. A mainstay of deli bakery cases across New York City, they were once spotlighted on the *Seinfeld* television show. Black and whites have a huge following and evoke fond memories, particularly among those who ate them as children. Recalls Sue Spataro, an enthusiastic home cook who grew up on Long Island and now lives in North Carolina: "I had an afternoon paper route when I was about thirteen years old. After I collected my fees on Friday afternoons, I would ride my bicycle the three miles to Di Monda's bakery. The black and whites stood out from the other cookies because of their striking color and size. I would buy one and eat it as I rode home. I was in heaven. My biggest problem was which side to eat first; the chocolate or vanilla? In the long run, it didn't matter, because it was *all* good."

Since many who grew up enjoying black and whites still hanker for them, some folks who have moved away from New York now make their own. Sue says she bakes them for her daughters and shares a few with her neighbors, who are from New Jersey and also enjoy "a taste of home." Sue tested my black-and-whites recipe, and she and her husband approved the final version. "He especially liked the icings—exactly like he remembered," she adds. (Incidentally, the fondants are easy to make, spread readily, and lend a nice, smooth finish to the black and whites.)

3 cups all-purpose white flour

Scant ³/₄ teaspoon salt

¹/₄ teaspoon baking soda

1¹/₃ cups sugar

²/₃ cup (1 stick plus 2²/₃ tablespoons) unsalted butter, slightly softened

¹/₂ cup white vegetable shortening

2 large eggs

2¹/₂ teaspoons vanilla extract

2 teaspoons light corn syrup

Scant ³/₄ teaspoon lemon extract

¹/₃ cup sour cream

QUICK VANILLA AND CHOCOLATE FONDANTS

¹/₄ cup light corn syrup

5 cups powdered sugar, sifted after measuring, plus more if needed

³/₄ teaspoon vanilla extract

2 ounces unsweetened chocolate, chopped

Preheat the oven to 350 degrees F. Grease several baking sheets or coat with nonstick spray.

In a medium bowl, thoroughly stir together the flour, salt, and baking soda; set aside. In a large bowl, with an electric mixer on medium speed,

beat together the sugar, butter, and shortening until well blended and fluffy, about 2 minutes. Add the eggs, vanilla, corn syrup, and lemon extract and beat until evenly incorporated. Beat in half of the flour mixture until evenly incorporated. On low speed, beat in the sour cream. Beat or stir in the remaining flour mixture, just until well blended and smooth. Let the dough stand to firm up for about 5 minutes.

Using a scant ¼-cup measure of dough, shape into balls with lightly greased hands. Place on the baking sheets, spacing about 3½ inches apart. Using your hand, press and pat the balls to about 3¼ inches in diameter.

Bake the cookies, one sheet at a time, in the middle of the oven for 10 to 14 minutes, or until lightly browned at the edges and the tops just spring back when lightly pressed in the centers. Reverse the sheet from front to back halfway through baking to ensure even browning. Transfer the sheet to a wire rack and let stand until the cookies firm up slightly, 1 to 2 minutes. Using a spatula, transfer the cookies to wire racks. Let stand until completely cooled.

FOR THE FONDANTS

In a medium, heavy saucepan, bring ½ cup water and the corn syrup just to a boil over medium-high heat. Remove from the heat and stir in the powdered sugar and vanilla until completely smooth. Place the chocolate in a small, deep bowl. Pour ⅔ cup of the hot vanilla fondant over the chocolate. Stir until the chocolate is partially melted. Pour another ½ cup of the vanilla fondant over the chocolate. Stirring constantly, thin the chocolate fondant to a fluid but not runny consistency by adding 3 to 4 teaspoons of hot water, a little at a time. Stir until the chocolate melts completely and the water is thoroughly incorporated.

Set the wire racks with the cookies over wax paper to catch drips. Using a small, wide-bladed spatula, spreader, or table knife, immediately ice half of each cookie with the chocolate fondant. (If the fondant stiffens as you work, thin it by thoroughly stirring in a few drops of hot water. If the fondant cools completely, rewarm it over low heat, stirring.)

If necessary, adjust the consistency of the vanilla fondant by stirring in additional powdered sugar or hot water until fluid but not runny. Ice the second half of each cookie with the vanilla fondant. Let the cookies stand until the icing sets, at least 2 hours and preferably 4 hours.

Store the cookies in a single layer or layered between wax paper in an airtight container for up to 1 week or freeze for up to 1 month.

Black-and-white memories

As Mary Jane Grauso, a home cook originally from Paterson, New Jersey, but who now lives in Maryland, points out, New Yorkers aren't the only ones who recall black and whites fondly: "My mother and I used to take walks in a park that was right by the Hillcrest Bakery in Paterson. On special occasions, she'd let me buy a cookie. I liked the black and whites because they looked so neat and tasted so good."

Tip

For a tidy dividing line between the black and white icings, put a small amount of chocolate fondant in a paper cone or pastry bag fitted with a fine writing tip. Pipe a straight chocolate line across the cookies, so they are divided in half. Ice one side up to the line with chocolate and the other side with vanilla.

watkins vanilla sugar cookies

makes about 60
(2½-to-3-inch)
cookies.

After testing many different sugar cookies, I discovered this exceptionally tasty version in the *Watkins Cook Book,* an influential product promotion cookbook first published in 1936 by the Minnesota-based J. R. Watkins Company. The company was founded in 1868 by liniment maker and traveling salesman Joseph R. Watkins. By the 1930s, the firm had become the nation's largest food and medicinals distributor, with 10,000 "dealers" selling more than 300 products door-to-door.

According to Jeff Severnson, copywriter and unofficial historian for the restructured descendant firm, Watkins, Inc., the company presence was so strong in the rural Midwest that the *Watkins Cook Book* became the standard. "That was my grandmother's everyday cookbook. If you were from western Wisconsin and your grandmother baked sugar cookies, they probably tasted like the Watkins recipe, because everybody used that book," he says. He adds that many cooks also used the Watkins vanilla the book specified, because it was one of the company's most highly touted products.

With the need for legions of traveling salesmen carrying goods into America's hinterlands now past, a downsized Watkins, Inc., distributes its products—including vanilla—through independent local representatives. Although the original recipe specifically called for Watkins vanilla, it isn't essential for this buttery, tender-crisp cookie—any high-quality brand will do. I particularly like to bake these cookies at Christmas.

2½ cups all-purpose white flour, sifted after
    measuring
1 teaspoon baking powder
1 cup (2 sticks) unsalted butter, slightly softened
1 cup sugar
2 large egg yolks

Generous pinch of salt
2 teaspoons vanilla extract

2–3 tablespoons sugar or Colored Decorating Sugars
    (page 375), for topping

In a large bowl, thoroughly stir together the flour and baking powder; set aside. In another large bowl, with an electric mixer on medium speed, beat together the butter and sugar until well blended and fluffy. Beat in the egg yolks, then the salt and vanilla, until evenly incorporated. Gradually beat or stir in the flour mixture to form a smooth dough.

THE ALL-AMERICAN COOKIE BOOK

Divide the dough in half. Place each portion between large sheets of wax paper. Roll out each portion ⅛ inch thick; check the underside of the dough and smooth out any wrinkles that form. Stack the rolled portions (paper still attached) on a baking sheet. Refrigerate for about 30 minutes, or until cold and firm, or freeze for about 15 minutes to speed the chilling.

Preheat the oven to 375 degrees F. Grease several baking sheets or coat with nonstick spray.

Working with one portion at a time and leaving the remaining dough chilled, gently peel away, then pat one sheet of wax paper back into place. Flip the dough over, then peel off and discard the second sheet. Using assorted 2½-to-3-inch cutters, cut out the cookies. (If at any point the dough softens too much to handle easily, transfer the paper and cookies to a baking sheet and refrigerate or freeze until firm again.) Using a spatula, carefully transfer the cookies to the baking sheets, spacing about 1¼ inches apart. Reroll any dough scraps. Continue cutting out the cookies until all the dough is used. Sprinkle the cookies with the sugar or colored sugar.

Bake the cookies, one sheet at a time, in the upper third of the oven for 8 to 11 minutes, or until lightly colored on top and slightly darker at the edges. Reverse the sheet from front to back halfway through baking to ensure even browning. Transfer the sheet to a wire rack and let stand until the cookies firm up slightly, 1 to 2 minutes. Using a spatula, transfer the cookies to wire racks. Let stand until completely cooled.

Store in an airtight container for up to 2 weeks or freeze for up to 1 month.

THE WATKINS MAN

Jim Dullenty, proprietor of the Rocky Mountain House bookshop in Hamilton, Montana, remembers the salesman from Watkins fondly: "When I was a child, rural families relied on visits by 'the Watkins man' for supplies like spices, extracts, ointment, and soap. Of course, he carried the company's cookbook, too. It was so widely distributed, I think influenced what a generation of Montana ranch families ate."

MapLe sugar cookies

Makes 30 to 35
(2½-to-3-inch)
Leaf-shaped cookies.

The secret to intense maple flavor in baked goods is using granular maple sugar rather than the less concentrated syrup. New England cooks, including the creator of a 1909 cookie recipe that inspired this one, figured out this trick long ago.

It is said that Native Americans introduced the early colonists to maple sugar. In the seventeenth and eighteenth centuries, maple sugar was far more commonplace than maple syrup, because the dry product was compact and easier to store and, like cane sugar, could be kept for long periods without fear of spoilage. Today, maple sugar is not seen much, though it is available from Dakin Farm, Route 7, Ferrisburg, VT 05456 (800-993-2546).

It's well worth tracking down maple sugar to make these unusual rolled cookies. (Be sure it's pure maple sugar; some maple-flavored sugars contain cane sugar, which alters the consistency and flavor.) If the sugar is coarse, grind it in a food processor or blender until it's the consistency of granulated sugar. The cookies have a crispy texture and a seductive butter-and-maple flavor that is exceptional. Garnish them with a sprinkling of maple sugar or crystal sugar or decorate with the optional maple icing.

1½ cups all-purpose white flour
¼ teaspoon baking powder
½ cup granular maple sugar (see above)
½ cup (1 stick) unsalted butter, slightly softened
½ cup sugar
1 large egg
⅛ teaspoon salt
1½ teaspoons vanilla extract
    Powdered sugar, for rolling

MAPLE ICING (OPTIONAL)
¼ cup granular maple sugar
½ teaspoon light corn syrup
⅛ teaspoon vanilla extract
    About ¼ cup powdered sugar

In a medium bowl, thoroughly stir together the 1½ cups flour and the baking powder; set aside. If the maple sugar is coarse, grind it in a food processor until it is the consistency of granulated sugar. In a large bowl, with an electric mixer on medium speed, beat together the butter, maple sugar, and sugar until very light and well blended. Add the egg, salt, and vanilla and beat until evenly incorporated. Beat or stir in the flour mixture just until evenly incorporated; the dough will be fairly soft. If too soft to handle, let stand for 5 to 10 minutes, or until firmed up slightly.

Divide the dough in half. Place each portion between large sheets of wax paper. Roll out each portion ⅛ inch thick; check the underside of the dough and smooth out any wrinkles that form. Stack the rolled portions (paper still attached) on a baking sheet. Refrigerate for about 1 hour, or until cold and firm, or freeze for about 30 minutes to speed chilling.

Preheat the oven to 350 degrees F. Grease several baking sheets or coat with nonstick spray.

Working with one portion at a time and leaving the remaining dough chilled, gently peel away, then pat one sheet of wax paper back into place. Flip the dough over, then peel off and discard the second sheet. Using a 2½-to-3-inch maple leaf-shaped cutter, cut out the cookies; if the cutter sticks, occasionally dip it into powdered sugar, tapping off the excess. (If at any point the dough softens too much to handle easily, transfer the paper and cookies to a baking sheet and refrigerate or freeze until firm again.) Using a spatula, carefully transfer the cookies to the baking sheets, spacing about 1½ inches apart. Reroll any dough scraps. Continue cutting out the cookies until all the dough is used.

Bake the cookies, one sheet at a time, in the upper third of the oven for 6 to 9 minutes, or until just slightly colored on top and faintly tinged with brown at the edges. Reverse the sheet from front to back halfway through baking to ensure even browning. Using a spatula, immediately transfer the cookies to wire racks. If topping the cookies with maple sugar or coarse crystal sugar, sprinkle it over while the cookies are still hot. Let stand until completely cooled. Cool the baking sheets between batches.

FOR THE ICING, IF USING

In a small, deep bowl, thoroughly stir together the maple sugar, 1 teaspoon hot water, corn syrup, and vanilla until the maple sugar dissolves and the mixture is well blended and smooth. Gradually stir in enough powdered sugar to stiffen the icing to piping consistency; stir until completely smooth. Spoon the icing into a paper cone or a small pastry bag fitted with a moderately fine writing tip. Pipe leaf-vein lines on the cookies. Let stand until the icing sets, at least 1 hour.

Store in an airtight container for up to 10 days or freeze for up to 1 month.

TIP

To make maple leaf–shaped cookies without a cutter, make a pattern by tracing or scoring around a real (or silk) maple leaf on a sheet of medium-weight plastic (the clear sheet on a greeting card box, for example) or thin cardboard. Cut out the pattern, place it on the rolled-out dough, and cut around it with a paring knife to form cookies. Plastic patterns can be washed, dried, and used again.

words of kitchen wisdom

"Use a caldron deeper than it is wide [for the sap] and never fill it more than half full to allow room for boiling up. Prepare a thick bed of faggots for fast, hot kindling. Since few people have new sugaring-off houses, pile some brush to break the wind. He who figures to get more than one gallon of syrup from less than 35 gallons of sap is not good at figuring nor at making maple syrup."

– *Old Farmer's Almanac* (1798), quoted in Evan Jones, *American Food: The Gastronomic Story*, 1975

New Mexican Anise sugar cookies (Biscochitos)

Biscochitos are considered so important in New Mexican culture that in 1989, the state legislature officially designated them the state cookie. Invariably, these sweets contain aniseed, an intensely aromatic, licorice-flavored herb popular in European baked goods but not often seen in American ones. This lends credence to the belief that Spanish priests coming north from Chihuahua, Mexico, introduced the herb to the region. Biscochitos are always baked at Christmas and offered as part of the traditional holiday meal. They are often served with Mexican hot chocolate.

I got this recipe from Susan Curtis, proprietor of the Santa Fe School of Cooking. Prepared at the school for a number of years, these biscochitos are wonderfully crisp and flavored with brandy and cinnamon as well as aniseed. The recipe calls for toasting the seeds, which makes their fragrance and flavor even more pronounced than usual.

Traditional recipes usually call for lard, but unless fresh, good-quality lard is available in your area, vegetable shortening is a better choice.

1–1½ teaspoons aniseed, to taste
1 cup sugar (divided)
3 cups all-purpose white flour
1½ teaspoons baking powder
Scant ½ teaspoon salt
1 cup white vegetable shortening or good-quality lard
1 large egg

3½ tablespoons good-quality brandy
½ teaspoon finely grated lemon zest (colored part of the skin; optional)

3 tablespoons sugar combined with ½ teaspoon ground cinnamon, for topping

Spread the aniseed in a small, heavy saucepan over medium heat. Toast, frequently stirring or shaking the pan, until very fragrant and just slightly darker in color, 3 to 5 minutes. Immediately turn out into a small bowl; let cool. Combine the aniseed and ½ cup of the sugar in a food processor. Process until the seed is ground fairly fine. (Alternatively, combine the aniseed and ½ cup of the sugar in a blender and blend for 1 to 2 minutes, stopping and stirring to redistribute the contents several times.) Set aside.

In a large bowl, thoroughly stir together the flour, baking powder, and salt; set aside. In another large bowl, with an electric mixer on medium speed, beat together the shortening or lard, sugar-aniseed mixture, remaining ½ cup sugar, and egg until well blended and fluffy. Add the

brandy, 2 tablespoons water, and lemon zest, if using, and beat until well blended and smooth. Gradually beat or stir in the flour mixture until well blended. If the dough seems too moist, let it stand to firm up for about 5 minutes before proceeding.

Divide the dough into thirds. Place each portion between large sheets of wax paper. Roll out each portion a scant ¼ inch thick; check the under-side of the dough and smooth out any wrinkles that form. Stack the por-tions (paper still attached) on a baking sheet. Refrigerate for 25 to 30 minutes, or until chilled and slightly firm, or freeze for about 15 minutes to speed chilling.

Preheat the oven to 350 degrees F. Grease several baking sheets or coat with nonstick spray.

Working with one portion at a time and leaving the remaining dough chilled, gently peel away, then pat one sheet of wax paper back into place. Flip the dough over, then peel off and discard the second sheet. Using assorted 2½-to-3-inch cutters or a single cutter, cut out the cook-ies. (If at any point the dough softens too much to handle easily, transfer the paper and cookies to a baking sheet and refrigerate or freeze until firm again.) Using a spatula, carefully transfer the cookies to the baking sheets, spacing about 1¼ inches apart. Reroll any dough scraps. Con-tinue cutting out the cookies until all the dough is used. Sprinkle the cookies with the cinnamon-sugar.

Bake the cookies, one sheet at a time, in the upper third of the oven for 8 to 11 minutes, or until just faintly tinged with brown at the edges. Re-verse the sheet from front to back halfway through baking to ensure even browning. Transfer the sheet to a wire rack and let stand until the cookies firm up slightly, 1 to 2 minutes. Using a spatula, carefully trans-fer the cookies to wire racks. Let stand until completely cooled.

Store in an airtight container for up to 2 weeks or freeze for up to 2 months.

caramel-frosted Brown sugar drops

makes about 30 (2½-to-2¾-inch) cookies.

This is one of those "nothing fancy" but devastatingly good recipes that shows off the genius and resourcefulness of traditional American home bakers. It calls for simple kitchen staples, with brown sugar and butter in the starring roles. The full, rich caramel flavor of the frosting combined with the mild, buttery softness of the cookies is truly inspired. They remind me of a heavenly caramel-frosted yellow cake my mother often baked for my birthday when I was a child. She never made brown-sugar drop cookies, although I've since tried similar recipes in cookbooks from the 1940s and 1950s. The cookies were very satisfying, but my mother's caramel frosting is better, so I've adapted it for use in this recipe.

2¾ cups all-purpose white flour

1 teaspoon baking soda

Generous ¼ teaspoon salt

1 cup (2 sticks) unsalted butter, slightly softened

1⅓ cups packed light brown sugar

2 large eggs

1½ teaspoons vanilla extract

⅔ cup sour cream

1 cup (4 ounces) chopped pecans (divided; optional)

CARAMEL FROSTING

7 tablespoons unsalted butter, cut into chunks

¾ cup packed light brown sugar

1 tablespoon light corn syrup

1⅔ cups powdered sugar, sifted after measuring

1¼ teaspoons vanilla extract

Preheat the oven to 350 degrees F. Grease several baking sheets or spray with nonstick spray.

In a medium bowl, sift together the flour, baking soda, and salt; set aside. In a large bowl, with an electric mixer on medium speed, beat together the butter and brown sugar until well blended and fluffy. Add the eggs and vanilla and beat until evenly incorporated. Lightly beat in half of the flour mixture. Add the sour cream and beat until well blended. Stir in the remaining flour mixture and a generous ¾ cup of the pecans, if using, until evenly incorporated.

Using a heaping ⅛-cup measure or coffee scoop, drop the dough onto the baking sheets into evenly shaped mounds, spacing about 2½ inches apart. Using a greased hand, pat down the cookies until flattened on top.

TIP
These cookies are equally good with or without the pecans.

Bake the cookies, one sheet at a time, in the upper third of the oven for 9 to 12 minutes, or until lightly tinged with brown at the edges and barely firm when pressed in the centers. Reverse the sheet from front to back halfway through baking to ensure even browning. Transfer the sheet to a wire rack and let stand until the cookies firm up slightly, 1 to 2 minutes. Using a spatula, carefully transfer the cookies to wire racks. Let stand until completely cooled.

FOR THE FROSTING

In a medium saucepan, melt the butter over medium-high heat. Bring to a boil and gently simmer, stirring occasionally, until it smells very fragrant and turns slightly golden, about 3 minutes; watch carefully. Stir in the brown sugar and cook, stirring, for 1 minute more. Stir in 2½ tablespoons hot water and the corn syrup until the mixture is well blended and the sugar dissolves. Vigorously stir in the powdered sugar and vanilla until well blended and completely smooth. Set the frosting aside, stirring occasionally, until it cools and stiffens just enough to spread, 2 to 4 minutes.

Set the wire racks with the cookies over wax paper to catch drips. Using a small, wide-bladed spatula, spreader, or table knife, generously swirl the cookie tops with the frosting. If pecans were added to the dough, sprinkle a few of the remaining scant ¼ cup pecans over the top of each cookie before the frosting sets. (If at any point the frosting stiffens too much to spread, stir in just enough hot water to make it spreadable.) Let the cookies stand until the frosting sets, about 45 minutes.

Store in a single layer or layered with wax paper in an airtight container for up to 1 week or freeze for up to 1 month.

words of kitchen wisdom
"For stirring . . . [butter and sugar], nothing is so convenient as a round hickory stick about a foot and a half long, and somewhat flattened at one end."

– A Lady of Philadelphia (Eliza Leslie), *Seventy-Five Receipts for Pastry, Cakes and Sweetmeats,* 1828

Butterscotch crunch cookies

Unpretentious butterscotch cookies have been popular with Americans for at least 75 years. Folding crushed butterscotch candy into the dough gives these cookies a wonderful crunchy-chewiness.

8 ounces butterscotch hard candy (about 1 generous cup crushed)

1³/₄ cups all-purpose white flour

¹/₂ teaspoon baking soda

¹/₄ teaspoon salt

9¹/₂ tablespoons (1 stick plus 1¹/₂ tablespoons) unsalted butter, slightly softened

²/₃ cup packed light brown sugar

1 large egg

2 teaspoons vanilla extract

³/₄ cup chopped walnuts or pecans

Preheat the oven to 350 degrees F. Lightly grease several baking sheets or coat with nonstick spray. Line the sheets with aluminum foil. Heavily grease the foil or heavily coat with nonstick spray.

Put the candy in a heavy-duty plastic bag or a double layer of regular plastic bags. Using a kitchen mallet or a large, heavy spoon, pound the candy until finely cracked; some ¹/₈-to-¹/₄-inch bits can remain, but most should be very fine.

In a medium bowl, thoroughly stir together the flour, baking soda, and salt; set aside. In a large bowl, with an electric mixer on medium speed, beat together the butter and brown sugar until well blended and fluffy. Add the egg and vanilla and beat until evenly incorporated. Add the candy pieces and beat for 1 minute more. Beat or stir in the flour mixture and walnuts or pecans just until evenly incorporated. Drop the dough onto the baking sheets by heaping measuring tablespoonfuls, spacing about 3 inches apart.

Bake the cookies, one sheet at a time, in the upper third of the oven for 8 to 11 minutes, or until golden on top and slightly darker at the edges; be careful not to overbake. Reverse the sheet from front to back halfway through baking to ensure even browning. Transfer the sheet to a wire rack and let stand until completely cooled; very carefully peel the cookies from the foil.

Store in a single layer or layered with wax paper in an airtight container for up to 2 weeks or freeze for up to 2 months.

cornmeal sables

Sables (pronounced SAB-blay), meaning "sandies," are classic French butter cookies with a distinctive sandy-crisp texture. Except in the Basque region, where crewmen returning from one of Columbus's voyages are said to have introduced corn several hundred years ago, cornmeal is little used in France. However, this New World ingredient not only accentuates the sandy texture with its slight graininess, but it rounds out the buttery flavor with its gentle, mellow taste. These American sables are reminiscent of rolled shortbread or thick sugar cookies.

1 cup (2 sticks) cold unsalted butter, cut into chunks

2 cups all-purpose white flour

¾ cup yellow or white cornmeal

¾ cup powdered sugar

3 large egg yolks

1½ tablespoons milk

1½ teaspoons vanilla extract

½ cup sugar

⅛ teaspoon salt

In a food processor, combine the butter, flour, cornmeal, and powdered sugar. Process in on/off pulses until the mixture is the consistency of fine crumbs. Turn out the mixture into a large bowl. (Alternatively, in a large bowl, thoroughly stir together the butter, flour, cornmeal, and powdered sugar. Using forks, a pastry blender, or your fingertips, cut in the butter until the mixture is the consistency of fine crumbs.) In a small bowl, beat together the egg yolks, milk, vanilla, sugar, and salt until well blended. Stir, then knead, the egg-yolk mixture into the flour mixture to form a smooth dough. If the dough is too dry, knead in a little water.

Divide the dough in half. Place each portion between large sheets of wax paper. Roll out each portion a generous ⅜ inch thick; check the underside of the dough and smooth out any wrinkles that form. Stack the rolled portions (paper still attached) on a baking sheet. Freeze for 30 minutes, or until chilled and slightly firm. (The dough may be frozen for up to 24 hours; let thaw slightly before using.)

Preheat the oven to 350 degrees F. Grease several baking sheets or coat with nonstick spray.

Working with one portion at a time and leaving the remaining dough chilled, gently peel away, then pat one sheet of wax paper back into place. Flip the dough over, then peel off and discard the second sheet. Using a fluted, scalloped, or plain round 2-inch cutter, cut out the cookies. (If at any point the dough softens too much to handle easily, transfer the paper and cookies to a baking sheet and refrigerate or freeze until firm again.) Using a spatula, carefully transfer the cookies to the baking sheets, spacing about 1 inch apart. Reroll any dough scraps. Continue cutting out the cookies until all the dough is used.

While the cookies are still slightly chilled, bake, one sheet at a time, in the upper third of the oven for 12 to 16 minutes, or until barely colored on top and just slightly darker at the edges. Reverse the sheet from front to back halfway through baking to ensure even browning. Transfer the sheet to a wire rack and let stand until the cookies firm up slightly, 1 to 2 minutes. Using a spatula, transfer the cookies to wire racks. Let stand until completely cooled.

Store in an airtight container for up to 2 weeks or freeze for up to 1 month.

Mrs. Porter's improved jumbles

Makes 30 to 35
(2½-inch) cookies.

Recipes for jumbles (originally jumbals) appeared frequently in eighteenth- and nineteenth-century American cookbooks, though they have almost completely disappeared from the scene today. Dating at least to early-seventeenth-century Europe and brought to this country by colonists, they are a good example of how recipes are transferred and adapted from one culture to another and may go in and out of favor over time. Nineteenth-century American jumble recipes often called for shaping the dough into rings by forming it into little ropes and pinching them together at the ends.

These jumbles are appealingly crisp, well flavored (from an uncharacteristically generous amount of butter), and faintly fragrant with nutmeg. Mrs. M. E. Porter, who created them, noted in her 1871 *New Southern Cookery Book* that these are "very delicate, will keep a long time, and are a decided improvement on the old sorts." Other than halving the batch and converting the quantities from pounds to cups, I've left this outstanding old receipt alone.

Most jumbles were not decorated in Mrs. Porter's day, but during the holidays, I like to capitalize on the ring shape and turn them into colorful wreath cookies, using some green and red powdered-sugar icings. Presented this way, they make a tempting seasonal gift. For an easier, yet elegant, decorating touch, use homemade colored sugar when you shape the cookies.

2¼ cups all-purpose white flour
1 teaspoon freshly grated nutmeg or ¾ teaspoon ground nutmeg
¼ teaspoon salt
1 cup (2 sticks) unsalted butter, just slightly softened

⅔ cup sugar
1 large egg plus 1 large egg yolk

About ¼ cup sugar or Colored Decorating Sugars (page 375), for shaping cookies

Preheat the oven to 350 degrees F. Grease several baking sheets or coat with nonstick spray.

In a medium bowl, thoroughly stir together the flour, nutmeg, and salt; set aside. In a large bowl, with an electric mixer on medium speed, beat together the butter and sugar until light and well blended. Beat in the egg and egg yolk until evenly incorporated. Beat or stir in the flour mixture until evenly incorporated; the dough will be slightly soft. If the dough is too soft to handle, let stand for 10 minutes, or until firmed up slightly.

Tip
The butter should be just barely softened for this recipe. Otherwise, the dough will be too warm and soft to shape without chilling.

Sprinkle a work surface with sugar or colored sugar. With lightly greased hands, pull off pieces of dough the size of walnuts—generous 1-inch balls. Roll each ball back and forth between your palms to form an evenly thick 2-inch-long rope. Lay the rope on the work surface and roll back and forth until it is about 5 inches long. Bring the ends of each rope together and press firmly to create a ring. Place on the baking sheets, spacing about 1½ inches apart. Sprinkle the work surface with more sugar, as needed.

Bake the cookies, one sheet at a time, in the upper third of the oven for 10 to 14 minutes, or until almost firm on top and lightly browned at the edges. Reverse the sheet from front to back halfway through baking to ensure even browning. Transfer the sheet to a wire rack and let stand until the cookies firm up, about 5 minutes. Using a spatula, transfer the cookies to wire racks. Let stand until completely cooled.

Store the cookies in an airtight container for up to 3 weeks or freeze for up to 2 months.

VARIATION Holiday Wreath Jumbles

To keep the decorated jumbles from being too sweet, do not sprinkle the work surface with sugar. Instead, lightly oil the work surface or coat with nonstick spray. Shape and bake the jumbles as directed.

In a small bowl, stir together 1½ cups powdered sugar and 1½ table-spoons water until smooth and well blended. If the icing is too stiff to stir, add a few more drops of water, but keep the consistency stiff though very smooth. Transfer about 2 tablespoons of the icing to a small cup. Stir enough red food coloring into the smaller amount to yield a berry red shade (paste coloring works best, but liquid coloring can be used). Add enough green food coloring to the remaining icing to yield an ever-green shade. If necessary, adjust the icing consistency; it needs to be stiff enough to hold its shape when piped, but just soft enough to go through a fine piping tip.

Spoon each icing in a paper cone or a small pastry bag fitted with a fine writing tip. Using the green icing, pipe fine, closely spaced zigzag lines horizontally all the way around each ring to suggest the wreath greens. Then randomly pipe small clusters of red dots on the wreath to suggest berries. Let stand until the icing completely sets, about 1 hour.

A JUMBLED HISTORY

Early forerunners of these sweets were shaped into double rings or knots. The word *jumble* comes from Latin. Originally spelled *jom-bil* or *jumbal*, it was related to *gemel*, which means twin, and *gimbel*, an unusual double-ringed finger ring sometimes worn during the period. Somewhere along the way, the two circlets turned into a single ring, but the name continued on. Since the cookies were named for their shape and not for their ingredients, jumbles came in many flavors—almond, coconut, spice, anise, caraway, and lemon were especially common.

Lemon Jumbles

These crisp, slightly buttery sugar cookies make a festive and somewhat unusual addition to a cookie tray, particularly if they are dipped in glaze.

Since rolling dough into the characteristic ring shape of the seventeenth and eighteenth century was a bit time-consuming, by the late nineteenth century, some cooks took shortcuts by simply rolling out the dough, cutting it into thick rounds, and punching away a smaller center hole (as for doughnuts). Gradually, the convention of the ring shape began to fade, and some jumbles were simply rolled out and cut into solid rounds. Such was the case with the following recipe, which is roughly based on one in the 1879 book *Housekeeping in Old Virginia,* edited by Marion Cabell Tyree. Today, only culinary historians seem aware of the early convention.

I like the idea of jumbles having a hole in the middle—that was why they were called jumbles, after all—so I've gone back to hand-shaping the rings. The dough is easy to work with, which makes the task go quickly. Moreover, this shaping gives the finished cookies an appealing handmade look. However, if you wish to roll and cut out plain rounds as called for in Mrs. Tyree's version, I've given alternative directions.

2¾ cups all-purpose white flour

1 teaspoon cream of tartar

½ teaspoon baking soda

¼ teaspoon salt

1 cup (2 sticks) unsalted butter, slightly softened

Scant 1 cup sugar

1 large egg

Generous 1 tablespoon finely grated lemon zest (colored part of the skin)

1 tablespoon fresh lemon juice

1 teaspoon almond extract (optional)

GLAZE (OPTIONAL)

1½ cups powdered sugar

1 tablespoon unsalted butter, very warm but not melted

1–2 tablespoons fresh lemon juice, at room temperature or slightly warm

½ teaspoon light corn syrup

2 drops almond extract (optional)

1–2 drops yellow liquid food coloring (optional)

2 tablespoons chopped, sliced, or slivered unblanched or blanched almonds, for topping (optional)

Preheat the oven to 350 degrees F. Grease several baking sheets or coat with nonstick spray.

In a large bowl, thoroughly stir together the flour, cream of tartar, baking soda, and salt; set aside. In another large bowl, with an electric mixer on medium speed, beat together the butter, sugar, egg, lemon zest, lemon juice, and almond extract (if preparing lemon-almond jumbles) until light and well blended. Beat or stir in the flour mixture until evenly incorporated.

Gather up the dough and shape it into a ball. Cut it into quarters. Shape each quarter into a flat disk. Score each disk into quarters, then cut into 12 wedges. Roll each wedge between your palms or on a work surface to form an evenly thick 4½-to-5-inch-long rope. Bring the ends of each rope together and press firmly to create a ring. Place on the baking sheets, spacing about 1¼ inches apart.

Bake the cookies, one sheet at a time, in the middle third of the oven for 8 to 12 minutes, or until just faintly browned at the edges. Reverse the

sugar cookies and shortbreads

sheet from front to back halfway through baking to ensure even browning. Using a spatula, immediately transfer the cookies to wire racks. Let stand until completely cooled.

FOR THE GLAZE, IF USING

In a small bowl, stir together the powdered sugar, butter, 2 to 3 teaspoons lemon juice, corn syrup, almond extract (if preparing lemon-almond jumbles), and food coloring, if using, until smooth and well blended. Thin the mixture with enough additional lemon juice to produce a thin glaze. Set the wire racks with the cookies over wax paper to catch drips. Dip the top of each cookie into the glaze; shake off the excess. If preparing lemon-almond jumbles, immediately sprinkle a few bits of almond over the glaze. Let stand until the glaze completely sets, about 1 hour.

Store in an airtight container for up to 2 weeks or freeze for up to 2 months.

FOR PLAIN ROLLED JUMBLES

Divide the dough in half. Place each portion between large sheets of wax paper. Roll out each portion ⅜ inch thick; check the underside of the dough and smooth out any wrinkles that form. Stack the rolled portions (paper still attached) on a baking sheet. Refrigerate for 45 minutes, or until chilled and firm, or freeze for 25 minutes to speed chilling.

Working with one portion at a time and leaving the remaining dough chilled, gently peel away, then pat one sheet of wax paper back into place. Flip the dough over, then peel off and discard the second sheet. Using a 2-to-2½-inch round cutter, cut out the cookies. (If at any point the dough softens too much to handle easily, transfer the paper and cookies to a baking sheet and refrigerate or freeze until firm again.) Reroll any dough scraps. Continue cutting out the cookies until all the dough is used. Note that the yield and baking time will vary depending on the cutter used.

TIP

Once the cookies are glazed, add a little food coloring to the leftover icing to intensify the hue just slightly. Then pipe or drizzle random zigzagged lines across the cookie tops for an easy but effective contrasting garnish.

MRS. Lee's ROLLed shortbread cookies

It's surprising that a cookie this good isn't in every modern American cookie baker's repertoire. It is rolled and cut out like an ordinary sugar cookie but is richer and more tender, with an outstanding buttery shortbread taste. And although the mixing method is not typical for either sugar cookies or classic shortbread, the recipe is just as undemanding to make.

The cookie comes from an 1832 work, *The Cook's Own Book,* a 2,500-recipe tome by "A Boston Housekeeper" named Mrs. N. K. M. Lee. As she noted on her title page, Mrs. Lee collected most of the recipes from several other cookbooks of the time.

The original dough for these "sugar cakes" was too rich, although removing just 2 tablespoons of butter solved this problem. As was typical in that era, the original receipt relied on rose water for flavoring. I've substituted vanilla extract, which is readily available and more appealing to modern tastes.

2 cups all-purpose white flour	1 large egg yolk
²/₃ cup sugar	1¹/₂ tablespoons light cream
³/₄ cup plus 2 tablespoons (1³/₄ sticks) cold unsalted butter, cut into chunks	2 teaspoons vanilla extract
	¹/₄ teaspoon salt

In a large bowl, thoroughly stir together the flour and sugar. Using forks, a pastry blender, or your fingertips, cut the butter into the flour mixture until the mixture is the consistency of coarse meal. In a small bowl, beat together the egg yolk, cream, vanilla, and salt with a fork until well blended and smooth. Stir, then knead, the egg-yolk mixture into the flour mixture until evenly incorporated.

Divide the dough in half. Place each portion between large sheets of wax paper. Roll out each portion ¼ inch thick; check the underside of the dough and smooth out any wrinkles that form. Stack the rolled portions (paper still attached) on a baking sheet. Refrigerate for 30 minutes, or until chilled and firm, or freeze for about 15 minutes to speed chilling.

Preheat the oven to 325 degrees F. Grease several baking sheets or coat with nonstick spray.

Working with one portion at a time and leaving the remaining dough chilled, gently peel away, then pat one sheet of wax paper back into place. Flip the dough over, then peel off and discard the second sheet. Using a 2½-inch fluted round cutter or other desired shape, cut out the cookies. (If at any point the dough softens too much to handle easily, transfer the paper and cookies to a baking sheet and refrigerate or freeze until firm again.) Using a spatula, carefully transfer the cookies to the baking sheet, spacing about 1¼ inches apart. Reroll any dough scraps. Continue cutting out the cookies until all the dough is used.

Bake the cookies, one sheet at a time, in the middle third of the oven for 9 to 13 minutes, or until just lightly browned at the edges. Reverse the sheet from front to back halfway through baking to ensure even browning. Using a spatula, immediately transfer the cookies to wire racks. Let stand until completely cooled.

Store in an airtight container for up to 2 weeks or freeze for up to 2 months.

carolina stamped shortbread

North Carolina has a significant ethnic Scottish population, thanks in part to the large-scale deportations that occurred after rebellions were put down in Scotland in 1745 and 1746. During the Clearings, inhabitants were rounded up and forcibly shipped to the New World. A considerable number of Scots arrived at the port of Wilmington, North Carolina, and eventually moved west and settled the state. Ties to the homeland have always remained, however, and today, many Scottish Tarheels still enjoy making traditional shortbread.

This fine recipe was shared with me years ago by a coworker in Raleigh, North Carolina. Although it's fairly typical for Scottish shortbread rounds to be stamped with a thistle design using a large, hand-carved wooden mold, this Americanized recipe calls for an unusual shaping and stamping method. First, the dough is rolled and cut out just as for sugar cookies, instead of being baked in one large round as Scottish versions often are. More important, the cookies are stamped after they have been in the oven a few minutes instead of prior to baking, as is usually done. Stamping after the cookies have begun to set helps keep the imprinted designs clear and sharp, although it does sometimes cause the cookie edges to crack slightly. The cookies are fragrant and tender without being crumbly.

Any of the small, modern ceramic or plastic cookie stamps sold in kitchenware shops will work with these cookies. And if you don't have a stamp, you can improvise by pressing in the design from a cut-glass vase or bowl; the starburst pattern etched into the bottom of some bowls and drinking glasses produces a particularly pretty design.

1¹/₂ cups (3 sticks) unsalted butter, slightly softened

1 cup powdered sugar

²/₃ cup cornstarch

2 tablespoons sugar

Scant ¹/₂ teaspoon salt

1¹/₂ teaspoons vanilla extract

2³/₄ cups all-purpose white flour

In a large bowl, with an electric mixer on low, then medium, speed, beat together the butter, powdered sugar, cornstarch, sugar, salt, and vanilla until light and well blended, about 3 minutes. Beat or stir in the flour until evenly incorporated. Let the dough stand for 5 minutes, or until firmed up slightly.

Divide the dough in half. Place each portion between large sheets of wax paper. Roll out each portion ¹/₃ inch thick; check the underside of the dough, and smooth out any wrinkles that form. Stack the rolled portions (paper still attached) on a baking sheet. Refrigerate for 30 minutes or until chilled and firm, or freeze for 20 minutes to speed chilling.

Preheat the oven to 300 degrees F. Set out several baking sheets.

Working with one portion at a time and leaving the remaining dough chilled, gently peel away, then pat one sheet of wax paper back into place. Flip the dough over, then peel off and discard the second sheet. Using a 2½-to-2¾-inch fluted, daisy, or plain round cutter or other desired size or shape needed to accommodate the stamp used, cut out the cookies. (If at any point the dough softens too much to handle easily, transfer the paper and cookies to a baking sheet and refrigerate or freeze until firm again.) Using a spatula, carefully transfer the cookies to the baking sheets, spacing about 1½ inches apart. Reroll any dough scraps. Continue cutting out the cookies until all the dough is used.

Bake the cookies, one sheet at a time, in the upper third of the oven for 10 minutes. Remove the cookies from the oven. Using a cookie stamp, press a design into the top of each cookie. Return the cookies to the oven and bake for 15 to 20 minutes more, or until just tinged with color all over and faintly darker at the edges. Reverse the sheet from front to back halfway through baking to ensure even browning. Transfer the sheet to a wire rack and let stand until the cookies firm up, about 10 minutes. Using a spatula, transfer the cookies to wire racks. Let stand until completely cooled.

If desired, the designs stamped into the cookies can be highlighted by painting with a color wash (see page 331).

Store in an airtight container for up to 2 weeks or freeze for up to 2 months.

VARIATION Molded Shortbread

An 8-inch-diameter or similar ceramic shortbread mold—designed for actually baking in rather than just imprinting a design—requires half a recipe of dough. (You can use the remaining dough half by baking in the mold twice. Or bake the other half in an 8-inch square baking pan or use it for making individual stamped shortbreads as directed above.) After the dough is prepared, divide it in half; reserve one half for another purpose. Press the dough evenly into the mold. Lay a sheet of wax paper on the dough, then press out the dough to form a very smooth, even layer.

Refrigerate for 30 minutes, or until chilled and firm. Peel off and discard the paper.

Preheat the oven to 300 degrees F.

Bake the shortbread in the middle of the oven for 55 to 65 minutes, or until just pale golden all over and faintly darker at the edges. Reverse the mold from front to back halfway through baking to ensure even browning. Transfer the mold to a wire rack and let stand until cooled to barely warm. Gently tip the shortbread out of the mold and transfer it, imprinted side up, to a cutting board. Using a large, sharp knife, cut the shortbread into portions using the imprinted design as a guide.

VARIATION Shortbread Fingers

Preheat the oven to 300 degrees F. Set out a 9-by-13-inch baking dish.

Pat and press the dough into a rough layer in the baking dish. Lay a sheet of wax paper on the dough, then press out the dough to form a very smooth, even layer. Refrigerate for 30 minutes, or until chilled and firm. Peel off and discard the paper. Using a large, sharp knife, cut the dough crosswise into quarters and lengthwise into eighths. Using a fork, prick the dough all over in an attractive pattern.

Bake the shortbread in the middle of the oven for 60 to 75 minutes, or until just pale golden all over and faintly darker at the edges. Reverse the baking dish from front to back halfway through baking to ensure even browning. Transfer the baking dish to a wire rack and let stand until cooled to warm. Using a large, sharp knife, retrace the cuts previously made. Let stand until completely cooled before removing the bars from the pan.

For a decorative touch, you can dip the ends of the shortbread fingers into melted chocolate. Store in the refrigerator.

TIP
The dough can also be baked in a modern ceramic shortbread mold or a flat, rectangular pan and cut into fingers. See the alternative directions at the end of the recipe.

vanilla
shortbread
domes

These rich, tender, not-too-sweet shortbread domes are quickly and easily hand-shaped or scooped into balls instead of being rolled out as most shortbreads are. They have a pleasant, understated appearance, a mellow vanilla-butter taste, and a meltingly tender texture. The inspiration for them came from a sophisticated little cookie called Vanilla Bean Shortbread Domes, which I recently sampled at the City Bakery in Manhattan.

1½ cups all-purpose white flour
½ cup plus 1 tablespoon powdered sugar
¼ cup cornstarch
¼ teaspoon salt
1 cup (2 sticks) cold unsalted butter, cut into chunks

1 2½-to-3-inch-long vanilla bean, split in half lengthwise
1½ teaspoons vanilla extract

About 2 tablespoons powdered sugar, for topping (tossed with the scraped vanilla bean for a few minutes, if desired)

Preheat the oven to 325 degrees F. Set out two baking sheets.

In a food processor, combine the flour, powdered sugar, cornstarch, and salt. Process in on/off pulses to blend. Sprinkle the butter chunks over the flour mixture. Using a paring knife, scrape out all the pulp from the vanilla bean and add the pulp and the vanilla extract to the flour mixture. Process in on/off pulses until the mixture is just evenly blended and smooth, stopping and stirring to redistribute the contents several times, if necessary. If the dough seems too soft too handle, let it stand for 5 to 10 minutes, or until firmed up slightly.

Shape portions of the dough into generous 1-inch balls with lightly greased hands, or scoop it into neat 1-inch balls with a small ice cream scoop. Place on the baking sheets, spacing about 2 inches apart.

Place the cookies on separate racks in the middle of the oven for 11 minutes; switch the position of the sheets and continue baking for 10 to 12 minutes more, or until the cookies are faintly colored on top and browned at the edges. Using a spatula, immediately transfer the cookies to wire racks. Let stand until completely cooled. Sift powdered sugar over the cookie tops; use a light to heavy hand, depending on the amount of sweetness desired.

Store in an airtight container for up to 1 week or freeze for up to 1 month. If freezing, dust the cookies with powdered sugar after they have completely thawed.

TIP
If you don't have a vanilla bean, these cookies are still well worth making (though slightly less fragrant, of course). Just increase the vanilla extract to 2 teaspoons.

marguerites

Recipes for these frosted Victorian-era cookies circulated from the latter half of the nineteenth century to the early twentieth century. *Miss Leslie's New Cookery Book,* published by Philadelphia author Eliza Leslie in 1857, included a general description of how to make them, calling them "Marmalade Meringues." Later, three very similar recipes turned up in the 1879 cookbook *Housekeeping in Old Virginia* under the name "Marguerites."

Recipes for marguerites involve preparing round sugar cookies, spreading their tops with a layer of marmalade, and encasing each in a fluffy meringue frosting. (The frosted cookies look rather like miniature cakes.) The marguerites are then returned to the oven briefly to firm up the meringue. The cookie bases are fairly good keepers, but once the marmalade and frosting are added, the marguerites should be eaten within a day or so.

These have a romantic, old-fashioned appearance and are pretty for a spring garden party, shower, tea, or little girl's birthday party.

3 cups all-purpose white flour

½ teaspoon salt

¼ teaspoon ground cinnamon

¼ teaspoon ground nutmeg or mace

1 cup (2 sticks) unsalted butter, slightly softened

1 cup sugar

3 large egg yolks, at room temperature

½ teaspoon finely grated lemon zest (colored part of the skin)

MERINGUE FROSTING

3 large egg whites, free of yolk and at room temperature

½ teaspoon fresh lemon juice

2½ cups powdered sugar, sifted after measuring, if lumpy

About ⅓ cup orange marmalade or apricot preserves

Preheat the oven to 375 degrees F. Grease several baking sheets or coat with nonstick spray.

In a large bowl, thoroughly stir together the flour, salt, cinnamon, and nutmeg or mace; set aside. In another large bowl, with an electric mixer on medium speed, beat together the butter and sugar until light and well blended. In another bowl, with an electric mixer on high speed, beat the egg yolks and 3 tablespoons warm water until light colored and thickened, 2 to 3 minutes. Beat the egg-yolk mixture and lemon zest into the butter mixture until well blended and smooth. Gradually beat or stir in the flour mixture until evenly incorporated.

Divide the dough in half. Place each portion between large sheets of wax paper. Roll out each portion ⅓ inch thick; check the underside of the dough and smooth out any wrinkles that form. Working with one portion at a time, gently peel away, then pat one sheet of wax paper back into place. Flip the dough over, then peel off and discard the second sheet. Using a 2-inch round cutter, cut out the cookies. (If at any point the dough softens too much to handle easily, transfer the paper and cookies to a baking sheet and refrigerate or freeze until firm again.) Using a spatula, carefully transfer the cookies to the baking sheets, spacing about 1¼ inches apart. Reroll any dough scraps. Continue cutting out the cookies until all the dough is used.

Bake the cookies, one sheet at a time, in the upper third of the oven for 8 to 12 minutes, or until faintly colored on top and just slightly darker at the edges. Reverse the sheet from front to back halfway through baking to ensure even browning. Transfer the sheet to a wire rack and let stand until the cookies firm up slightly, 1 to 2 minutes. Using a spatula, transfer the cookies to wire racks. Let stand until completely cooled.

FOR THE FROSTING
In a large bowl, with an electric mixer on low speed, beat the egg whites, lemon juice, and powdered sugar until blended. Increase the speed to high and beat for 2 to 3 minutes more, or until the mixture is glossy and stiffened.

Preheat the oven to 325 degrees F. Grease several baking sheets or coat with nonstick spray.

Thinly spread the cookie tops with a layer of marmalade or preserves. Spread the cookies with frosting, using enough to completely cover their sides. Place the cookies on the baking sheets, spacing about 1 inch apart. Bake for 8 to 11 minutes, or until the frosting is just tinged with brown. If desired, fix a candied violet or rose petal in place on the top of each marguerite using a dab of frosting "glue" created by stirring together a little powdered sugar and water. Let stand for at least 15 minutes before serving.

Store the cookie bases in an airtight container for up to 10 days or freeze for up to 1 month. Once frosted, the marguerites should be eaten within 2 days. Store the frosted cookies in a single layer in an airtight container.

TIP
For a decorative touch, top each marguerite with a candied violet or a tiny fresh or candied rose petal. These should be added after the meringue layer has been baked.

Apricot sandwich tea cakes

Makes 35 to 40
(2½-inch)
sandwich cookies.

This old-fashioned southern tea cake is gussied up by sandwiching pairs of cookies around apricot preserves or jam. The cookies are a nice choice for the sandwiches because they look attractive and their distinctive fruit flavor goes well with the apricot filling. Since the cookies gradually absorb the moisture from the preserves and become soft, it's best not to assemble the sandwiches more than 24 hours ahead. The cookies can be readied well in advance, however.

3 cups all-purpose white flour

½ teaspoon baking soda

1 cup plus 2 tablespoons (2¼ sticks) cold unsalted butter, cut into chunks

2 large egg yolks

2 tablespoons peach or apricot brandy or schnapps, *or* orange juice, if preferred

2 teaspoons vanilla extract

1 teaspoon almond extract

⅔ cup sugar

1 teaspoon finely grated lemon zest (colored part of the skin)

½ teaspoon finely grated orange zest (colored part of the skin)

¼ teaspoon salt

Generous ¾ cup apricot preserves or jam, processed in a food processor or chopped by hand, if chunky

In a food processor, combine the flour and baking soda. Process in on/off pulses to blend. Sprinkle the butter chunks over the flour mixture. Process in on/off pulses until the mixture is the consistency of fine crumbs. Turn out the mixture into a large bowl. (Alternatively, in a large bowl, thoroughly stir together the flour and baking soda. With forks, a pastry blender, or your fingertips, cut in the butter until the mixture is the consistency of fine crumbs.)

In a medium bowl, using a fork, beat together the egg yolks, brandy or orange juice, vanilla, almond extract, sugar, lemon and orange zests, and salt until well blended. Stir, then knead, the egg-yolk mixture into the flour mixture until evenly incorporated. If the dough seems dry, add up to 2 tablespoons water a bit at a time and continue kneading until evenly incorporated.

Divide the dough in half. Place each portion between large sheets of wax paper. Roll out each portion ⅛ inch thick; check the underside of the dough and smooth out any wrinkles that form. Stack the rolled portions (paper still attached) on a baking sheet. Freeze for 15 minutes, or until chilled and slightly firm.

Preheat the oven to 350 degrees F. Grease several baking sheets or coat with nonstick spray.

Working with one portion at a time and leaving the remaining dough chilled, gently peel away, then pat one sheet of wax paper back into place. Flip the dough over, then peel off and discard the second sheet. Using a fluted, scalloped, or plain round 2¼-inch cutter, cut out the cookies. Using a mini cutter, the larger end of a pastry piping tip, or a thimble, cut away a small circle, heart, oval, or other decorative shape from the center of half of the cookies. (If at any point the dough softens too much to handle easily, transfer the paper and cookies to a baking sheet and refrigerate or freeze until firm again.) Using a spatula, carefully transfer the cookies to the baking sheets, spacing about 1 inch apart; place the solid rounds on one sheet and the rounds with the cutaway centers on another. Reroll any dough scraps. Continue cutting out the cookies until all the dough is used.

Bake the cookies, one sheet at a time, in the upper third of the oven for 8 to 12 minutes, or until just slightly colored on top and slightly darker at the edges. Reverse the sheet from front to back halfway through baking to ensure even browning. The cookies with the cutaways will bake faster than the solid ones, so watch carefully to avoid burning. Transfer the sheet to a wire rack and let stand until the cookies firm up slightly, 1 to 2 minutes. Using a spatula, transfer the cookies to wire racks. Let stand until completely cooled.

Spread about 1 teaspoon of the preserves or jam on the underside of each cookie bottom. Center the tops over the bottoms. Very lightly press down until the preserves or jam shows through the cutaway tops.

Store in an airtight container for up to 1 week. The cookies can be frozen for up to 2 months but should not be filled and sandwiched together until shortly before serving.

TIP
Cutting away the centers from the sandwich tops and letting the preserves show through makes a pretty presentation with relatively little fuss. The "cakes" will look even fancier if the wafers are cut out using a small fluted, scalloped, or daisy cutter.

jam jewels

These exceptionally tender and appealing thumbprint cookies are decorated with dabs of assorted colorful jams in the center and, if you like, with bits of pistachios and almonds as well. The cookies look wonderfully festive and jewel-like but are actually easy to prepare.

2¼ cups all-purpose white flour

Scant ½ teaspoon baking soda

¼ teaspoon baking powder

¼ teaspoon salt

1 cup (2 sticks) unsalted butter, slightly softened

Scant 1 cup powdered sugar

1 large egg yolk

1 3-ounce package cream cheese, slightly softened and cut into chunks

1½ teaspoons vanilla extract

1 teaspoon finely grated lemon zest (colored part of the skin)

About ⅔ cup (about 2¾ ounces) chopped pistachios or chopped slivered almonds, or a combination, for topping (optional)

Assorted seedless jams, such as cherry, plum, raspberry, blackberry, and apricot, for topping

Preheat the oven to 350 degrees F. Grease several baking sheets or coat with nonstick spray.

In a medium bowl, thoroughly stir together the flour, baking soda, baking powder, and salt; set aside. In a large bowl, with an electric mixer on medium speed, beat together the butter, sugar, and egg yolk until fluffy and well blended. Beat in the cream cheese, vanilla, and lemon zest until evenly incorporated. Beat or stir in the flour mixture until well blended and smooth. Let stand for 5 to 10 minutes, or until the dough firms up just slightly.

Shape portions of the dough into scant 1-inch balls with lightly greased hands. Dip the tops of the balls into the pistachios or almonds, if using. Place, nut side up, on the baking sheets, spacing about 1½ inches apart. Using your thumb or knuckle, press a deep well into the center of each ball. Place about ¼ teaspoon jam in each well.

Bake the cookies, one sheet at a time, in the upper third of the oven for 9 to 12 minutes, or until the cookies are tinged with brown at the edges. Reverse the sheet halfway through baking to ensure even browning. Transfer the sheet to a wire rack and let stand until the cookies firm up slightly, 2 to 3 minutes. Using a spatula, transfer the cookies to wire

tip

Be sure to fill the cookie indentations with jam or preserves, not jelly. Most jellies are too thin and will bubble over and run during baking.

racks. Let stand until completely cooled. Wipe off the sheets and re-grease them before reusing.

Store in an airtight container for up to 2 weeks or freeze for up to 2 months.

3

Chocolate and White Chocolate Chip Cookies

classic chocolate chip cookies

Makes 45 to 50
(2½-to-2¾-inch)
cookies.

This is the cookie that launched a thousand chips! It was devised in 1930, in Whitman, Massachusetts, when Mrs. Ruth Wakefield discovered she was out of nuts and added some chopped chocolate to a cookie dough. She assumed the chocolate pieces would melt, but instead they remained as intact, munchable bits. Since Mrs. Wakefield and her husband owned the Toll House Inn in Whitman, she dubbed her creation the "Toll House Chocolate Crunch Cookie."

Mrs. Wakefield's chocolate-studded cookies became so popular around the country that the Nestlé company began manufacturing prescored chocolate bars so cooks could conveniently break them into small pieces for cookie baking. In 1939, Nestlé bought the rights to Mrs. Wakefield's creation and came up with an even more appealing solution— little packages containing the first ready-to-use chocolate morsels and the "authentic" Toll House cookie recipe.

Today, chocolate chip cookies are far and away America's favorite; we eat an estimated several billion of them annually. (Which means that, over the years, this cookie has actually launched trillions of chips!) In honor of the phenomenal success, Massachusetts has declared the Toll House cookie its state cookie.

The following recipe is very close to Mrs. Wakefield's original. I have doubled the vanilla extract to 2 teaspoons and omitted the 1 teaspoon of water she called for. I've also changed the proportions of brown sugar and sugar slightly because I like a more prominent brown-sugar taste. I make the cookies twice as large as Ruth Wakefield did, though mine are still not big by modern standards. (She dropped the dough by teaspoonfuls and said the recipe yielded 100 cookies!) I do follow Mrs. Wakefield's advice on doneness: "They should be brown through, and crispy, not white and hard as I have sometimes seen them."

2¼ cups all-purpose white flour

1 teaspoon baking soda

1 teaspoon salt

1 cup (2 sticks) unsalted butter, slightly softened

¾ cup plus 2 tablespoons packed light brown sugar

½ cup plus 2 tablespoons sugar

2 large eggs

2 teaspoons vanilla extract

2 cups (12 ounces) semisweet chocolate morsels

2 cups (8 ounces) chopped walnuts or pecans (optional)

Preheat the oven to 375 degrees F. Grease several baking sheets or coat with nonstick spray.

In a medium bowl, sift together the flour, baking soda, and salt; set aside. In a large bowl, with an electric mixer on medium speed, beat together the butter, brown sugar, and sugar until well blended and fluffy. Add the eggs and vanilla and beat until evenly incorporated. Stir in the flour mixture, chocolate morsels, and walnuts or pecans, if using, just until evenly incorporated.

Drop the dough onto the baking sheets by heaping measuring tablespoonfuls, spacing about 2 inches apart.

Bake the cookies, one sheet at a time, in the upper third of the oven for 8 to 11 minutes, or until golden brown all over and slightly darker at the edges. Reverse the sheet from front to back halfway through baking to ensure even browning. Transfer the sheet to a wire rack and let stand until the cookies firm up slightly, 1 to 2 minutes. Using a spatula, transfer the cookies to wire racks. Let stand until completely cooled. Let the baking sheets cool between batches to keep the cookies from spreading too much.

Store in an airtight container for up to 2 weeks or freeze for up to 1 month.

words of kitchen wisdom
"All systematic housekeepers will hail the day when some enterprising Yankee or Buckeye girl shall invent a stove or range with a thermometer attached."

–Estelle Woods Wilcox (ed.), *Buckeye Cookery and Practical Housekeeping,* 1880

chocolate and white chocolate chip cookies

chewy chocolate chunk monster cookies

Monster cookies came into fashion in the late 1980s and have been popular with the young—and the hungry—ever since. The idea is to turn out single cookies that pack a four- or five-cookie wallop, perhaps to save people the time previously spent going back for seconds, or perhaps so they can claim they ate only one.

At any rate, these monsters fit with the current spirit of overindulgence; they are nearly 5 inches across and loaded with a whole pound of chocolate chunks. They are also crispy and brown on the edges and chewy everywhere else—just the way many fans think chocolate chip cookies should be.

2¾ cups all-purpose white flour

2 teaspoons cream of tartar

1 teaspoon baking soda

½ teaspoon salt

1 cup (2 sticks) unsalted butter, slightly softened

¾ cup plus 2 tablespoons sugar

¾ cup packed light brown sugar

2½ tablespoons light corn syrup

2 large eggs

2½ teaspoons vanilla extract

2¾ cups (about 16 ounces) semisweet chocolate chunks (divided)

In a large bowl, thoroughly stir together the flour, cream of tartar, baking soda, and salt; set aside. In another large bowl, with an electric mixer on medium speed, beat together the butter, sugar, brown sugar, and corn syrup until well blended and fluffy, about 2 minutes. Add the eggs and vanilla and beat until evenly incorporated. Beat in half of the flour mixture until evenly incorporated. Stir in the remaining flour mixture and a generous 1 cup chocolate chunks until evenly incorporated. Refrigerate the dough for 30 to 40 minutes, or until firm enough to shape into balls. (If necessary, the dough can chill for 1 to 2 hours, but the cookies will spread less and be smaller.) Place the remaining chocolate chunks in a shallow bowl.

Preheat the oven to 350 degrees F. Grease several baking sheets or coat with nonstick spray.

Working on a sheet of wax paper, shape the dough into a disk, then divide it into quarters. Divide each quarter into 5 or 6 equal portions. Shape the portions of dough into balls with lightly greased hands (the dough will be soft). Dip half of each ball into the reserved chocolate

tip

Prepare the cookies with either ready-to-use semisweet chocolate chunks or semisweet chocolate bars chopped into ⅛-to-¼-inch pieces.

chunks to generously embed the top of the cookie with them; don't worry if it looks like too many, as the chunks will disperse as the cookies spread. Place on the baking sheets, chocolate chunk side up, spacing about 4 inches apart. Using your hands, pat down the tops of the balls until flattened.

Bake the cookies, one sheet at a time, in the upper third of the oven for 9 to 12 minutes, or until golden brown at the edges but still slightly soft and underdone in the centers. Reverse the sheet from front to back halfway through baking to ensure even browning. Transfer the sheet to a wire rack and let stand until the cookies firm up slightly, 1 to 2 minutes. Using a spatula, transfer the cookies to wire racks. Let stand until completely cooled. Let the baking sheets cool between batches to keep the cookies from spreading too much.

Store in an airtight container for up to 10 days or freeze for up to 2 months.

NOt
Neiman marcus's
chocolate chip cookies

makes 20 to 24
(3¾-inch)
cookies.

Have you heard the story about the woman who thought she'd bought a $2.50 Neiman Marcus chocolate chip cookie recipe, only to realize the charge on her credit card had been $250 instead? To get even, she supposedly gave out the recipe to everybody she could. So many people have heard the anecdote that it's become an urban legend. Neiman Marcus, however, says the incident never occurred.

Even if it didn't happen, the notion of getting a $250 recipe for nothing is appealing enough to keep the tale alive. The following recipe is not exactly like the one said to be Neiman Marcus's; I've modified it by replacing some of the granulated sugar with brown sugar. But whatever its origin, this is a great cookie—big, thick, chewy-crispy, and well flavored from the ground oats, grated milk chocolate, and an abundance of semisweet chocolate morsels.

2 cups old-fashioned rolled oats

2 cups all-purpose white flour

1 teaspoon baking powder

1 teaspoon baking soda

1/2 teaspoon salt

1 cup (2 sticks) unsalted butter, slightly softened

3/4 cup packed light brown sugar

1/2 cup sugar

2 tablespoons light corn syrup

2 large eggs

2 teaspoons vanilla extract

2 cups (12 ounces) semisweet chocolate morsels

1 3¹/₂-to-4-ounce bar top-quality milk chocolate, coarsely grated or finely chopped

1 cup (4 ounces) chopped walnuts or pecans (optional)

Preheat the oven to 350 degrees F. Grease several baking sheets or coat with nonstick spray.

In a food processor or blender, grind the oats to a very fine powder. (If using a blender, stop the motor and stir the oats several times.) In a large bowl, thoroughly stir together the oats, flour, baking powder, baking soda, and salt; set aside. In another large bowl, with an electric mixer on medium speed, beat the butter until light and fluffy. Add the brown sugar, sugar, and corn syrup and beat until well blended and fluffy. Add the eggs and vanilla and beat until evenly incorporated. Beat in about half of the flour mixture. Beat or stir in the chocolate morsels, grated or chopped chocolate, walnuts or pecans (if using), and remaining flour mixture until evenly incorporated. Let stand for 5 to 10 minutes, or until the dough firms up just slightly.

Divide the dough into quarters. Divide each quarter into 5 or 6 equal portions. Shape them into balls with lightly greased hands. Place on the baking sheets, spacing about 3 inches apart. Using your hands, pat down the balls to 1 inch thick.

Bake the cookies, one sheet at a time, in the upper third of the oven for 9 to 12 minutes, or until tinged with brown and just beginning to firm up in the centers; for very moist cookies, be careful not to overbake. Reverse the sheet from front to back halfway through baking to ensure even browning. Transfer the sheet to a wire rack and let stand until the cookies firm up slightly, 3 to 4 minutes. Using a spatula, transfer the cookies to wire racks. Let stand until completely cooled.

Store in an airtight container for up to 1 week or freeze for up to 1 month.

Toffee-chocolate chip drop cookies

Makes about 30
(2½-to-2¾-inch)
cookies.

Up until the 1990s, if you wanted to add toffee pieces to cookies, you had to buy toffee candy and chop it up yourself. Now, a manufacturer sells bags of small bits.

Though it might seem like gilding the lily, I think the toffee bits are particularly good folded into chocolate chip cookies. They add a hint of butterscotch flavor, plus a slight crunch and chew. In this recipe, they also make the dough more spreadable, which contributes to the appealing tender-crispness of these cookies.

Even hard-core fans of traditional chocolate chip cookies have found this variation difficult to resist.

2 cups all-purpose white flour
Scant ½ teaspoon salt
¼ teaspoon baking soda
1 cup (2 sticks) unsalted butter, slightly softened
2½ tablespoons corn oil or other flavorless vegetable oil

¾ cup packed light brown sugar
⅔ cup packed dark brown sugar
1 large egg
2 teaspoons vanilla extract
1½ cups (9 ounces) semisweet chocolate morsels
½ cup Heath bar or other milk chocolate toffee bits

Preheat the oven to 350 degrees F. Generously grease several baking sheets or coat with nonstick spray.

In a medium bowl, thoroughly stir together the flour, salt, and baking soda; set aside. In a large bowl, with an electric mixer on low, then medium, speed, beat together the butter, oil, and brown sugars until well blended and fluffy, about 2 minutes. Add the egg and vanilla and beat until well blended. Beat or stir in the flour mixture until evenly incorporated. Stir in the chocolate morsels and toffee bits until evenly incorporated.

Drop the dough onto the baking sheets using a ⅛-cup measure or coffee scoop, spacing about 2½ inches apart; keep the portions as round as possible. With oiled fingertips, pat down the cookies slightly.

Bake the cookies, one sheet at a time, in the upper third of the oven for 10 to 12 minutes, or until tinged with brown, slightly darker at the edges, and almost firm when pressed in the centers. Reverse the sheet from front to back halfway through baking to ensure even browning. Transfer the sheet to a wire rack and let stand until the cookies firm up slightly, 3 to 4 minutes. Using a spatula, transfer the cookies to wire racks. Let stand until completely cooled.

Store in an airtight container for up to 1 week or freeze for up to 6 weeks.

words of kitchen wisdom
"It is said that 'good cooks never measure anything.' They do. They measure by judgment and experience; and until *you* have a large share of both these essential qualities, use your spoon and cup or scales."

—Mrs. D .A. Lincoln, *The Boston Cooking-School Cook Book,* 1883

chocolate and white chocolate chip cookies

oregon Hazelnut-chocolate chip cookies

makes about 30 (3-inch) cookies.

This recipe is adapted from one created by my Oregonian friend Lucy Gerspacher, who included it in her *Hazelnuts and More Cookbook.* Lucy was born and raised in America's premier hazelnut-growing region, the Willamette Valley, and there was a hazelnut tree in her family's backyard. When she grew up and married, her first home was in a hazelnut orchard, which she admits she took for granted until she moved away.

Lucy's cookies are crispy like typical chocolate chip cookies, but ground and chopped toasted hazelnuts give them a distinctive nutty flavor. This isn't your mother's classic recipe, but the cookies are just as terrific in their own way.

Hazelnuts are not often called for in early American cookbooks or in our old-fashioned cookie recipes. Native hazelnut trees produced only small nuts with thick shells and rough-textured husks. The more productive, thinner-shelled European type was introduced to the Willamette Valley in 1876, when a French settler named David Grenot planted 50 trees. Apparently, the valley afforded ideal growing conditions, because it now provides nearly the entire U.S. hazelnut crop.

1 1/3 cups (about 7 ounces) whole hazelnuts

2 cups all-purpose white flour

1/2 teaspoon baking powder

1/4 teaspoon baking soda

Generous 1/4 teaspoon salt

1/2 cup (1 stick) unsalted butter, slightly softened

1/2 cup white vegetable shortening

2/3 cup packed light brown sugar

1/2 cup sugar

1 large egg

2 tablespoons milk

2 teaspoons vanilla extract

1 cup (6 ounces) semisweet chocolate morsels

Preheat the oven to 350 degrees F. Grease several baking sheets or coat with nonstick spray.

Spread the hazelnuts in a small baking pan and toast in the oven, stirring occasionally, for 15 to 19 minutes, or until the hulls loosen and the nuts are lightly browned; be careful not to burn. Immediately turn out into a small bowl and let stand until cool enough to handle. Rub the hazelnuts between your hands or in a clean kitchen towel, loosening and discarding as much hull as possible. By hand, chop half the nuts moderately fine; set aside. In a food processor, process the remaining nuts in on/off pulses until ground to a powder but not clumped together or oily looking.

In a large bowl, thoroughly stir together the flour, ground hazelnuts, baking powder, baking soda, and salt; set aside. In another large bowl, with an electric mixer on medium speed, beat together the butter and shortening until light and well blended. Add the brown sugar and sugar and beat until fluffy and smooth. Add the egg, milk, and vanilla and beat until evenly incorporated. Beat or stir in the flour mixture, then the chopped hazelnuts and chocolate morsels, until evenly incorporated.

Using an ice cream scoop or spoons, drop the dough onto the baking sheets in golf-ball-sized mounds, spacing about 3½ inches apart. Using lightly greased hands, slightly pat down the tops of the mounds until flat.

Bake the cookies, one sheet at a time, in the upper third of the oven for 9 to 12 minutes, or until the tops are golden, the edges are lightly browned, and they are still slightly soft when pressed in the centers. Reverse the sheet from front to back halfway through baking to ensure even browning. Transfer the sheet to a wire rack and let stand until the cookies firm up slightly, 2 to 3 minutes. Using a spatula, transfer the cookies to wire racks. Let stand until completely cooled.

Store in an airtight container for up to 1 week or freeze for up to 1 month.

chocolate chip iceboxcookies

These are simple, convenient, and very, very good. They have not only a nice flavor but an outstanding, tender-crisp texture. Make the dough up to two months ahead. Then, for great homemade chocolate chip cookies in about 15 minutes, remove from the freezer, slice, and bake.

1²/₃ cups all-purpose white flour

1¹/₂ teaspoons baking powder

¹/₄ teaspoon salt

¹/₂ cup (1 stick) unsalted butter, slightly softened

¹/₄ cup corn oil or other flavorless vegetable oil

¹/₃ cup packed light brown sugar

¹/₃ cup sugar

1 large egg

2 teaspoons vanilla extract

1 cup (6 ounces) semisweet chocolate minimorsels

³/₄ cup (about 3 ounces) finely chopped walnuts or pecans (optional)

In a medium bowl, thoroughly stir together the flour, baking powder, and salt; set aside. In a large bowl, with an electric mixer on medium speed, beat together the butter, oil, brown sugar, and sugar until fluffy and well blended. Add the egg and vanilla and beat until evenly incorporated. Beat or stir in the flour mixture, then the chocolate morsels and walnuts or pecans, if using, until evenly incorporated.

Spoon half of the dough onto a sheet of wax paper, forming a rough log about 7 inches long. Repeat with the second dough portion. Smooth the wax paper around the dough to help form the logs. Refrigerate the dough for 30 to 40 minutes, or until firmed up and easier to handle. Re-shape the logs, smoothing them further. Roll the logs up in sheets of plastic wrap, twisting the ends to keep the wrap from unrolling. Freeze the logs until completely frozen, at least 3 hours. Bake immediately, or transfer to an airtight plastic bag and freeze for up to 2 months.

Preheat the oven to 375 degrees F. Grease several baking sheets or coat with nonstick spray.

Carefully peel the plastic wrap from a dough log. Using a large, sharp knife, cut crosswise into generous ¼-inch-thick slices; due to the morsels, the dough won't cut neatly, so it may be necessary to pat and smooth the slices back into shape. Using a spatula, carefully transfer the slices to the baking sheets, spacing about 2 inches apart. If desired, repeat with the second log, or save it to bake another time.

tip

Be sure to use chocolate mini-morsels — regular morsels make the frozen dough too difficult to slice.

Bake the cookies, one sheet at a time, in the upper third of the oven for 7 to 10 minutes, or until golden all over and just slightly darker around the edges. Reverse the sheet from front to back halfway through baking to ensure even browning. Transfer the sheet to a wire rack and let stand until the cookies firm up slightly, 1 to 2 minutes. Using a spatula, transfer the cookies to wire racks. Let stand until completely cooled.

Store in an airtight container for up to 1 week or freeze for up to 1½ months.

words of kitchen wisdom
"When your druggist . . . is not to be relied upon, use a baking powder which has been tested and proved pure. Pure baking powders are soda and cream of tartar mixed by weight in the proper proportion, and combined with rice flour, cornstarch, or some harmless ingredient to insure their keeping."

—Mrs. D. A. Lincoln, *The Boston Cooking-School Cook Book,* 1883

chocolate and white chocolate chip cookies

banana-chocolate chip Drop cookies

Makes about 30 (2¾-inch) cookies.

Set aside your skepticism: the banana–chocolate chip combination is downright addictive. The slightly soft, slightly chewy banana-flavored dough is terrific studded with chocolate morsels, especially the mild milk chocolate variety.

1½ cups all-purpose white flour

¼ teaspoon baking soda

¼ teaspoon salt

¾ cup (1½ sticks) unsalted butter, slightly softened

⅔ cup sugar

⅓ cup packed light brown sugar

1 large egg

2 teaspoons vanilla extract

½ cup thoroughly mashed or pureed overripe banana (1 medium banana)

1 cup old-fashioned rolled oats

1 cup (6 ounces) milk chocolate morsels, chopped

Preheat the oven to 350 degrees F. Grease several baking sheets or coat with nonstick spray.

In a medium bowl, thoroughly stir together the flour, baking soda, and salt; set aside. In a large bowl, with an electric mixer on medium speed, beat together the butter, sugar, and brown sugar until very well blended, about 2 minutes. Add the egg and vanilla and beat until evenly incorporated. Beat in the banana, then the flour mixture, until evenly incorporated. Stir in the oats and chocolate morsels until evenly incorporated.

Using an ice cream scoop or spoons, drop the dough onto the baking sheets in scant golf-ball-sized mounds, spacing about 2½ inches apart.

Bake the cookies, one sheet at a time, in the upper third of the oven for 10 to 14 minutes, or until lightly tinged with brown all over and almost firm when pressed in the centers. Reverse the sheet from front to back halfway through baking to ensure even browning. Transfer the sheet to a wire rack and let stand until the cookies firm up slightly, 2 to 3 minutes. Using a spatula, transfer the cookies to wire racks. Let stand until completely cooled.

These cookies are best when fresh but may be stored in an airtight container for up to 4 days or frozen for up to 1 month.

Tip

For the best flavor and texture, be sure to use an extremely ripe banana. One that is too soft and brown to eat fresh is ideal for this recipe.

white chocolate-macadamia nut cookies

makes 25 to 30
(3¼-to-3½-inch)
cookies.

I don't know who first declared white chocolate-macadamia nut cookies trendy, but in the mid-1980s, suddenly every shopping-mall cookie kiosk in the country was selling them. The cookies were such a favorite with my son that he often requested a batch of them in place of a birthday cake.

Like the cookie-kiosk versions, my cookies are large, rich, and chewy-crispy. They also have a light, delicate taste that lets the mild white chocolate and macadamia nut flavors come through.

1¹/₂ cups old-fashioned rolled oats

1¹/₃ cups all-purpose white flour

³/₄ teaspoon baking soda

¹/₄ teaspoon salt

1 cup minus 2 tablespoons (1³/₄ sticks) unsalted butter, slightly softened

1 cup sugar

¹/₃ cup packed dark brown sugar

1 large egg

1¹/₂ tablespoons milk

2¹/₂ teaspoons vanilla extract

¹/₈ teaspoon almond extract

8 ounces top-quality white chocolate, coarsely chopped, *or* 1¹/₃ cups (8 ounces) top-quality white chocolate morsels

1¹/₃ cups (about 6 ounces) coarsely chopped macadamia nuts

tip

If salted macadamia nuts are used, wipe them with paper towels to remove as much salt as possible before chopping.

Preheat the oven to 325 degrees F. Grease several baking sheets or coat with nonstick spray.

In a food processor, process the oats in on/off pulses until ground to a powder. (Alternatively, grind the oats to a powder in a blender, stopping and stirring a number of times to redistribute the contents.) In a medium bowl, thoroughly stir together the ground oats, flour, baking soda, and salt; set aside. In a large bowl, with an electric mixer on medium speed, beat the butter until lightened, about 1 minute. Add the sugar and brown sugar and beat until very fluffy and smooth. Add the egg, milk, vanilla, and almond extract and beat until evenly incorporated. Beat or stir in the flour mixture until evenly incorporated. Stir in the white chocolate and macadamia nuts until evenly incorporated.

Using an ice cream scoop or spoons, drop the dough onto the baking sheets in generous golf-ball-sized mounds, spacing about 3 inches apart. Or shape the dough into generous golf-ball-sized balls using well-greased hands. Pat the mounds or balls down slightly.

Bake the cookies, one sheet at a time, in the middle of the oven for 12 to 17 minutes, or until the tops are pale golden and the edges are just lightly browned; be very careful not to overbake. Reverse the sheet halfway through baking to ensure even browning. Transfer the sheet to a wire rack and let stand until the cookies firm up slightly, 2 to 3 minutes. Using a spatula, transfer the cookies to wire racks. Let stand until completely cooled.

Store in an airtight container for up to 1 week or freeze for up to 1 month.

white chocolate-macadamia nut cookies (page 73) and chocolate-espresso white chocolate chunk cookies (page 76)

chocolate-espresso white chocolate chunk cookies

The American culinary scene was awash with white chocolate in the late 1980s and with gourmet coffees in the 1990s. Now, these two trendy ingredients often appear together, and the pairing usually works exceedingly well.

Here, a chocolatey dough is infused with espresso and generously studded with white chocolate chunks. The chocolate-coffee flavor and mellow white chocolate are a great foil for one another in these big, chewy, rich-as-sin rounds. I created them after sampling similar cookies at a number of coffee bars and bakeries on both the East and West coasts.

5 ounces bittersweet (*not* unsweetened) or semisweet chocolate, broken up or coarsely chopped

1/2 cup (1 stick) unsalted butter, cut into chunks

1/4 cup plus 1 tablespoon all-purpose white flour

2 tablespoons unsweetened cocoa powder, Dutch-process or American-style, sifted after measuring, if lumpy

3/4 cup sugar

1/8 teaspoon salt

2 large eggs

1 tablespoon plus 1 teaspoon instant espresso powder or granules, dissolved in 1 tablespoon hot water

1 1/2 teaspoons vanilla extract

8 ounces top-quality white chocolate, coarsely chopped, *or* 1 1/2 cups (about 9 ounces) top-quality white chocolate morsels, very coarsely chopped

In a medium, microwave-safe bowl, microwave the bittersweet or semi-sweet chocolate and butter on 100-percent power for 1 minute. Stir well. Continue microwaving on 50-percent power, stirring at 30-second intervals. Stop microwaving before the chocolate completely melts and let the residual heat finish the job. (Alternatively, in a small, heavy saucepan, melt the chocolate and butter over lowest heat, stirring frequently; be very careful not to burn. Immediately remove from the heat.) Let cool to warm.

In a medium bowl, thoroughly stir together the flour and cocoa powder; set aside. In a large bowl, with an electric mixer on medium, then high, speed, beat together the sugar, salt, eggs, espresso mixture, and vanilla for 2 to 3 minutes, or until well blended, slightly thick, and lightened. Beat in the melted chocolate mixture, then the flour mixture, until well blended. Stir in the white chocolate until evenly incorporated. Refrigerate the dough for at least 1½ hours, or until firm enough to shape.

Preheat the oven to 350 degrees F. Line several baking sheets with parchment paper.

Divide the dough into quarters. Divide each quarter into 5 or 6 equal portions. Shape them into balls with lightly greased hands. Place on the baking sheets, spacing about 3 inches apart. Pat down the balls just slightly.

Bake the cookies, one sheet at a time, in the middle of the oven for 9 to 12 minutes, or until barely firm when pressed in the centers. Reverse the sheet from front to back halfway through baking to ensure even browning. Transfer the sheet to a wire rack and let stand until the cookies firm up slightly, 2 to 3 minutes. Slide the cookies, still attached to the parchment, onto a wire rack. Let stand until completely cooled. Carefully peel the cookies from the parchment.

These cookies are best when fresh but may be stored in an airtight container for up to 4 days or frozen for up to 1 month.

Death-by-chocolate white chocolate chip cookies

Makes about 30 (2½-inch) cookies.

It was proximity to the cattle-drive trails that attracted gunmen like Wyatt Earp and Bat Masterson and hundreds of rowdy cowpunchers to Dodge City, Kansas, in the 1880s. These dense, dark, take-no-prisoners chocolate cookies would be the big draw today. Adapted from a recipe featured at the Boot Hill Bed & Breakfast, they are nearly black, robustly chocolatey, and heavily studded with white chocolate bits. The original recipe was created by the proprietor, Jacques Laurent, a former professional pastry chef.

Though the original recipe doesn't call for any semisweet chocolate bits, I think adding some makes these cookies even more decadent. They are best eaten the day they are made, which in most households is not going to be a problem!

1 cup (2 sticks) unsalted butter, slightly softened
Scant 1¼ cups sugar
1 cup unsweetened American-style cocoa powder, sifted after measuring, if lumpy
½ teaspoon baking soda
⅛ teaspoon salt
2 large eggs
1 tablespoon light or dark corn syrup

2 teaspoons vanilla extract
2½ cups all-purpose white flour
1½ cups (9 ounces) top-quality white chocolate morsels
½ cup (3 ounces) semisweet chocolate morsels (optional)

Preheat the oven to 350 degrees F. Grease several baking sheets or coat with nonstick spray.

In a large bowl, with an electric mixer on medium speed, beat together the butter and sugar until very fluffy and smooth. Reduce the speed to low and beat in the cocoa powder, baking soda, and salt until evenly incorporated. Add the eggs, corn syrup, and vanilla and beat until smooth and well blended. Beat or stir in the flour until evenly incorporated. Stir in the white and semisweet chocolate morsels, if using, until evenly incorporated.

Using an ice cream scoop or spoons, drop the dough in generous golf-ball-sized mounds, spacing about 2½ inches apart.

Bake the cookies, one sheet at a time, in the middle of the oven for 9 to 12 minutes, or until the centers are almost firm when pressed; be very careful not to overbake. Reverse the sheet from front to back halfway through baking to ensure even browning. Transfer the sheet to a wire rack and let stand until the cookies firm up slightly, 2 to 3 minutes. Using a spatula, transfer the cookies to wire racks. Let stand until completely cooled.

Store in an airtight container for up to 2 days or freeze for up to 1 month.

pecan fudgies

I have come across versions of these easy, incredibly creamy-chewy drop cookies in community cookbooks from several different towns along Florida's west coast, though they appear to be adaptations of test-kitchen recipes nationally circulated over a number of years to promote Eagle Brand sweetened condensed milk. Perhaps fudgies turned up here because sweetened condensed milk has long been a staple ingredient in many Florida kitchens—it's used in the ever-popular key lime pie.

In any case, in combination with chocolate, the condensed milk gives these chocolate-chocolate chip cookies a uniquely fudgy quality. Note that the recipe doesn't call for sugar; the condensed milk and semisweet chocolate morsels provide all the sweetness needed.

1½ cups (6 ounces) chopped pecans

2 cups (12 ounces) semisweet chocolate morsels (divided)

¼ cup (½ stick) unsalted butter

1 14-ounce can sweetened condensed milk

1 large egg

1½ teaspoons vanilla extract

Pinch of salt

⅔ cup all-purpose white flour

1 cup (about 3 ounces) shredded or flaked sweetened coconut (optional)

Preheat the oven to 350 degrees F. Line several baking sheets with parchment paper or coat with nonstick spray.

Spread the pecans in a small baking pan and toast in the oven, stirring occasionally, for 7 to 9 minutes, or until nicely browned; be careful not to burn. Immediately turn out into a small bowl and let cool; set aside.

In a large, microwave-safe bowl, microwave 1½ cups of the chocolate morsels and the butter on 100-percent power for 1½ minutes. Stir well. Continue microwaving on 50-percent power, stirring at 30-second intervals. Stop microwaving before the chocolate completely melts and let the residual heat finish the job. (Alternatively, in a large, heavy saucepan, melt the chocolate and butter over lowest heat, stirring frequently; be very careful not to burn. Immediately remove from the heat.) Let cool to warm.

Thoroughly stir the condensed milk, egg, vanilla, and salt into the chocolate mixture until well blended. Stir in the flour, pecans, remaining ½ cup chocolate morsels, and coconut, if using, until evenly incorporated.

Tip
Be sure to use sweetened condensed milk and not evaporated milk in this recipe. Evaporated milk will not work!

Drop the dough onto the baking sheets by heaping measuring table-spoonfuls, spacing about 2 inches apart.

Bake the cookies, one sheet at a time, in the middle of the oven for 6 to 8 minutes, or until barely firm when pressed in the centers; be careful not to overbake. Reverse the sheet from front to back halfway through baking to ensure even browning. Transfer the sheet to a wire rack and let stand until the cookies firm up slightly, about 5 minutes. Using a spatula, transfer the cookies to wire racks. Let stand until completely cooled.

Store in an airtight container for up to 4 days or freeze for up to 1 month.

peppermint road chocolate chipsters

Makes 40 to 45
(2¼-inch) cookies.

Considering that nobody thought to put chocolate bits into cookies until the 1930s, it's amazing how far we've taken the idea. Now all sorts of candy, from M&M's to broken-up toffee bars to chopped gumdrops, get tossed in—with varying degrees of success.

These unusual cookies feature crushed peppermint candy and chocolate morsels in a chocolatey dough, a combination that children and most adult fans of chocolate-mint confections love. Besides providing flecks of color and an appealing crunch, the peppermint candy delivers a potent minty punch to the cookies that peppermint extract cannot. (This is because peppermint candy is flavored not with peppermint extract, but with oil of peppermint, a much more concentrated form of the herb.)

Obviously, these are a nice choice for holiday baking. Children enjoy breaking the peppermint candy into pieces, as well as embedding the candy shards in the cookies, giving them a "peppermint road" look. And, of course, part of the fun is snitching a few chocolate and peppermint bits to eat.

1½ cups (9 ounces) semisweet chocolate minimorsels or semisweet chocolate morsels, chopped (divided)

1 cup crushed peppermint hard candy or candy canes (divided)

1¾ cups all-purpose white flour

½ cup minus 1 tablespoon unsweetened Dutch-process cocoa powder

1 teaspoon baking powder

¾ cup (1½ sticks) unsalted butter, slightly softened

2½ tablespoons corn oil or other flavorless vegetable oil

¾ cup sugar

1 large egg

Scant ½ teaspoon salt

1½ teaspoons vanilla extract

Preheat the oven to 350 degrees F. Line several baking sheets with aluminum foil. Grease the foil or coat with nonstick spray.

In a food processor, combine ¾ cup of the chocolate morsels, a generous ⅓ cup of the peppermint candy, the flour, cocoa, and baking powder. Process in on/off pulses until the chocolate and candy are finely ground; set aside. In a large bowl, with an electric mixer on medium speed, beat together the butter, oil, and sugar until lightened and fluffy. Add the egg, salt, and vanilla and beat until well blended and smooth. Beat or stir in the flour mixture and the remaining ¾ cup chocolate morsels until evenly incorporated.

TIP

Crush the candy into chocolate-minimorsel-sized pieces by placing it in a double layer of plastic bags and smashing with a kitchen mallet or the back of a large, heavy metal spoon.

Shape portions of the dough into scant 1¼-inch balls with lightly greased hands. Place on the baking sheets, spacing about 2½ inches apart. Dip a large, flat-bottomed glass into cold water; shake off the excess water. Using the bottom of the glass, press the balls into 2-inch rounds, dipping the glass into the water between cookies.

Bake the cookies, one sheet at a time, in the upper third of the oven for 8 to 10 minutes, or until almost firm when pressed in the centers. Reverse the sheet from front to back halfway through baking to ensure even browning. Remove from the oven and immediately sprinkle some of the remaining peppermint candy over the cookies; don't sprinkle too heavily, and discard (or eat!) any candy chunks larger than chocolate-chip size. Using a large, lightly greased, flat-bottomed glass, press down on one cookie at a time to embed the candy. Regrease the bottom of the glass as needed. Return the sheet to the oven and bake for 2 minutes more, or until the candy barely melts.

Transfer the sheet to a wire rack and let stand until the cookies firm up slightly, 3 to 4 minutes. Using a spatula, transfer the cookies to wire racks. Let stand until completely cooled.

Store in an airtight container for up to 10 days or freeze for up to 1 month.

cocoa-spice chocolate chip cookies

These slightly exotic cocoa-spice cookies incorporate the basic flavor combination that gave nineteenth-century spiced-chocolate jumbles their appeal, yet are entirely modern.

2 cups all-purpose white flour

1/4 cup unsweetened American-style cocoa powder, sifted after measuring, if lumpy

1 teaspoon baking powder

3/4 teaspoon ground ginger

3/4 teaspoon ground cinnamon

Generous 1/8 teaspoon ground cloves

1/8 teaspoon salt

2/3 cup (1 stick plus 2 2/3 tablespoons) unsalted butter, slightly softened

1 cup plus 2 tablespoons sugar

1/4 cup light molasses

1 large egg

1/2 teaspoon finely grated orange zest (colored part of the skin)

1/2 cup (3 ounces) semisweet chocolate minimorsels or semisweet chocolate morsels, chopped

Preheat the oven to 350 degrees F. Grease several baking sheets or coat with nonstick spray.

In a large bowl, thoroughly stir together the flour, cocoa powder, baking powder, ginger, cinnamon, cloves, and salt; set aside. In another bowl, with an electric mixer on medium speed, beat together the butter, sugar, and molasses until well blended and fluffy, about 2 minutes. Add the egg and orange zest and beat until well blended and smooth. Beat in half of the flour mixture until evenly incorporated. Beat or stir in the remaining flour mixture and the chocolate morsels until evenly incorporated. Refrigerate the dough for 10 minutes, or until it firms up just slightly.

Shape portions of the dough into 1¼-inch balls with lightly greased hands. Place on the baking sheets, spacing about 2 inches apart. With your hands, pat down the balls into ½-inch-thick rounds.

Bake the cookies, one sheet at a time, in the upper third of the oven for 7 to 9 minutes, or until barely firm when touched in the centers. Reverse the sheet from front to back halfway through baking to ensure even browning. Transfer the sheet to a wire rack and let stand until the cookies firm up slightly, 1 to 2 minutes. Using a spatula, transfer the cookies to wire racks. Let stand until completely cooled.

Store in an airtight container for up to 10 days or freeze for up to 2 months.

chocolate-peanut-raisin chunkies

MAKES 20 TO 25
(2½-inch)
cookies.

I first saw a recipe for cookies something like these in a *Farm Journal* cookbook back in the 1970s. They were called "clusters," not chunkies, and they didn't contain raisins or chocolate chips. I was intrigued because they were more candy-like than any chocolate cookies I'd ever seen—sort of like Chunky candy bars in cookie form. Little did I know that they were the forerunner of many chocolate cookies to come.

These are plain looking and not at all subtle, but if the bold taste of dark chocolate, raisins, and peanuts appeals to you, they are likely to become a favorite. (If you wish, omit the raisins. However, the cookies will not stay as moist.)

1¼ cups (6¼ ounces) raisins
2 ounces unsweetened chocolate, broken up or coarsely chopped
¼ cup (½ stick) unsalted butter, cut into chunks
¾ cup sugar
¼ teaspoon salt
1 tablespoon light corn syrup

1½ teaspoons vanilla extract
1 large egg
¼ cup all-purpose white flour
1½ cups (about 7 ounces) coarsely chopped unsalted peanuts
1 cup (6 ounces) semisweet chocolate morsels

Preheat the oven to 350 degrees F. Heavily grease several baking sheets or coat with nonstick spray.

In a small bowl, cover the raisins with hot water. Let soak for 5 minutes. Turn out the raisins into a colander. Let stand until well drained.

Meanwhile, in a large, microwave-safe bowl, microwave the chocolate and butter on 50-percent power, stirring at 30-second intervals. Stop microwaving before the chocolate completely melts and let the residual heat finish the job. (Alternatively, in a medium, heavy saucepan, melt the chocolate and butter over lowest heat, stirring frequently; be very careful not to burn. Immediately remove from the heat.) Let cool to warm.

Stir the sugar, salt, corn syrup, and vanilla into the chocolate mixture until very well blended. Vigorously stir in the egg until evenly incorporated. Stir in the flour, then the peanuts, raisins, and chocolate morsels, until evenly incorporated.

chocolate and white chocolate chip cookies

85

Drop the dough onto the baking sheets by heaping measuring table-spoonfuls, spacing about 2½ inches apart. (Be sure to wipe off any bits of dough that drop onto the sheet, as they will stick and burn.)

Bake the cookies, one sheet at a time, in the middle of the oven for 7 to 10 minutes, or until just firm when pressed in the centers; they will look shiny and slightly underdone. Reverse the sheet from front to back halfway through baking to ensure even browning. Transfer the sheet to a wire rack and let stand until the cookies are firmed up, about 5 minutes. Using a spatula, transfer the cookies to wire racks. Let stand until completely cooled.

Store in an airtight container for up to 1 week or freeze for up to 1 month.

chocolate and white chocolate chip cookies

chocolate chubbies

With a whole pound of chocolate in the recipe, these cookies are deeply chocolatey. The dough is dark and heavily studded with pecan chunks and chocolate morsels and yields cookies that are almost candy-like.

In New York City, chocolate chubbies are right up there in popularity with chocolate chip cookies. My recipe was inspired by the chubbies from Sarabeth's Kitchen and the Mangia coffee and pastry bar, both in Manhattan. Chocolate chubbies are a customer favorite in both shops. And no wonder.

2 cups (8 ounces) coarsely chopped pecans

8 ounces bittersweet (not unsweetened) or semisweet chocolate, broken up or coarsely chopped

3 tablespoons cold unsalted butter, cut into chunks

¹/₃ cup all-purpose white flour

¹/₄ teaspoon baking soda

¹/₄ teaspoon salt

²/₃ cup sugar

2 large eggs

1¹/₂ teaspoons vanilla extract

1¹/₃ cups (8 ounces) semisweet chocolate morsels

Preheat the oven to 325 degrees F. Line several baking sheets with parchment paper or very heavily coat with nonstick spray.

Spread the pecans in a medium baking pan and toast in the oven, stirring occasionally, for 7 to 9 minutes, or until nicely browned; be careful not to burn. Immediately turn out into a medium bowl and let cool.

Meanwhile, in large, microwave-safe bowl, microwave the bittersweet or semisweet chocolate and butter on 100-percent power for 1 minute. Stir well. Continue microwaving on 50-percent power, stirring at 30-second intervals. Stop microwaving before the chocolate completely melts and let the residual heat finish the job. (Alternatively, in a medium, heavy saucepan, melt the chocolate and butter over lowest heat, stirring frequently; be very careful not to burn. Immediately remove from the heat.) Let cool to warm.

In a small bowl, thoroughly stir together the flour, baking soda, and salt; set aside. In a large bowl, with an electric mixer on medium speed, beat together the sugar, eggs, and vanilla until well blended, thickened, and lightened. Beat the melted chocolate mixture, then the flour mixture, into the egg mixture until thoroughly blended. Stir in the pecans and chocolate morsels until evenly incorporated. Refrigerate the dough for at least 1½ hours or up to 8 hours, or until it firms up slightly.

Drop the dough onto the baking sheets by heaping measuring tablespoonfuls, spacing about 2½ inches apart.

Bake the cookies, one sheet at a time, in the middle of the oven for 11 to 14 minutes, or until just firm at the edges but still slightly soft in the centers; be careful not to overbake. Reverse the sheet from front to back halfway through baking to ensure even browning. Transfer the sheet to a wire rack and let stand until the cookies are firmed up, about 5 minutes. Using a spatula, transfer the cookies to wire racks. Let stand until completely cooled.

These cookies are best when fresh but may be stored in an airtight container for up to 4 days or frozen for up to 1 month.

Double-chocolate cranberry cookies

From the nation's earliest days, new products have inspired American cooks to create new recipes. I devised this chewy, super-rich cookie when dried, sweetened cranberries —one brand is Craisins—first came on the market in the 1990s. (Plain dried cranberries are not a modern product; Lewis and Clark mentioned purchasing some from Pacific Coast Indians during the winter of 1806.)

It occurred to me that, like cherries, cranberries might pair well with chocolate. They do—especially when soaked in cherry brandy to mellow their flavor. The dough is dark and rich and the cranberries fruity and succulent. The resulting cookies have a taste vaguely reminiscent of chocolate-covered cherries.

2½ cups (about 10 ounces) dried, sweetened cranberries

¼ cup kirsch (cherry brandy)

12 ounces bittersweet (not unsweetened) or semisweet chocolate, broken up or coarsely chopped

⅓ cup (5⅓ tablespoons) unsalted butter

1 cup minus 2 tablespoons packed light brown sugar

¼ teaspoon baking powder

2 large eggs, plus 1 large egg yolk

1½ teaspoons vanilla extract

Scant ½ teaspoon almond extract

⅔ cup all-purpose white flour

1½ cups (9 ounces) semisweet or milk chocolate morsels

1 cup (about 4 ounces) blanched slivered almonds, chopped (optional)

In a large bowl, stir together the cranberries and kirsch and let stand until most of the liquid is absorbed, about 5 minutes.

Meanwhile, in a medium, microwave-safe bowl, microwave the bitter-sweet or semisweet chocolate and butter on 100-percent power for 1½ minutes. Stir well. Continue microwaving on 50-percent power, stopping and stirring at 30-second intervals. Stop microwaving before the chocolate completely melts and let the residual heat finish the job. (Alternatively, in a medium, heavy saucepan, melt the chocolate and butter over lowest heat, stirring frequently; be very careful not to burn. Immediately remove from the heat.) Let cool to warm.

TIP

Be sure to use dried, *sweetened* cranberries; dried, unsweetened cranberries are too tart for this recipe.

Stir the brown sugar, baking powder, eggs and egg yolk, vanilla, and almond extract into the cranberry mixture until the sugar dissolves and the mixture is very well blended. Stir in the chocolate mixture, then the flour, chocolate morsels, and almonds, if using, until evenly incorporated. Refrigerate the dough for 1½ hours, or until it firms up slightly.

Preheat the oven to 350 degrees F. Line several baking sheets with parchment paper.

Drop the dough onto the baking sheets using a ⅛-cup measure or coffee scoop, spacing about 2½ inches apart.

Bake the cookies, one sheet at a time, in the middle of the oven for 8 to 11 minutes, or until dry in the centers and almost firm when pressed. Reverse the sheet from front to back halfway through baking to ensure even browning. Transfer the sheet to a wire rack and let stand until the cookies are firmed up slightly, 1 to 2 minutes. Slide the cookies, still attached to the parchment, onto a wire rack. Let stand until completely cooled. Carefully peel the cookies from the parchment.

Store in a single layer or layered with wax paper in an airtight container for up to 4 days or freeze for up to 1 month.

Tutti-Frutti chocolate fruitcake drops

A new take on an old tradition, these incredibly chocolatey, fruit-studded cookies are guaranteed to banish fruitcake's fuddy-duddy image forever. The colorful mix of dried fruit, nuts, and chocolate morsels complements the dough beautifully, lending lively flavor and gratifying chew. Great-Aunt Gertrude may turn over in her grave at the idea of replacing her heirloom holiday fruitcake with these, but everyone else will be overjoyed.

1/2 cup (2 ounces) chopped dried, sweetened cranberries

1/3 cup (about 1 3/4 ounces) finely chopped dried apricots

1/3 cup (about 1 3/4 ounces) golden raisins

1/4 cup orange juice

3/4 cup all-purpose white flour

1/2 teaspoon baking powder

1/8 teaspoon salt

3 ounces bittersweet (not unsweetened) or semisweet chocolate, broken up or coarsely chopped

1 ounce unsweetened chocolate, broken up or coarsely chopped

1/2 cup (1 stick) unsalted butter, cut into chunks

3/4 cup sugar

3/4 teaspoon finely grated orange zest (colored part of the skin)

1 1/2 teaspoons vanilla extract

1 large egg, plus 1 large egg white

1/2 cup (2 ounces) chopped pecans

1/2 cup (3 ounces) semisweet chocolate morsels

32–36 candied-cherry or pecan halves, or a combination, for topping

In a medium bowl, stir together the cranberries, apricots, raisins, and orange juice and let stand for 15 minutes, or until most of the liquid is absorbed.

In a medium bowl, thoroughly stir together the flour, baking powder, and salt; set aside. In a large, microwave-safe bowl, microwave the bittersweet or semisweet and unsweetened chocolates and butter on 100-percent power for 1 minute. Stir well. Continue microwaving on 50-percent power, stirring at 30-second intervals. Stop microwaving before the chocolates completely melt and let the residual heat finish the job. (Alternatively, in a medium, heavy saucepan, melt the chocolates and butter over lowest heat, stirring frequently; be very careful not to burn. Immediately remove from the heat.) Let cool to warm.

Stir the sugar, orange zest, and vanilla into the chocolate mixture until well blended. Vigorously stir in the egg and egg white until well blended. Stir in the flour mixture, then the pecans, fruit mixture, and chocolate morsels, until evenly incorporated. Refrigerate for at least 2 hours or up to 12 hours, or until firmed up.

Preheat the oven to 350 degrees F. Generously grease several baking sheets or coat with nonstick spray.

Shape the dough into a disk, then divide it into quarters. Working with one quarter at a time and keeping the remaining dough refrigerated, divide the dough into 8 or 9 equal portions. Shape the portions of dough into balls with lightly greased hands. Place on the baking sheets, spacing about 2½ inches apart. Firmly press a candied-cherry half or pecan half into the center of each ball.

Bake the cookies, one sheet at a time, in the middle of the oven for 9 to 12 minutes, or until just barely firm when pressed in the centers. Reverse the sheet from front to back halfway through baking to ensure even browning. Transfer the sheet to a wire rack and let stand until the cookies firm up slightly, about 2 minutes. Using a spatula, transfer the cookies to wire racks. Let stand until completely cooled.

Store in an airtight container for up to 1 week or freeze for up to 1 month.

chocolate and white chocolate chip cookies

chocolate thumbprint crackles

These late-twentieth-century cookies are named for their dramatic, crackled-looking tops. Balls of fudgy dough are coated with powdered sugar prior to baking, and when dark cracks later form, they stand out in bold contrast to the powdery white surface. Unlike usual crackles, indentations in the centers are filled with a dab of either green mint jelly or red raspberry preserves. These are always well received on any holiday cookie tray. A batch also makes a nice gift.

6¹/₂ ounces bittersweet (not unsweetened) or semisweet chocolate, broken up or coarsely chopped

¹/₂ cup (1 stick) unsalted butter

²/₃ cup sugar

3 large eggs

1¹/₂ teaspoons vanilla extract

2 tablespoons mint jelly or reduced-sugar seedless raspberry preserves

1 teaspoon peppermint extract (optional; use if preparing mint thumbprints)

1³/₄ cups all-purpose white flour

3 tablespoons unsweetened American-style cocoa powder

¹/₄ teaspoon baking powder

¹/₄ teaspoon salt

1 cup (6 ounces) semisweet chocolate minimorsels or chopped regular semisweet chocolate morsels

About ¹/₂ cup sifted powdered sugar, for topping

About ¹/₂ cup mint jelly or reduced-sugar seedless raspberry preserves, for filling thumbprints

tip

I like to use reduced-sugar raspberry preserves, because their slight tartness goes better with the rich chocolate dough than regular raspberry preserves.

In a large, microwave-safe bowl, microwave the bittersweet or semisweet chocolate and butter on 100-percent power for 1 minute. Stir well. Continue microwaving on 50-percent power, stirring at 30-second intervals. Stop microwaving before the chocolate completely melts and let the residual heat finish the job. (Alternatively, in a large, heavy saucepan, melt the chocolate and butter over lowest heat, stirring frequently; be very careful not to burn. Immediately remove from the heat.) Let cool to warm.

Stir the sugar into the chocolate mixture until well blended. Using a spoon, beat in the eggs, one at a time. Stir in the vanilla. In a small, microwave-safe bowl, microwave the 2 tablespoons mint jelly or raspberry preserves on 50-percent power just until fluid but not bubbling, about 1 minute. (Or heat in a small saucepan over low heat.) Stir the mint jelly and peppermint extract into the chocolate mixture if making mint thumbprints, or stir in the raspberry preserves if preparing raspberry thumbprints. Set aside.

In a medium bowl, thoroughly stir together the flour, cocoa powder, baking powder, and salt. Add the flour mixture and chocolate morsels to the chocolate mixture and stir just until well blended. Refrigerate the dough for at least 1½ hours or up to 8 hours, or until firmed up, or freeze for 45 to 60 minutes to speed chilling.

Preheat the oven to 325 degrees F. Generously grease several baking sheets or heavily coat with nonstick spray.

Place half of the powdered sugar in a medium bowl. Shape portions of the dough into 1-inch balls with lightly greased hands. Drop several balls at a time into the powdered sugar and rotate the bowl until they are heavily coated and no chocolate shows through. Lift out the balls with a slotted spoon, tapping off the excess powdered sugar against the side of the bowl. Place on the baking sheets, spacing about 1½ inches apart. Frequently wipe buildup from your hands with paper towels. Replenish the bowl of powdered sugar as needed. Using your thumb or knuckle, press a deep well into the center of each ball. Place about ¼ teaspoon of mint jelly or raspberry preserves into each well.

Bake the cookies, one sheet at a time, in the middle of the oven for 7 to 9 minutes, or until just beginning to feel firm when pressed in the centers; be careful not to overbake. Reverse the sheet from front to back halfway through baking to ensure even browning. Transfer the sheet to a wire rack and let stand until the cookies firm up slightly, 3 to 4 minutes. Using a spatula, transfer the cookies to wire racks. Let stand until completely cooled. Wipe off the sheets and regrease them before reusing.

Store the cookies in a single layer in an airtight container for up to 3 days. Due to the powdered-sugar coating (which can become soggy during defrosting), these cookies don't freeze well.

4

Chocolate and Mocha Cookies

The First chocoLate cookie

makes about 30
(1¾-inch) cookies.

Prior to the mid-1800s, chocolate cookies were largely unknown in this country. The first chocolate cookie I've found is a sketchy receipt for rich, candy-like, chocolate-almond macaroons in an 1832 cookbook, *The Cook's Own Book,* by "A Boston House-keeper" named Mrs. N. K. M. Lee. It would be nice to credit Mrs. Lee with a great American cookie breakthrough, but I can't: she copied her recipe word for word from *The Cook's Dictionary and Housekeeper's Directory,* written by a British author of the same period, Richard Dolby. Nevertheless, Mrs. Lee's introduction of a chocolate cookie to the American public was the first step in a long "chocolafication" process that has ultimately resulted in a complete cookie paradigm shift. In two hundred years, we have gone from no chocolate cookies to nearly all our favorite cookies containing chocolate.

The best news about Mrs. Lee's purloined chocolate-almond macaroon recipe is the cookie itself. I suspect that any adventuresome nineteenth-century cook who made it was utterly thrilled and instantly won over to baking with chocolate. By loosely adapting the instructions to melt "a quarter of a pound of chocolate on a tin-plate," and then by following directions to combine it with "a sweet almond paste, made as for macaroons," I was able to produce remarkably good results. These are dense and have an intense, pleasing chocolate-and-almond flavor.

4 ounces unsweetened chocolate, broken up or coarsely chopped

1½ cups (about 4½ ounces) blanched or unblanched sliced almonds

¼ cup sugar

7–8 ounces almond paste, cut into chunks

⅔ cup powdered sugar, plus a little more for topping

3 large egg whites

½ teaspoon vanilla extract

About ¾ cup (about 3 ounces) very finely chopped blanched slivered almonds or chocolate jimmies, or some powdered sugar, for topping (optional)

In a small, microwave-safe bowl, microwave the chocolate on 100-percent power for 1 minute. Stir well. Continue microwaving on 50-percent power, stirring at 30-second intervals. Stop microwaving before the chocolate completely melts and let the residual heat finish the job. (Alternatively, in a small, heavy saucepan, melt the chocolate over low heat, stirring frequently; be very careful not to burn. Immediately remove from the heat.)

In a food processor, process the almonds and sugar until the almonds are very finely ground, about 1½ minutes. Add the almond paste, powdered sugar, and chocolate and process for 2 to 3 minutes more, stopping and scraping down the bowl as necessary, until very well blended; the mixture will be crumbly. Add the egg whites and vanilla and process in on/off pulses just until the mixture stiffens and the processor motor labors; immediately stop the processor. If the mixture is not thoroughly blended, turn out the dough into a medium bowl and vigorously stir until well blended. Refrigerate the dough for at least 2 hours or up to 12 hours, or until the dough firms up.

Preheat the oven to 325 degrees F. Line several baking sheets with parchment paper or aluminum foil.

Shape portions of the dough into scant 1¼-inch balls with lightly greased hands. Roll the balls in the chopped almonds or chocolate jimmies, if using, until thoroughly coated. Place on the baking sheets, spacing about 2 inches apart.

Bake the cookies, one sheet at a time, in the middle of the oven for 10 to 14 minutes, or until barely firm when pressed in the centers. Reverse the sheet from front to back halfway through baking to ensure even browning. Slide the cookies, still attached to the parchment or foil, onto a wire rack. Let stand until completely cooled. Carefully peel the cookies from the parchment or foil. If the macaroons have not been decorated with almonds or jimmies, sift a little powdered sugar over them.

Store in an airtight container for up to 4 days or freeze for up to 1 month.

Health Food

The notion that chocolate was healthful was widespread in eighteenth- and nineteenth-century America, as Mrs. D. A. Lincoln's 1884 comments in *The Boston Cooking-School Cook Book* suggest: "[Chocolate] is the most nutritious and convenient form of cocoa: a small cake of it will satisfy hunger. It is a very good lunch for travellers [*sic*]. . . . Chocolate does not produce the injurious effects which render tea and coffee objectionable, and is far better for children and working-people."

chocolateHearts

These unusual, tempting chocolate meringue cutout cookies are a hit whenever I serve them, but especially on Valentine's Day. They are adapted from a 1909 edition of *The Good Housekeeping Everyday Cookbook.* Because the original recipe was a bit sugary for modern tastes, I've made several changes to reduce the sweetness. I've also added a little vanilla to round out the flavor. Additionally, I've provided a baking temperature to replace the cook's thoughtful, but for most modern readers unenlightening, guidance: "The oven should not be as cool as for meringues, but not quite so hot as for sponge cakes."

These cookies have a pleasing chewy texture, an intense chocolate flavor, and, due to the way the meringue bakes, a puffy, layered look that always provokes comments. As appealing as they are, it's surprising they aren't a standard in cookie bakers' repertoires today. Now, perhaps they will be.

3¹/₂ ounces unsweetened chocolate, broken up or coarsely chopped

2²/₃ cups powdered sugar (divided), plus more if needed

2 tablespoons unsweetened American-style cocoa powder

¹/₃ cup egg whites (about 3 large egg whites), at room temperature

1 teaspoon vanilla extract

Sugar, for topping (optional)

Preheat the oven to 325 degrees F. Line several baking sheets with parchment paper.

In a small, microwave-safe bowl, microwave the chocolate on 100-percent power for 1 minute. Stir well. Continue microwaving on 50-percent power, stirring at 30-second intervals. Stop microwaving before the chocolate completely melts and let the residual heat finish the job. (Alternatively, in a small, heavy saucepan, melt the chocolate over lowest heat, stirring frequently; be very careful not to burn. Immediately remove from the heat.) Let cool to warm.

In a large bowl, with an electric mixer on low speed, beat together the chocolate, about one-third of the powdered sugar, and the cocoa powder until well blended. Gradually add about one-third of the egg whites and beat until evenly incorporated. Add another one-third of the powdered sugar, then another one-third of the egg whites, and beat until smooth. Repeat the process, adding the remaining one-third of the powdered

Tip

Be sure to use room-temperature egg whites. Cold egg whites will lower the temperature of the chocolate and cause it to set in small bits, which will yield a lumpy dough. To warm up the egg whites in a hurry, place them in a small bowl set in a slightly larger bowl of barely hot tap water.

sugar, then the remaining one-third of the egg whites, and the vanilla. Increase the speed to high and beat for 2 minutes more, or until very smooth and well blended. Let the dough stand for 5 minutes to allow the egg whites to be more fully absorbed. At this point, if the dough seems dry and crumbly, beat in 1 to 2 teaspoons water until it holds together. If the dough seems sticky and wet, beat in 1 to 2 tablespoons more powdered sugar to stiffen it just slightly. Beat the dough for 1 minute more, or until very well blended.

Divide the dough in half. Place each portion between large sheets of wax paper. Roll out the portions a scant ¼ inch thick; check the underside of the dough and smooth out any wrinkles that form. Working with one portion at a time, gently peel away, then pat one sheet of wax paper back into place. Flip the dough over, then peel off and discard the second sheet. Using a 2-to-2¼-inch or similar small, heart-shaped cutter, cut out the cookies; if the cutter sticks, occasionally dip it into powdered sugar, tapping off the excess. Using a spatula, carefully transfer the cookies to the baking sheets, spacing about 1¼ inches apart. Reroll any dough scraps. Continue cutting out the cookies until all the dough is used.

Bake the cookies, one sheet at a time, in the middle of the oven for 9 to 13 minutes, or until dry on the surface but soft in the centers when very lightly pressed. Slide the cookies, still attached to the parchment, onto a wire rack. If desired, immediately sprinkle the tops of the cookies with sugar. Let stand until completely cooled. Carefully peel the cookies from the parchment.

Store in an airtight container for up to 2 days or freeze for up to 1 month.

old-Fashioned ROLLed chocoLate cookies

Early chocolate cookies were invariably made with unsweetened chocolate. It was the first chocolate to come on our market and the one Americans baked with almost exclusively until the 1920s. The earliest chocolate manufacturer in America was Baker's, which in 1780 began producing the same bitter, intensely flavored blocks that cooks still use today.

These cookies, from the *1902 Cook Book,* "A Collection of Tried Recipes Contributed by Estherville (Iowa) Housewives," showcase the robust, slightly rough taste of unsweetened chocolate. They have an emphatically chocolatey aroma and a bittersweet edge, as well as a pleasant toothsomeness, that goes well with a strong cup of coffee.

Originally, the cookies were presented plain, but I like to dress them up with a quick sprinkling of chocolate jimmies.

4 ounces unsweetened chocolate, broken up or coarsely chopped

½ cup (1 stick) unsalted butter, slightly softened

½ cup sugar

1 large egg

1 teaspoon vanilla extract

⅛ teaspoon salt

1⅓ cups powdered sugar

1 cup all-purpose white flour

2–3 tablespoons chocolate jimmies, for topping (optional)

In a small, microwave-safe bowl, microwave the chocolate on 100-percent power for 1 minute. Stir well. Continue microwaving on 50-percent power, stirring at 30-second intervals. Stop microwaving before the chocolate completely melts and let the residual heat finish the job. (Alternatively, in a small, heavy saucepan, melt the chocolate over lowest heat, stirring frequently; be very careful not to burn. Immediately remove from the heat.) Let cool to warm.

In a large bowl, with an electric mixer on medium speed, beat together the butter and sugar until well blended and lightened. Add the egg, vanilla, and salt and beat until well blended and smooth. Reduce the speed to low and beat in the powdered sugar and ½ cup of the flour, then the chocolate, until well blended. Beat or stir in the remaining ½ cup flour until evenly incorporated.

Divide the dough in half. Place each portion between large sheets of wax paper. Roll out the portions ⅛ inch thick; check the underside of the dough and smooth out any wrinkles that form. Stack the rolled portions (paper still attached) on a baking sheet. Refrigerate for 45 minutes, or until chilled and firm, or freeze for about 20 minutes to speed chilling.

Preheat the oven to 350 degrees F. Grease several baking sheets or coat with nonstick spray.

Working with one portion at a time and leaving the remaining dough chilled, gently peel away, then pat one sheet of wax paper back into place. Flip the dough over, then peel off and discard the second sheet. Using a 2½-to-2¾-inch fluted round cutter (or any shape desired), cut out the cookies. (If at any point the dough softens too much to handle easily, transfer the paper and cookies to a baking sheet and refrigerate until firm again.) Using a spatula, carefully transfer the cookies to the baking sheets, spacing about 1¼ inches apart. Reroll any dough scraps. Continue cutting out the cookies until all the dough is used. Sprinkle a few chocolate jimmies, if using, over the cookie tops, patting down just slightly.

Bake the cookies, one sheet at a time, in the middle of the oven for 6 to 9 minutes, or until just barely firm when pressed in the centers. Reverse the sheet from front to back halfway through baking to ensure even browning. Transfer the sheet to a wire rack and let stand until the cookies firm up slightly, 3 to 4 minutes. Using a spatula, transfer the cookies to wire racks. Let stand until completely cooled.

Store in an airtight container for up to 2 weeks or freeze for up to 1 month.

words of kitchen wisdom
"New laid eggs appear semi-transparent when placed between the eye and a strong light, and have a small and perceptible division of skin from shell which is filled with air."

– J. Thompson Gill, Manager, Confectioner and Baker Publishing Company, *The Complete Bread, Cake and Cracker Baker*, 1881

savannah chocolate chewies

Chocolate chewies were once the most popular cookie at Gottlieb's Bakery, a Savannah institution that opened in 1884. One hundred years later, the company published a small, spiral-bound recipe book. Sadly, Gottlieb's went out of business in the early 1990s, but its favorite cookie lives on. The recipe is easy, but the cookies must be baked on parchment paper. My version is a tad less sweet and more chocolatey than the original. I also make these cookies normal-sized instead of large as Gottlieb's did.

2 cups (about 8 ounces) chopped pecans

2¼ cups powdered sugar

¼ cup plus 2 tablespoons unsweetened American-style cocoa powder

2 tablespoons all-purpose white flour

Generous pinch of salt

3 large egg whites

¾ teaspoon vanilla extract

1 ounce bittersweet (not unsweetened) or semisweet chocolate, grated

Preheat the oven to 325 degrees F. Line several baking sheets with parchment paper.

Spread the pecans in a medium baking pan and toast in the oven, stirring occasionally, for 7 to 9 minutes, or until fragrant and faintly tinged with brown; be careful not to burn. Immediately turn out into a medium bowl and let cool.

In a large bowl, thoroughly stir together the powdered sugar, cocoa powder, flour, and salt. With an electric mixer on low speed, beat the egg whites, one at a time, into the powdered-sugar mixture. Add the vanilla and beat for 1½ minutes on high speed, scraping down the sides several times. Fold in the pecans and chocolate until evenly incorporated.

Drop the dough onto the baking sheets by heaping measuring tablespoonfuls, spacing about 2 inches apart.

Bake the cookies, one sheet at a time, in the middle of the oven for 15 to 18 minutes, or until dry on the surface but soft in the centers when pressed. Reverse the sheet from front to back halfway through baking to ensure even browning. Slide the cookies, still attached to the parchment, onto a wire rack. Let cool completely. Carefully peel the cookies from the parchment.

Store in an airtight container for up to 3 days or freeze for up to 1 month.

cocoa-mocha macs

makes about 24
(2¾-inch) cookies.

Macadamia nut cookies are among America's best baking inventions of the late twentieth century. In part, we have Hawaii's flourishing macadamia industry to thank. Originally, macadamia trees were planted in Hawaii for ornamental purposes, though people quickly began to value the nuts for home use or sale to local markets. In the late 1930s, University of Hawaii horticulturists recognized the macadamia nut's commercial potential and began selecting the best varieties and encouraging large-scale production.

By the 1950s, the cultivated Hawaiian macadamia trees were beginning to bear, and pricey little jars of these exotic nuts began showing up on American supermarket shelves. Hawaii now produces well over 90 percent of the world crop. As a result of increased availability and successful marketing, macadamias gradually made their way into mainstream baking by the 1980s, when white chocolate–macadamia nut cookies became the rage at high-end shopping-mall cookie bars and bakeries.

Since then, the macadamia-cookie repertoire has broadened considerably due to experimentation by both home bakers and pastry chefs. My Cocoa-Mocha Macs pair macadamias with two of Hawaii's other premium products, coffee and chocolate, in an airy, chewy-soft meringue that contrasts nicely with the creamy-crunchy texture of the nuts. The drizzled chocolate is a fitting visual embellishment for these slightly extravagant cookies, but since they taste almost as good plain, consider it entirely optional.

2¼ teaspoons instant espresso powder or granules

1½ teaspoons vanilla extract

⅛ teaspoon coconut or almond extract

1 ounce unsweetened chocolate, broken up or coarsely chopped

½ cup egg whites (4 large egg whites), free of yolk and at room temperature

¼ teaspoon cream of tartar

⅛ teaspoon salt

¼ cup packed light brown sugar

1¾ cups powdered sugar

2 tablespoons unsweetened American-style cocoa powder

2 tablespoons all-purpose white flour

1⅓ cups (about 6 ounces) coarsely chopped macadamia nuts, wiped with paper towels, if salted

CHOCOLATE DRIZZLE (OPTIONAL)

2 ounces semisweet or bittersweet (*not* unsweetened) chocolate (divided)

1½ teaspoons white vegetable shortening

Preheat the oven to 325 degrees F. Line two large baking sheets with parchment paper.

In a cup, stir together the instant espresso powder or granules, vanilla, and coconut or almond extract. Let stand until the espresso completely dissolves.

In a small, microwave-safe bowl, microwave the chocolate on 50-percent power for 1 minute. Stir well. Continue microwaving on 50-percent power, stirring at 30-second intervals. Stop microwaving before the chocolate completely melts and let the residual heat finish the job. (Alternatively, in a small, heavy saucepan, melt the chocolate over lowest heat, stirring frequently; be very careful not to burn. Immediately remove from the heat.) Let cool to warm.

In a large bowl, with an electric mixer on low speed (use a whisk attachment, if available), beat together the egg whites, cream of tartar, and salt until frothy. Increase the speed to medium-high and beat just until the mixture is opaque and forms soft peaks. Add the brown sugar, 1½ tablespoons at a time, beating after each addition. Gradually beat in the powdered sugar on low speed until evenly incorporated. Add the espresso mixture. Increase the speed to high and beat until the mixture stands in firm, glossy (but not dry) peaks, 2 to 3 minutes more. Combine the cocoa powder and flour in a sieve or sifter and sift over the meringue. Add the chocolate to the meringue. On low speed, beat just until evenly incorporated; avoid overmixing, or the meringue may lose too much volume. Lightly fold in the macadamia nuts.

Immediately drop the meringue onto the baking sheets by heaping measuring tablespoonfuls, spacing about 3 inches apart.

Bake the cookies, one sheet at a time, in the middle of the oven for 12 to 16 minutes, or until barely firm when lightly pressed in the centers; the interior that shows through the surface cracks will not look done. Reverse the sheet from front to back halfway through baking to ensure even browning. Transfer the sheet to a wire rack and let the cookies stand until completely cooled. Carefully peel the cookies from the parchment.

FOR THE DRIZZLE, IF USING

In a medium, microwave-safe bowl, microwave 1½ ounces of the chocolate and the shortening on 50-percent power for 1 minute. Stir well. Continue microwaving on 50-percent power, stirring at 30-second intervals. Stop microwaving before the chocolate is completely melted and let the residual heat finish the job. (Alternatively, in a small, heavy saucepan,

TIPS
The meringue may deflate if allowed to stand, so bake the cookies promptly. Also, if possible, use large baking sheets, so all the cookies can be baked in only two batches.

chocolate and mocha cookies

melt 1½ ounces of the chocolate and the shortening over low heat, stirring frequently; be very careful not to burn. Immediately remove from the heat.) Stir the remaining ½ ounce chocolate into the chocolate mixture until it at least partially melts and the mixture has cooled to barely warm; this step helps ensure that the chocolate will set properly. Arrange the cookies slightly apart on a wax-paper-lined baking sheet.

If necessary, discard the unmelted piece of chocolate. Spoon the chocolate mixture into a paper cone or a small pastry bag fitted with a fine writing tip. Drizzle the chocolate back and forth over all the cookies. Immediately transfer the baking sheet to the refrigerator. Refrigerate for about 10 minutes, or until the chocolate sets. Let the cookies return to room temperature before serving.

Store in a single layer or layered with wax paper in an airtight container for up to 3 days or freeze for up to 1 month.

MACADAMIA ROAD

Hawaii's Big Island and Maui are the world's largest producers of macadamia nuts. However, the trees actually originated in Australia and didn't arrive in Hawaii until 1878. Also called Queensland nuts, macadamias were named for Dr. John Macadam, a chemist who worked on cultivating the trees in Australia.

mocha-espresso wafers

An espresso-flavored cookie served in a Seattle restaurant was the starting point for the following recipe. Because I particularly like the taste of mocha, I decided to include a little cocoa powder to mellow and round out the coffee flavor. Then I decided to change the cookies' texture and shape. By the time I'd finished, my cookies bore no resemblance to the original, except in their use of espresso beans!

These dark, slightly bittersweet wafers are absolutely perfect for enjoying with coffee.

1²/₃ cups all-purpose white flour

3½ tablespoons unsweetened Dutch-process cocoa powder

¼ teaspoon salt

¾ cup (1½ sticks) unsalted butter, slightly softened

½ cup sugar

⅓ cup powdered sugar

1 tablespoon plus 2½ teaspoons instant espresso powder or granules, dissolved in 1 tablespoon hot water

1¼ teaspoons vanilla extract

Scant 2 tablespoons very finely ground espresso beans

BITTERSWEET CHOCOLATE ICING

1 cup powdered sugar

2 tablespoons unsweetened Dutch-process cocoa powder

In a medium bowl, sift together the flour, cocoa, and salt; set aside. In a large bowl, with an electric mixer on medium speed, beat together the butter, sugar, powdered sugar, espresso mixture, and vanilla until well blended. Beat in the ground espresso beans. Beat or stir in the flour mixture until evenly incorporated.

Divide the dough in half. Place each portion between large sheets of wax paper. Roll out the portions ⅛ inch thick; check the underside of the dough and smooth out any wrinkles that form. Stack the rolled portions (paper still attached) on a baking sheet. Refrigerate for about 45 minutes or until cold and firm, or freeze for about 20 minutes to speed chilling.

Preheat the oven to 350 degrees F. Grease several baking sheets or coat with nonstick spray.

Working with one portion at a time, gently peel away, then pat one sheet of wax paper back into place. Flip the dough over, then peel off and dis-

card the second sheet. Using a 2¼-to-2½-inch round or oval cutter, cut out the cookies. (If at any point the dough softens too much to handle easily, transfer the paper and cookies to a baking sheet and refrigerate until firm again.) Using a spatula, carefully transfer the cookies to the baking sheets, spacing about 1½ inches apart. Reroll any dough scraps. Continue cutting out the cookies until all the dough is used.

Bake the cookies, one sheet at a time, in the upper third of the oven for 5 to 8 minutes, or until just beginning to firm up when pressed in the centers; be careful not to burn. Reverse the sheet from front to back halfway through baking to ensure even browning. Transfer the sheet to a wire rack and let stand until the cookies firm up slightly, about 2 minutes. Using a spatula, transfer the cookies to wire racks set over sheets of wax paper. Let stand until completely cooled.

FOR THE ICING

Sift the powdered sugar and cocoa together into a small, deep bowl. Stir in 1½ tablespoons hot water, or enough to make a smooth, slightly runny icing. Using a piping cone or small pastry bag fitted with a fine writing tip, decoratively drizzle fine lines of icing back and forth over the cookies. (Alternatively, put the icing in a small, sturdy plastic bag, squeezing the icing into one corner and twisting the top of the bag closed. Snip the point of the corner to produce a small hole. Then drizzle fine lines of icing back and forth across the cookies.) Let the cookies stand until the icing sets, about 1 hour.

Store in an airtight container for up to 1 week or freeze for up to 1 month.

fantastic Fudgewiches

As a child, I was always intrigued by the idea of fudge sandwich cookies, but even then, I never felt that the commercial versions lived up to their name. I experimented to see if I could create ones that met my early expectations, and these definitely made the grade. They were a big hit with my taste testers, particularly with my son, who insisted I give him the recipe immediately. All my testers liked the creamy richness of the filling and the bittersweet edge and tender-crispness of the chocolate wafers. For me, the key to these cookies is the fudge filling. It has a full, mellow flavor that an ordinary chocolate crème just can't match. And it's easy and virtually foolproof to prepare.

It's best not to make the cookies too large, as two wafers and an ample amount of filling yield a generous serving. For convenience, the fudge may be made ahead and reheated when needed to fill the sandwiches.

1³/₄ cups all-purpose white flour

   ¹/₃ cup unsweetened Dutch-process cocoa powder, sifted after measuring, if lumpy

   1 teaspoon baking powder

   ²/₃ cup (1 stick plus 2²/₃ tablespoons) unsalted butter, slightly softened

   2 tablespoons corn oil or other flavorless vegetable oil

³/₄ cup sugar

   1 large egg

   2 teaspoons vanilla extract

   Scant ¹/₂ teaspoon salt

QUICK FUDGE

   1 14-ounce can sweetened condensed milk

1¹/₂ cups (9 ounces) semisweet chocolate morsels

1¹/₂ ounces unsweetened chocolate, broken up or coarsely chopped

1¹/₂ tablespoons unsalted butter, slightly softened

   1 teaspoon vanilla extract

   About 1 tablespoon unsweetened Dutch-process cocoa powder, for topping (optional)

In a large bowl, thoroughly stir together the flour, cocoa powder, and baking powder; set aside. In another large bowl, with an electric mixer on low, then medium, speed, beat together the butter, oil, and sugar until lightened and fluffy. Add the egg, vanilla, and salt and beat until well blended and smooth. Beat or stir in the flour mixture until evenly incorporated.

Divide the dough in half. Place each portion between large sheets of wax paper. Roll out each portion ¹/₈ inch thick; check the underside of the dough and smooth out any wrinkles that form. Stack the rolled portions (paper still attached) on a baking sheet. Refrigerate for 45 minutes, or until chilled and firm but not hard, or freeze for about 20 minutes to

TIP

Be sure to use Dutch-process cocoa, such as Droste or European-style Hershey's, in this recipe. Nonalkalized American cocoa won't lend the right taste, color, or texture to the dough.

speed chilling. (If desired, the dough may be held for up to 24 hours; let warm up slightly before using.)

Preheat the oven to 350 degrees F. Grease several baking sheets or coat with nonstick spray.

Working with one portion at a time and leaving the remaining dough chilled, gently peel away, then pat one sheet of wax paper back into place. Flip the dough over, then peel off and discard the second sheet. Using a 2-inch round or square cutter, cut out the cookies. If desired, using a mini cutter, the larger end of a pastry piping tip, or a thimble, cut away a small hole from the center of half the cookies. (If at any point the dough softens too much to handle easily, transfer the paper and cookies to a baking sheet and refrigerate or freeze until firm again.)

chocolate and mocha cookies

Using a spatula, carefully transfer the cookies to the baking sheets, spacing about 1½ inches apart. Place the solid rounds on one sheet and the rounds with the cutaway centers on another. Reroll any dough scraps. Continue cutting out the cookies until all the dough is used.

Bake the cookies, one sheet at a time, in the upper third of the oven for 6 to 9 minutes, or until almost firm when pressed in the centers; cutaways will bake faster. Reverse the sheet from front to back halfway through baking to ensure even browning. Transfer the sheet to a wire rack and let stand until the cookies firm up slightly, 1 to 2 minutes. Using a spatula, transfer the cookies to wire racks. Let stand until completely cooled.

FOR THE FUDGE

In a 1-quart or similar heavy saucepan, stir together the condensed milk, chocolate morsels, unsweetened chocolate, and butter over medium-low heat. Heat, stirring constantly, until the chocolates melt and the mixture is completely smooth; be careful not to burn. Immediately remove from the heat. Stir in the vanilla. Let cool until thickened just enough to spread. (The fudge may be prepared a day or so in advance, then refrigerated in an airtight container. Before using, reheat it over low heat, stirring, until spreadable.)

Immediately spread the fudge about ⅓ inch thick on the underside of each cookie bottom. (If the fudge stiffens as you work, warm it just slightly over low heat, stirring constantly.) Center the tops over the bottoms. Very lightly press down. Lightly dust the cookie tops with cocoa powder, if desired.

Store in an airtight container for up to 1 week. The cookies can be frozen for up to 1 month but should not be filled and sandwiched together until shortly before serving.

chocolate-malt sandwich cookies

I sometimes wonder whether today's youth are growing up with a sufficient appreciation of malted milk. When I was a child, people thought that malted milk powder was nutritious, kept it in their cupboards, and encouraged their youngsters to make drinks with it. (Presumably, the fact that malt is a dried, germinated barley product accounts for its healthful reputation.)

Since many children seem to be maltless nowadays, I wanted to do my part to keep this comfortable, old-fashioned flavoring from fading from the scene. These are generous, decadent sandwich cookies, made with crispy-chewy chocolate rounds and a fluffy, creamy chocolate-malt filling that's guaranteed to generate—or rekindle—chocolate-malt enthusiasm. The idea for the filling came from the frosting of a popular T.G.I. Friday's chocolate-malt cake.

2 cups all-purpose white flour

¹/₂ cup unsweetened American-style cocoa powder, sifted after measuring, if lumpy

2 tablespoons plain (*not* chocolate-flavored) malted milk powder

1 teaspoon baking soda

¹/₂ teaspoon salt

1³/₄ cups sugar

²/₃ cup (1 stick plus 2²/₃ tablespoons) unsalted butter, slightly softened

¹/₃ cup corn oil or other flavorless vegetable oil

¹/₄ cup sour cream

1 large egg

2 teaspoons vanilla extract

CHOCOLATE-MALT FILLING

1²/₃ cups (10 ounces) semisweet chocolate morsels

¹/₄ cup plus 1 tablespoon unsalted butter, cut into chunks

³/₄ cup plus 2 tablespoons plain (*not* chocolate-flavored) malted milk powder

1 3-ounce package cream cheese, softened slightly and cut into chunks

¹/₄ cup plus 2 tablespoons milk

2 teaspoons vanilla extract

Preheat the oven to 350 degrees F. Grease several baking sheets or coat with nonstick spray.

In a medium bowl, thoroughly stir together the flour, cocoa powder, malted milk powder, baking soda, and salt; set aside. In a large bowl, with an electric mixer on medium speed, beat together the sugar, butter, and oil until well blended. Add the sour cream, egg, and vanilla and beat until well blended; the mixture may look curdled. Beat in half of the flour mixture, scraping down the sides several times. Beat in 3 tablespoons hot water, then beat or stir in the remaining flour mixture until evenly incorporated.

Drop the dough onto the baking sheets using a ¹/₈-cup measure or coffee

tip

Note that the recipe calls for *plain* malted milk powder, not chocolate-flavored; I add the chocolate as a separate ingredient. Also, use American-style, not Dutch-process, unsweetened cocoa powder.

scoop, spacing about 2½ inches apart. Using a lightly greased hand, pat down the tops just slightly.

Bake the cookies, one sheet at a time, in the middle of the oven for 10 to 12 minutes, or until the tops begin to flatten and the cookies are just barely firm in the centers. Reverse the sheet from front to back halfway through baking to ensure even browning. Transfer the sheet to a wire rack and let stand until the cookies are slightly firm, about 3 minutes. Using a spatula, transfer the cookies to wire racks. Let stand until completely cooled.

FOR THE FILLING

In a medium, microwave-safe bowl, microwave the chocolate morsels and butter on 100-percent power for 1½ minutes. Stir well. Continue microwaving on 50-percent power, stirring at 30-second intervals. Stop microwaving before the chocolate is completely melted and let the residual heat do the job. (Alternatively, in a small, heavy saucepan, melt the chocolate morsels and butter over lowest heat, stirring frequently; be very careful not to burn. Immediately remove from the heat.) Let cool to warm.

In a large bowl, with an electric mixer on medium speed, beat together the malted milk powder and cream cheese until well blended and completely smooth. Beat in half of the chocolate mixture just until incorporated. Beat in the milk, 1 tablespoon at a time, until well blended. Beat in the remaining chocolate mixture and the vanilla until evenly incorporated. Refrigerate for 30 minutes, or until somewhat thickened but not stiff. (Alternatively, if you are in a hurry, set the bowl in a larger bowl of ice water and stir until it cools and thickens.) Beat the filling on high speed until light in color and very fluffy, about 3 minutes more; scrape down the sides several times.

Spread about 2½ tablespoons of the filling on the underside of half of the cookies. Top each cookie with a second cookie about the same size. Press the two together until the filling squeezes out the edge. Let stand for at least 5 minutes so the flavors can mingle before serving.

Store in an airtight container for up to 4 days or freeze for up to 1 month.

A singular malt

Throughout the 1920s and 1930s, malt was a popular flavoring, and malt extract was widely sold to home cooks. (Although this was the Prohibition era and malt is a key ingredient in beer making, apparently no one sought to prohibit its sale.) The Premier Malt Products Company promoted its well-known Blue Ribbon brand by publishing test-kitchen recipes — including cookies — and claiming superior product quality:

"The only way to get Blue Ribbon Malt quality is to buy Blue Ribbon Malt Extract. If you have never tried Blue Ribbon you have a most delightful treat in store. . . . Its high standard of quality is at all times fully maintained. Pure barley malt is the only grain used in its manufacture. . . . The great factories where Blue Ribbon Malt Extract is made are models of modern specialized machinery and sanitation."

chocolate whoopie pies

Makes 7 or 8
(4-inch) sandwich cookies.

Whoopie pies are enormously popular modern sandwich cookies featuring large, cakey, saucer-shaped domes and a creamy, marshmallowy filling. Just about every bakery and farmers' market in eastern Pennsylvania's Amish country sells them, and in the western part of the state, they appear under the name "gobs." Whoopie pies are also very popular throughout New England.

Though the plump cookie sandwiches are occasionally prepared in home kitchens nowadays, they most likely began as a commercial bakery product. Peter Schlichting, a Dover, New Hampshire, dietitian whose hobby is sleuthing out whoopie-pie history, has traced the cookies back to the Depression era in several different states. He thinks there's a good chance that they originated in New England rather than Pennsylvania. He says that the Berwick Cake Company, located in the Roxbury section of Boston until it closed in 1977, seems to have been the first to make them; a retired employee has recalled that the firm began whoopie-pie production in 1926.

As for the name, the only story I've seen suggests that it originated with a cook who had some leftover cake batter and dropped it into generous cookie-sized rounds. The success of this experiment supposedly elicited the exclamation, "Whoopie! Pies!"

While the dough does seem to have evolved from a cake batter, my guess is that both recipe and name were created by a clever commercial baker seeking a cake-like product that could be individually packaged and easily eaten out of hand. Considering that there is a Boston connection, the "pie" part of the name may have come from the cookies' passing resemblance to Boston cream pie.

Whoopie pies come in several different flavors, including molasses, peanut butter, pumpkin, and, most often, chocolate. My chocolate whoopie pies are slightly darker, moister, and more devil's foody than some versions; I think the bolder flavor goes better with the frosting-like filling. This recipe may be doubled, if desired.

²/₃ cup unsweetened American-style cocoa powder, sifted after measuring, if lumpy

1 teaspoon baking soda

2 cups all-purpose white flour

1 teaspoon baking powder

³/₄ teaspoon salt

1¹/₃ cups packed light brown sugar

¹/₄ cup white vegetable shortening

¹/₄ cup (¹/₂ stick) unsalted butter, slightly softened

1 large egg

2 teaspoons vanilla extract

¹/₂ cup sour cream

FILLING

¹/₃ cup white vegetable shortening

¹/₃ cup (5¹/₃ tablespoons) unsalted butter, slightly softened

1 cup powdered sugar

1¹/₂ tablespoons light corn syrup

2 teaspoons vanilla extract

¹/₈ teaspoon salt

1 7-ounce jar (1¹/₃ cups) marshmallow creme

Preheat the oven to 350 degrees F. Grease several baking sheets or coat with nonstick spray.

In a medium bowl, beat together the cocoa powder, baking soda, and ¾ cup hot water with a fork until smooth; the mixture will foam up and darken. Let stand until the foaming subsides and the mixture cools. In a medium bowl, thoroughly stir together the flour, baking powder, and salt.

In a large bowl, with an electric mixer on medium speed, beat together the brown sugar, shortening, and butter until well blended, about 2 minutes; if necessary, scrape down the sides of the bowl several times. Add the egg and vanilla and beat until very light and fluffy, about 2 minutes more. Beat in half of the flour mixture; scrape down the sides several times. Stir the sour cream into the cocoa mixture. On low speed, beat the cocoa mixture, then the remaining flour mixture, into the brown-sugar mixture until evenly incorporated.

Using a ¼-cup measure, drop the dough onto the baking sheets, spacing about 3½ inches apart. Using a lightly greased knife, smooth out the tops slightly; don't make the rounds much larger, or they may spread too much during baking.

Bake the cookies, one sheet at a time, in the middle of the oven for 10 to 14 minutes, or until they just spring back when lightly pressed in the centers. Reverse the sheet from front to back halfway through baking to ensure even browning. Transfer the sheet to a wire rack and let stand until the cookies firm up, 4 to 5 minutes. Using a spatula, transfer the cookies to wire racks. Let stand until completely cooled.

FOR THE FILLING

In a large bowl, with an electric mixer on medium speed, beat together the shortening, butter, powdered sugar, corn syrup, vanilla, and salt until well blended and fluffy. Add the marshmallow creme and beat until evenly incorporated.

Spread about ⅓ cup of the filling on the underside of half of the cookies, leaving a ½-inch border around the edge. Top each cookie with a second cookie about the same size. Press the two together until the filling almost extends to the edges.

Store the cookies in individual plastic bags for up to 1 week. Do not freeze.

whoopies
for breakfast

Yankee magazine once humorously fashioned "The New England Food Pyramid," showing apple, pumpkin, blueberry, and whoopie pies as one of the major food groups and advising that this category "should be served for breakfast."

ice cream sandwiches

Recipes for homemade ice cream sandwiches didn't start turning up until the late 1970s. This is surprising, considering that they are easy to prepare and so much better than the typical store-bought ones. Not only are the cookies more chocolatey and satisfying, but the sandwiches can be filled with top-quality ice cream in any flavor desired.

These make a terrific do-ahead summer snack for both youngsters and adults. I've also served them as dessert after a casual company supper on the deck. For children's parties, it's fun to let the guests decorate their own sandwiches by pressing them into saucers of jimmies, colored sprinkles, assorted nuts, and chocolate minimorsels.

This recipe can be doubled, if desired.

2¼ cups all-purpose white flour

⅔ cup unsweetened Dutch-process cocoa powder, sifted after measuring, if lumpy

1 teaspoon baking powder

¾ cup plus 2 tablespoons (1¾ sticks) unsalted butter, slightly softened

2 tablespoons corn oil or other flavorless vegetable oil

Generous 1⅓ cups sugar

1 large egg

1 tablespoon coffee or water

2 teaspoons vanilla extract

½ teaspoon salt

About 1 quart ice cream, such as vanilla, fudge ripple, chocolate-chip mint, coffee, or fudge chunk

Chocolate jimmies, chopped nuts, or colored sprinkles, for topping (optional)

In a large bowl, thoroughly stir together the flour, cocoa, and baking powder; set aside. In a large bowl, with an electric mixer on low, then medium, speed, beat together the butter, oil, and sugar until lightened and fluffy. Add the egg, coffee or water, vanilla, and salt and beat until well blended and smooth. Beat or stir in the flour mixture until evenly incorporated. Let the dough stand for 10 to 15 minutes, or until firmed up slightly.

Divide the dough in half. Place each portion between large sheets of wax paper. Roll out each portion a scant ¼ inch thick; check the underside of the dough and smooth out any wrinkles that form. Stack the rolled portions (paper still attached) on a baking sheet. Refrigerate for 45 minutes, or until chilled and firm but not hard, or freeze for about 20 minutes to speed chilling. (If desired, the dough may be held for up to 24 hours; let warm up slightly before using.)

Preheat the oven to 350 degrees F. Grease several baking sheets or coat with nonstick spray.

Working with one portion at a time and leaving the remaining dough chilled, gently peel away, then pat one sheet of wax paper back into place. Flip the dough over, then peel off and discard the second sheet. Using a large, sharp knife, cut the dough into 1½-by-4-inch rectangles, or cut into rounds using a 3-inch or similar round or fluted cutter. (If at any point the dough softens too much to handle easily, transfer the paper and cookies to a baking sheet and refrigerate or freeze until firm again.) Using a spatula, carefully transfer the cookies to the baking sheets, spacing about 2 inches apart. Using the lightly oiled tines of a fork, deeply prick each cookie in a decorative design and score with a small, sharp knife as shown in the photograph, if desired. Reroll any dough scraps; chill the dough. Continue cutting out the cookies until all the dough is used.

Bake the cookies, one sheet at a time, in the upper third of the oven for 8 to 11 minutes, or until just firm when pressed in the centers. Reverse the sheet from front to back halfway through baking to ensure even browning. Transfer the sheet to a wire rack and let stand until the cookies firm up slightly, 1 to 2 minutes. Using a spatula, transfer the cookies to wire racks. Let stand until completely cooled.

Freeze the cookies for at least 1 hour or up to 1 month before assembling the sandwiches.

Spread ¼ to ⅓ cup ice cream on the underside of one cookie. Top with a second cookie about the same size. Press down slightly until the ice cream squeezes out to the edges. Pack the sandwiches in individual plastic bags, seal tightly, and return to the freezer for at least 3 hours or up to several days before serving. Serve the sandwiches as is or, if desired, dip the ice-cream edges into jimmies, nuts, or colored sprinkles before serving. Or provide saucers of toppings and let diners add their own treats.

Store the assembled sandwiches in the sealed plastic bags for up to 1 week; they will gradually lose some of their crispness after a few days.

TIP

It's difficult to tell when dark-colored cookies like these are done, because the telltale brown at the edges doesn't show. Nevertheless, it's important to avoid overbaking, or the chocolate will taste burned, and to avoid underbaking, or the cookies won't be crisp. I find that the best course is to start by baking these until they are just firm when pressed in the centers. If the cookies on the first sheet don't firm up and crisp when cooled, I return them to the oven to bake a bit longer. Then I leave the succeeding sheets in the oven a little longer than the first one.

5

Brownies, Blondies, and Other Bar Cookies

Lowney's
brownies

It's hard to imagine American baking without brownies, but so far as I can tell, not a single recipe for these fudgy, uniquely American favorites appeared in print before the twentieth century. (The first flurry of brownie-making activity was probably already under way in New England before the turn of the century, however.) The 1906 edition of *The Boston Cooking-School Cook Book* included a chocolate brownie recipe, and two more appeared in *Lowney's Cook Book,* published in 1907 by Boston chocolate and cocoa purveyor Walter M. Lowney. Lowney's brownies are winners: gratifyingly moist, dense, and, in keeping with the best of American baking tradition, remarkably uncomplicated to make.

Though it's often speculated that brownies were the happy accident resulting from somebody's cake falling, this isn't likely. Brownies are denser than cake not because they have fallen, but because they have almost no liquid. Maybe they were the fortunate result of someone forgetting the milk in a chocolate cake!

Note that the recipe calls for neither baking soda, baking powder, nor vanilla. The original sketchy instructions called only for creaming the butter and then mixing in the remaining ingredients. For clarity and to help ensure good results, I've indicated that the chocolate should be melted, the butter and sugar creamed together, and the chocolate added to them, before the remaining ingredients are stirred in. I've also specified the oven temperature, pan size, and baking time, which the original recipe omitted. The ingredients and quantities are left unchanged.

2 ounces unsweetened chocolate, broken up or coarsely chopped	2 large eggs
1/2 cup (1 stick) unsalted butter, slightly softened	1/2 cup all-purpose white flour
1 cup sugar	1/2 cup (2 ounces) chopped walnuts or pecans
	1/4 teaspoon salt

Preheat the oven to 350 degrees F. Lightly grease an 8-inch square baking pan or coat with nonstick spray. Line the pan with aluminum foil, letting the foil overhang two opposing sides of the pan by about 2 inches. Grease the foil or coat with nonstick spray.

In a small, microwave-safe bowl, microwave the chocolate on 50-percent power for 1 minute. Stir well. Continue microwaving on 50-percent power, stirring at 30-second intervals. Stop microwaving before the chocolate completely melts and let the residual heat finish the job. (Alternatively, in a small, heavy saucepan, melt the chocolate over lowest heat, stirring frequently; be very careful not to burn. Immediately remove from the heat.) Let cool to warm.

In a medium bowl, with a wooden spoon, mix together the butter and sugar until well blended and smooth. Stir in the chocolate until evenly incorporated. Stir in the eggs, then the flour, walnuts or pecans, and salt, until evenly incorporated. Turn out the batter into the baking pan, spreading to the edges.

Bake in the middle of the oven for 19 to 23 minutes, or until a toothpick inserted in the center comes out clean. Transfer the pan to a wire rack and let stand until the brownie is completely cooled. Refrigerate until chilled.

Using the overhanging foil as handles, transfer the brownie to a cutting board. Carefully peel off and discard the foil. Using a large, sharp knife, cut the brownie into 16 squares; wipe the knife clean between cuts.

Store in an airtight container for up to 4 days or freeze for up to 1 month. If freezing, leave the brownie slab whole, then cut into squares when partially thawed.

where's walter?

Whatever happened to Walter Lowney's chocolate company? Founded in the 1880s, it was a major competitor of the nearby Baker's chocolate firm by the early twentieth century. Gradually, Lowney's fortunes changed, and after being sold a number of times, the company was foreclosed by a bank in the 1930s. However, the Mansfield, Massachusetts, factory still makes chocolate for the Mercken's label, a brand now sold mainly wholesale to American candy makers.

fudge brownies supreme

These are the ones! The moistest, fudgiest, most succulent brownies ever. No frosting, no fruit, no crunchy munchies of any sort to distract from the mousse-like texture and deep, full-blown chocolate flavor. A friend commented that if great fudge were baked, it might taste like these brownies.

If you feel strongly that brownies should have nuts, you could add some walnuts to these. However, the effect will be similar to eating nuts in a chocolate mousse.

½ cup plus 2 tablespoons (1 stick plus 2 tablespoons) unsalted butter

5 ounces bittersweet (*not* unsweetened) or semisweet chocolate, broken up or coarsely chopped

⅔ cup all-purpose white flour

1½ tablespoons unsweetened American-style cocoa powder, sifted after measuring, if lumpy

¼ teaspoon salt

1 cup sugar

⅓ cup packed light brown sugar

3 large eggs

2½ teaspoons vanilla extract

Preheat the oven to 350 degrees F. Lightly grease an 8-inch square baking pan or coat with nonstick spray. Line the pan with aluminum foil, letting the foil overhang two opposing sides of the pan by about 2 inches. Grease the foil or coat with nonstick spray.

In a large, microwave-safe bowl, microwave the butter and chocolate on 100-percent power for 1 minute. Stir well. Continue microwaving on 50-percent power, stirring at 30-second intervals. Stop microwaving before the chocolate completely melts and let the residual heat finish the job. (Alternatively, in a large, heavy saucepan, melt the chocolate and butter over lowest heat, stirring frequently; be very careful not to burn. Immediately remove from the heat.) Let cool to warm.

In a small bowl, thoroughly stir together the flour, cocoa powder, and salt; set aside. Stir the sugar and brown sugar into the chocolate-butter mixture until well combined. Add the eggs and vanilla and stir until the sugar dissolves and the mixture is well blended and smooth. Stir in the flour mixture just until evenly incorporated. Turn out the batter into the baking pan, spreading to the edges.

Bake in the middle of the oven for 28 to 33 minutes, or until the center is almost firm when tapped and a toothpick inserted in the center comes out clean except for the bottom ¼ inch, which should still look moist. Transfer the pan to a wire rack and let stand until the brownie is completely cooled. Refrigerate until well chilled.

Using the overhanging foil as handles, transfer the brownie to a cutting board. Carefully peel off and discard the foil. If desired, cut away and discard any overbaked edges. Using a large, sharp knife, cut the brownie into 12 bars; wipe the knife clean between cuts.

Store in an airtight container for up to 3 days or freeze for up to 1 month. If freezing, leave the brownie slab whole, then cut into bars when partially thawed.

WHAT'S IN A NAME?

Nobody knows who created brownies, but they were not, as one colorful story goes, named for popular twentieth-century Maine food columnist "Brownie" Schrumpf. Mrs. Schrumpf was only a few years old when brownies first appeared! Moreover, other baked goods had been called brownies even before the bars we now refer to by that name came along. Some brown-sugar drop cookies in a 1902 Estherville, Iowa, community cookbook were titled "brownies," and so were some molasses cakes in the 1896 *Boston Cooking-School Cook Book*. Presumably the moniker resulted from the fact that these baked goods were brown.

chocolate chunk brownies

These brownies boast a moist crumb, shiny top, and shards of chocolate throughout. They are for traditionalists who demand something decadent.

6½ tablespoons unsalted butter

⅔ cup sugar

11 ounces bittersweet (*not* unsweetened) or semisweet chocolate (divided)

2½ teaspoons vanilla extract

2 large eggs

¾ cup all-purpose white flour

¼ teaspoon baking soda

¼ teaspoon salt

½ cup (2 ounces) chopped walnuts (optional)

Preheat the oven to 350 degrees F. Lightly grease an 8-inch square baking pan or coat with nonstick spray. Line the pan with aluminum foil, letting the foil overhang two opposing sides of the pan by about 2 inches. Grease the foil or coat with nonstick spray.

In a large saucepan over medium-high heat, bring the butter, sugar, and 2 tablespoons water just to a boil, stirring. Remove from the heat. Coarsely chop 7 ounces of the chocolate and stir into the sugar mixture until completely melted. Let cool to warm. Stir in the vanilla, then the eggs, until well blended.

In a small bowl, thoroughly stir together the flour, baking soda, and salt. Stir the flour mixture into the chocolate mixture just until evenly incorporated. Chop the remaining 4 ounces chocolate into ¼-inch chunks. Stir in the chocolate chunks and the walnuts, if using. Turn out the batter into the baking pan, spreading to the edges.

Bake in the middle of the oven for 22 to 27 minutes, or until the center is almost firm when tapped and a toothpick inserted in the center comes out clean except for the bottom ¼ inch, which should still look wet. Transfer the pan to a wire rack and let stand until the brownie is completely cooled. Refrigerate until well chilled.

Using the overhanging foil as handles, transfer the brownie to a cutting board. Carefully peel off and discard the foil. Using a large, sharp knife, cut the brownie into 16 bars; wipe the knife clean between cuts.

Store in an airtight container for up to 3 days or freeze for up to 1 month. If freezing, leave the brownie slab whole, then cut into bars when partially thawed.

The photograph is on page 124.

No-Bake Peanut Butter-chocolate crunch Bars

Makes 24 (2⅛-by-2¼-inch) bars.

I must have come across nearly 30 versions of this bar while looking at modern community cookbooks from the upper Midwest. And little wonder, since these are quick and easy enough for cooks as young as middle school age to whip up, yet tasty enough to proudly take to a picnic or bake sale. Kids generally love them; many adults like them, too.

It would be hard to go wrong with the peanut butter, peanuts, and chocolate combination, of course, and the corn flakes add a pleasant crunchy texture without being readily identifiable. The coconut is strictly optional. Those who like coconut will think it adds a lot to the recipe. I found that most versions of this recipe were too sweet, so I've reduced the sugar a bit. These bars keep well, though I don't think it's likely to matter.

1 cup smooth peanut butter
⅔ cup packed light brown sugar
1 tablespoon unsalted butter, cut into chunks
⅓ cup light corn syrup
4½ cups corn flakes, coarsely crushed
1 cup (4½ ounces) chopped peanuts, preferably unsalted (divided)

¾ cup (about 2 ounces) shredded or flaked sweetened coconut (optional)
¾ teaspoon vanilla extract
1 cup (6 ounces) semisweet chocolate minimorsels

Generously grease a 9-by-13-inch baking pan or coat with nonstick spray.

In a large, heavy saucepan, thoroughly stir together the peanut butter, brown sugar, butter, and corn syrup. Bring to a boil over medium-high heat, and boil, stirring constantly, for 1 minute. Remove from the heat. Stir in the corn flakes, ⅔ cup of the peanuts, the coconut (if using), and vanilla until evenly incorporated. Turn out the mixture into the baking pan, spreading to the edges. Immediately sprinkle the chocolate minimorsels over the top; let stand until they melt. Using a table knife, spread the melted chocolate evenly over the top. Sprinkle the remaining ⅓ cup peanuts over the chocolate. Refrigerate until the chocolate completely sets, about 30 minutes, or freeze for about 15 minutes to speed chilling. Using a large, sharp knife, cut into 24 bars

Store in an airtight container for up to 1 week or freeze for up to 1 month.

truffLebrownies

This recipe gives the all-American brownie a French accent. I've frosted the brownies with ganache—the same glorious cream-and-chocolate blend that's used in the centers of classic European truffles.

These brownies are dense, dark, moist, and supremely chocolatey, with a generous layer of bittersweet yet meltingly mellow ganache on top.

6½ ounces bittersweet (*not* unsweetened) or semisweet chocolate, broken up or coarsely chopped

1½ ounces unsweetened chocolate, broken up or coarsely chopped

½ cup (1 stick) unsalted butter, cut into chunks

¾ cup plus 2 tablespoons sugar

1½ tablespoons crème de cacao or other chocolate or coffee liqueur (or coffee, if preferred)

2 teaspoons vanilla extract

3 large eggs

½ cup all-purpose white flour

¼ teaspoon baking soda

¼ teaspoon salt

GANACHE

⅓ cup heavy (whipping) cream

1½ tablespoons crème de cacao or other chocolate or coffee liqueur (or coffee, if preferred)

6 ounces bittersweet (*not* unsweetened) or semisweet chocolate, broken up or coarsely chopped

Preheat the oven to 350 degrees F. Lightly grease a 9-inch square baking pan or coat with nonstick spray. Line the pan with aluminum foil, letting the foil overhang two opposing sides of the pan by about 2 inches. Grease the foil or coat with nonstick spray.

In a medium, microwave-safe bowl, microwave the chocolates and butter on 100-percent power for 1 minute. Stir well. Continue microwaving on 50-percent power, stirring at 30-second intervals. Stop microwaving before the chocolates completely melt and let the residual heat finish the job. (Alternatively, in a large, heavy saucepan over lowest heat, melt the chocolates and butter, stirring frequently; be very careful not to burn. Immediately remove from the heat.) Let cool to warm.

Stir the sugar, liqueur or coffee, and vanilla into the chocolate mixture until well blended. Vigorously stir in the eggs, one at a time, until they are evenly incorporated, the sugar is dissolved, and the mixture is smooth and shiny. In a small bowl, thoroughly stir together the flour, baking soda, and salt. Stir the flour mixture into the chocolate mixture just until evenly incorporated. Turn out the batter into the baking pan, spreading to the edges.

Bake in the middle of the oven for 18 to 22 minutes, or until the edges are just pulling away from the pan and a toothpick inserted in the center comes out clean except for the bottom ½ inch, which should still look moist. Transfer the pan to a wire rack and let stand until the brownie is completely cooled.

FOR THE GANACHE

In a small, microwave-safe bowl, microwave the cream and liqueur on 100-percent power until the mixture just comes to a boil, about 1 minute; set aside. In another small, microwave-safe bowl, microwave the chocolate on 100-percent power for 1½ minutes. Stir well. Continue microwaving on 50-percent power, stirring at 30-second intervals. Stop microwaving before the chocolate completely melts and let the residual heat finish the job. (Alternatively, in a small, heavy saucepan over medium-high heat, bring the cream and liqueur just to a boil. Melt the chocolate in the top of a double boiler set over gently simmering water.)

Stir the cream mixture into the chocolate until the mixture is well blended. Strain the ganache through a fine sieve. Let stand until cooled slightly.

Pour the ganache over the cooled brownie. Using a spatula or knife, spread to the edges. Let stand until the ganache is completely cooled and set, at least 1½ hours, or refrigerate for 45 minutes to speed cooling.

Using the overhanging foil as handles, transfer the brownie to a cutting board. Carefully peel off and discard the foil. Using a large, sharp knife, cut the brownie into 16 squares; wipe the knife clean between cuts.

Store in an airtight container for up to 3 days or freeze without the ganache for up to 1 month. If freezing, leave the brownie slab whole, then add the ganache and cut into squares when completely thawed.

white chocolate-chunk chocolate brownies

makes 16
(2¼-inch) squares.

Chockablock with white chocolate chunks and chocolate morsels, these dark, moist, and distinctive-looking brownies are a specialty of the Inn at Thorn Hill, a historic, century-old New Hampshire inn near the White Mountains. As Julie Dorman, the pastry chef who created the recipe, notes, the brownies are rich and fudge-like, with the white chocolate chunks embedded in the top lending a contrasting touch of sweetness. She says the brownies are a favorite Sunday dessert. She also often cuts them small and offers them at afternoon tea.

³/₄ cup (1¹/₂ sticks) unsalted butter, cut into chunks

4 ounces unsweetened chocolate, broken up or coarsely chopped

1¹/₂ cups sugar

2 teaspoons vanilla extract

4 large eggs

¹/₂ cup all-purpose white flour

¹/₄ teaspoon salt

1 cup (6 ounces) semisweet chocolate morsels

8 ounces top-quality white chocolate, coarsely chopped

Preheat the oven to 350 degrees F. Lightly grease a 9-inch baking pan or coat with nonstick spray. Line the pan with aluminum foil, letting the foil overhang two opposing sides of the pan by about 2 inches. Grease the foil or coat with nonstick spray.

In a large, microwave-safe bowl, microwave the butter and unsweetened chocolate on 100-percent power for 1 minute. Stir well. Continue microwaving on 50-percent power, stirring at 30-second intervals. Stop microwaving before the chocolate completely melts and let the residual heat finish the job. (Alternatively, in a medium, heavy saucepan over lowest heat, melt the butter and chocolate, stirring frequently; be very careful not to burn. Immediately remove from the heat.) Let cool to warm.

Stir the sugar and vanilla into the chocolate mixture until well blended. Vigorously stir in the eggs, one at a time, until they are evenly incorporated, the sugar is dissolved, and the mixture is smooth and shiny. In a small bowl, thoroughly stir together the flour and salt. Stir the flour mixture and the chocolate morsels into the chocolate mixture just until evenly incorporated. Turn out the batter into the baking pan, spreading to the edges. Sprinkle the white chocolate chunks over the top, patting them down to embed them just slightly.

Bake in the middle of the oven for 25 to 30 minutes, or until the white chocolate chunks are barely colored and a toothpick inserted in the center comes out clean except for the bottom ¾ inch, which should still look very moist; be careful not to overbake. Transfer the pan to a wire rack and let stand until the brownie is completely cooled. Refrigerate until well chilled.

Using the overhanging foil as handles, transfer the brownie to a cutting board. Carefully peel off and discard the foil. Using a large, sharp knife, cut the brownie into 16 squares; wipe the knife clean between cuts.

Store in an airtight container for up to 3 days or freeze for up to 1 month. If freezing, leave the brownie slab whole, then cut into squares when partially thawed.

ROCKY Road Brownies

The bumpy-lumpy "rocky road" pairing of chocolate and marshmallows is best known in American fudge recipes but has been around in American baking since at least the early twentieth century. The 1921 edition of the famous *Boston Cooking-School Cook Book* contains a surprisingly modern-sounding "Chocolate Marshmallow Cake," in which a still-warm chocolate cake layer is covered with cut-up marshmallows, then topped with chocolate fudge frosting.

My brownie variation on the rocky road theme calls for not only marshmallows but also chocolate minimorsels and chopped nuts. They are added to a partially baked brownie layer and heated until the marshmallows and chocolate morsels begin to melt into the brownie surface. Once cooled, the rocky road topping is a marvel of textural contrasts —gooey-soft from the marshmallows, crunchy from the nuts, and crispy from the chocolate morsels.

6 tablespoons (³/₄ stick) unsalted butter, cut into chunks

2¹/₂ ounces bittersweet (*not* unsweetened) or semisweet chocolate, broken up or coarsely chopped

2 ounces unsweetened chocolate, broken up or coarsely chopped

²/₃ cup sugar

²/₃ cup all-purpose white flour

¹/₄ teaspoon baking soda

¹/₄ teaspoon salt

2 large eggs, plus 1 large egg yolk

2 teaspoons vanilla extract

1 cup (4 ounces) chopped walnuts or pecans

1¹/₃ cups miniature marshmallows

³/₄ cup (4¹/₂ ounces) semisweet chocolate minimorsels

Preheat the oven to 350 degrees F. Lightly grease a 9-inch square baking pan or coat with nonstick spray. Line the pan with aluminum foil, letting the foil overhang two opposing sides of the pan by about 2 inches. Grease the foil or coat with nonstick spray.

In a medium, microwave-safe bowl, microwave the butter and chocolates on 100-percent power for 1 minute. Stir well. Continue microwaving on 50-percent power, stirring at 30-second intervals. Stop microwaving before the chocolates completely melt and let the residual heat finish the job. (Alternatively, in a medium, heavy saucepan, melt the butter and chocolates over lowest heat, stirring frequently; be very careful not to burn. Immediately remove from the heat.) Stir the sugar into the chocolate mixture until well blended. Let cool to warm.

In a small bowl, thoroughly stir together the flour, baking soda, and salt; set aside. Beat the eggs and egg yolk, one at a time, into the chocolate mixture. Add the vanilla, stirring vigorously until the mixture is completely smooth and shiny. Stir in the flour mixture until evenly incorporated. Turn out the batter into the baking pan, spreading to the edges.

Bake in the middle of the oven for 10 to 12 minutes, or until almost firm when pressed in the center. Immediately remove the pan from the oven. Reduce the oven temperature to 325 degrees F.

Sprinkle first the nuts, then the marshmallows, then the chocolate mini-morsels evenly over the brownie. Bake for 8 to 9 minutes more, or until the marshmallows are just lightly tinged with brown and a toothpick inserted in the center comes out clean except for the bottom ¼ inch, which should still look moist; be careful not to overbake. Transfer the pan to a wire rack and let stand until the brownie is completely cooled. Refrigerate until well chilled.

Using the overhanging foil as handles, transfer the brownie to a cutting board. Carefully peel off and discard the foil. Using a large, sharp knife, cut the brownie into 16 squares; wipe the knife clean between cuts.

Store in an airtight container for up to 4 days or freeze for up to 1 month. If freezing, leave the brownie slab whole, then cut into squares when partially thawed.

words of kitchen wisdom
"Have your materials measured or at hand, and all utensils ready before beginning the mixing, or putting the ingredients together. Keep a bucket or pan full of flour, freshly sifted each day, and ready for use."

– Mrs. D. A. Lincoln, *The Boston Cooking-School Cook Book*, 1883

Butterscotch-Toffee Brownies

Enhanced with ready-to-use chocolate toffee bits, these bars have a rich taste, golden color, and chewy texture. Though slightly updated, they were inspired by several recipes from the 1930s and 1940s (well before the "blondies" designation appeared), so I've kept the old-fashioned name.

1 cup (4 ounces) chopped pecans (optional)
1 cup all-purpose white flour
¹/₂ teaspoon baking powder
¹/₈ teaspoon salt
  Generous ³/₄ cup packed light brown sugar
¹/₂ cup (1 stick) unsalted butter, slightly softened

2 teaspoons vanilla extract
2 large eggs
¹/₃ cup Heath bar or other milk chocolate toffee bits
1 cup (about 3 ounces) sweetened shredded or flaked coconut (optional)

Preheat the oven to 325 degrees F.

Spread the pecans, if using, in a small baking pan and toast in the oven, stirring occasionally, for 7 to 9 minutes, or until nicely browned; be careful not to burn. Immediately turn out into a small bowl and let cool; set aside.

Lightly grease a 9-inch square baking pan or coat with nonstick spray. Line the pan with aluminum foil, letting the foil overhang two opposing sides of the pan by about 2 inches. Grease the foil or coat with nonstick spray.

In a medium bowl, thoroughly stir together the flour, baking powder, and salt; set aside. In a large bowl, with an electric mixer on medium speed, beat together the brown sugar, butter, and vanilla until well blended. Add the eggs, one at a time, and beat until well blended and smooth. Stir or beat in the flour mixture, toffee bits, pecans, and coconut, if using, until evenly incorporated. Turn out the batter into the baking pan, spreading to the edges.

Bake in the middle of the oven for 30 to 35 minutes, or until the top is golden and a toothpick inserted in the center comes out clean. Transfer the pan to a wire rack and let stand until the brownies are completely cooled.

Using the overhanging foil as handles, transfer the brownie to a cutting board. Carefully peel off and discard the foil. Using a large, sharp knife, cut the brownies into 12 bars; wipe the knife clean between cuts.

Store the brownies in an airtight container for up to 4 days or freeze for up to 1 month. If freezing, leave the brownie slab whole, then cut into bars when partially thawed.

words of kitchen wisdom
"All food materials are poor conductors of heat, and it takes time for the heat to penetrate. The length of time and temperature will depend upon the size and thickness of the food."

– Belle DeGraf,
Mrs. DeGraf's Cookbook, 1922

caramel swirl blondies

Blondies, also called butterscotch brownies or squares, are a twentieth-century American creation that started appearing in the 1920s—around the time chocolate brownies really began to catch on. The earliest version I've found appeared in the 1924 *Modern Priscilla Cookbook* and was called "Butterscotch Squares." Except that it lacked chocolate, it was very similar to early brownie recipes, suggesting that an inventive cook may have reinterpreted chocolate brownies in a nonchocolate form. The name "blondies" (presumably short for blond brownies) is much more modern than the bars themselves, first showing up in cookbooks and magazines in the 1970s and 1980s.

Whatever the name, these are chewy, gooey, brown-sugar bars with luscious swirls of caramel running through them. You'll need a candy thermometer for the recipe.

CARAMEL

- ⅔ cup heavy (whipping) cream
- 3 tablespoons light corn syrup
- Scant ⅔ cup packed light brown sugar
- ⅛ teaspoon salt
- 2½ tablespoons all-purpose white flour
- 1 teaspoon vanilla extract

BLONDIES

- 1⅓ cups all-purpose white flour
- ½ teaspoon baking powder
- ¼ teaspoon salt
- ¾ cup packed light brown sugar
- ⅔ cup (1 stick plus 2⅔ tablespoons) unsalted butter, slightly softened
- 2 large eggs
- 1½ tablespoons light corn syrup
- 1½ teaspoons vanilla extract
- ¾ cup (3 ounces) chopped pecans (optional)

Preheat the oven to 350 degrees F. Lightly grease an 8-inch square baking pan or coat with nonstick spray. Line the pan with aluminum foil, letting the foil overhang two opposing sides of the pan by about 2 inches. Grease the foil or coat with nonstick spray.

FOR THE CARAMEL

In a 2-quart heavy saucepan, thoroughly stir together the cream, corn syrup, brown sugar, and salt. Bring to a boil over medium-high heat, stirring. Insert a candy thermometer into the mixture, being sure the tip doesn't touch the bottom of the pan. Adjust the heat so the mixture boils briskly but not hard, and boil, stirring occasionally, until it reaches 240 degrees F, about 4 minutes. Reduce the heat slightly and continue gently boiling until the thermometer registers 245 degrees F. Immediately remove from the heat and stir in the flour until completely smooth. Stir in the vanilla. Set aside in a very warm spot while you prepare the batter.

FOR THE BLONDIES

In a medium bowl, thoroughly stir together the flour, baking powder, and salt; set aside. In a large bowl, with an electric mixer on medium speed, beat together the brown sugar and butter until light and fluffy. Add the eggs, corn syrup, and vanilla and beat until well blended and smooth. Stir or beat in the flour mixture and pecans, if using, until evenly incorporated. Turn out about two-thirds of the batter into the baking pan, spreading to the edges.

Reheat the caramel over medium heat, stirring, until warm and fluid. Spoon about 6 pools of caramel onto the batter, keeping them about ½ inch away from the sides of the pan (the caramel will burn if it comes in direct contact with the pan). Spoon the remaining batter in pools over the caramel. Using a table knife held vertically, slightly swirl the caramel and batter together; be careful to leave some large swirls and not to overmix.

Bake in the middle of the oven for 25 to 30 minutes, or until the top is golden and a toothpick inserted in the center comes out clean but moist. Transfer the pan to a wire rack. Carefully run a table knife around the edges of the pan to loosen any caramel from the sides. Let stand until the blondie is completely cooled.

Using the overhanging foil as handles, transfer the blondie to a cutting board. Carefully peel off and discard the foil. Using a large, sharp knife, cut into 12 bars; wipe the knife clean between cuts.

Store in an airtight container for up to 4 days or freeze for up to 1 month. If freezing, leave the blondie slab whole, then cut into bars when partially thawed.

congo Bars

I've never seen any information on why these succulent, chewy treats are called congo bars. I suppose it could be because they contain coconut, but, admittedly, this isn't a very compelling explanation. At any rate, they have been around since at least the late 1960s and continue to be popular.

The topping features nearly the same flavor combination as German chocolate cake —coconut, pecans, sweetened condensed milk, and chocolate—although in this case the chocolate is in the form of morsels.

1¹/₃ cups all-purpose white flour

¹/₃ cup packed light brown sugar

¹/₄ teaspoon salt

¹/₂ cup plus 2 tablespoons (1¹/₄ sticks) cold unsalted butter, cut into chunks

TOPPING

1 14-ounce can sweetened condensed milk

2 large eggs, plus 1 large egg yolk

¹/₄ cup plus 2¹/₂ tablespoons packed dark brown sugar

2¹/₂ teaspoons vanilla extract

¹/₄ teaspoon baking soda

Generous ¹/₈ teaspoon salt

2¹/₂ tablespoons all-purpose white flour

1¹/₂ cups (6 ounces) chopped pecans

1 cup (about 3 ounces) shredded or flaked sweetened coconut

²/₃ cup (4 ounces) semisweet chocolate morsels

Preheat the oven to 325 degrees F. Lightly grease a 9-by-13-inch baking pan or coat with nonstick spray. Line the pan with aluminum foil, letting the foil overhang the two narrow ends of the pan by about 2 inches. Grease the foil or coat with nonstick spray.

In a medium bowl, thoroughly stir together the flour, brown sugar, and salt. Using forks, a pastry cutter, or your fingertips, cut in the butter until the mixture is the consistency of coarse crumbs. Firmly press the mixture into an even layer in the baking pan; it is normal for flecks of brown sugar to show in the dough.

Bake in the middle of the oven for 20 to 23 minutes, or until barely browned at the edges. Transfer the pan to a wire rack and let cool slightly.

FOR THE TOPPING

In a large bowl, with an electric mixer on medium speed, beat together the condensed milk, eggs and egg yolk, brown sugar, vanilla, baking soda, and salt until the sugar dissolves and the mixture is well blended. Beat in the flour. Beat or stir in the pecans, coconut, and chocolate morsels. Spread the topping evenly over the crust.

Bake in the middle of the oven for 28 to 33 minutes, or until golden all over and barely baked through in the center. Transfer to a wire rack and let stand until completely cooled.

Using the overhanging foil as handles, transfer the slab to a cutting board. Carefully peel off and discard the foil. Using a large, sharp knife, cut the slab into 20 bars; wipe the knife clean between cuts.

Store in an airtight container for up to 4 days or freeze for up to 1 month. If freezing, leave the slab whole, then cut into bars when partially thawed.

TurTLe
Bars

To my mind, these chewy, gooey goodies are the ultimate bar cookie. My inspiration was a favorite American candy featuring what is without doubt one of the world's best sweet combinations—pecans, caramel, and chocolate.

2¹⁄₂ cups (10 ounces) coarsely chopped pecans

1¹⁄₄ cups all-purpose white flour
  3 tablespoons sugar
    Generous ¹⁄₄ teaspoon salt
 ¹⁄₂ cup (1 stick) cold unsalted butter, cut into chunks
1¹⁄₂ tablespoons milk, plus more if needed

CARAMEL LAYER
  1 cup heavy (whipping) cream
 ¹⁄₃ cup light corn syrup
 ¹⁄₄ cup (¹⁄₂ stick) unsalted butter
 ²⁄₃ cup packed light brown sugar
 ¹⁄₄ cup sugar
 ¹⁄₄ teaspoon salt
  2 teaspoons vanilla extract

  2 cups (12 ounces) semisweet chocolate morsels

Preheat the oven to 350 degrees F. Lightly grease or coat a 9-by-13-inch baking pan or coat with nonstick spray. Line the pan with aluminum foil, letting it overhang the two narrow ends of the pan by about 2 inches. Grease the foil or coat with nonstick spray.

Spread the pecans in a medium baking pan and toast in the oven, stirring occasionally, for 7 to 10 minutes, or until nicely browned; be careful not to burn. Immediately turn out into a small bowl and let cool; set aside.

In a medium bowl, thoroughly stir together the flour, sugar, and salt. Using forks, a pastry blender, or your fingertips, cut in the butter until the mixture is the consistency of coarse meal. Sprinkle the milk over the flour mixture. Lightly stir to mix. Gently knead until the mixture holds together. If necessary, add up to 3 teaspoons more milk until the mixture holds together but is not wet. (Alternatively, in a food processor, process the dry ingredients and the butter in on/off pulses until the mixture is the consistency of coarse meal; be careful not to overprocess. Add 2 teaspoons milk, a little at a time, and process in on/off pulses until the mixture begins to hold together; add just enough more milk so the mixture holds together but is not wet.)

Firmly press the dough in an even layer into the baking pan. Refrigerate for 30 minutes.

Bake in the middle of the oven for 21 to 25 minutes, or until browned at the edges and firm when pressed in the center. Set aside.

FOR THE CARAMEL LAYER

In a 3-quart heavy saucepan, thoroughly stir together the cream, corn syrup, butter, sugars, and salt. Bring to a boil over high heat, stirring; initially, it will boil up the pot sides, then gradually subside. Adjust the heat so the mixture boils briskly but not hard, and boil, stirring occasionally, for about 5 minutes, or until the mixture thickens somewhat. Reduce the heat to a simmer and insert a candy thermometer into the mixture, being sure the tip doesn't touch the bottom of the pan. Simmer, stirring occasionally and watching carefully to prevent burning, until the thermometer registers 245 to 246 degrees F. Immediately remove the pan from the heat. Stir in the vanilla and 1¾ cups of the pecans.

Spread the caramel evenly over the crust, all the way to the edges. Immediately sprinkle the chocolate morsels evenly over the caramel layer. Let stand until the morsels melt, then, using a table knife, spread the melted chocolate over the caramel. Chop the remaining ¾ cup pecans finely and sprinkle evenly over the chocolate. Refrigerate until completely cooled.

Using the overhanging foil as handles, transfer the slab to a cutting board. Carefully peel off and discard the foil. Using a large, sharp knife, cut the slab into 36 bars; wipe the knife clean between cuts.

Store in an airtight container for up to 1 week or freeze for up to 2 months. If freezing, leave the slab whole, then cut into bars when partially thawed.

Brownies, Blondies, and other Bar cookies

pecan brickle Bars

These bars feature a buttery shortbread crust and a pecan-studded, brown-sugar topping that is baked to a golden, chewy brickle stage. Then, to ensure their irresistibility, the bars are garnished with more pecans and some chocolate morsels.

They keep well, but, as one taster commented, only if stored under lock and key!

1¼ cups all-purpose white flour
3 tablespoons sugar
¼ teaspoon salt
½ cup (1 stick) cold unsalted butter, cut into chunks
1 tablespoon light cream, plus more if needed

TOPPING

3 cups (12 ounces) chopped pecans
¾ cup (1½ sticks) cold unsalted butter, cut into chunks
1 cup plus 2 tablespoons packed light brown sugar
¼ teaspoon salt
¼ cup light corn syrup
2 tablespoons light cream
2½ teaspoons vanilla extract

1 cup (6 ounces) semisweet chocolate morsels

Generously grease a 9-by-13-inch baking pan or coat with nonstick spray.

In a medium bowl, thoroughly stir together the flour, sugar, and salt. Using forks, a pastry blender, or your fingertips, cut in the butter until the mixture is the consistency of fine meal. Sprinkle the cream over the flour mixture. Lightly stir to mix. Gently knead until the mixture holds together. If necessary, add up to 3 teaspoons more cream until the mixture holds together but is not wet. (Alternatively, in a food processor, process the dry ingredients and the butter in on/off pulses until the mixture is the consistency of coarse meal; be careful not to overprocess. Add 1 tablespoon cream, a little at a time, and process in on/off pulses until the mixture begins to hold together; add just enough more cream so the mixture holds together but is not wet.)

Firmly press the dough in an even layer into the baking pan. Refrigerate for 30 minutes.

Preheat the oven to 350 degrees F.

Bake in the middle of the oven for 10 minutes, or until just tinged with brown at the edges. Transfer the pan to a wire rack and let stand until cooled to warm, about 5 minutes.

FOR THE TOPPING

Spread the pecans in a medium baking pan and toast in the oven, stirring occasionally, for 6 to 8 minutes, or until nicely browned; be careful not to burn. Immediately turn out into a medium bowl and let cool; set aside.

In a medium, heavy saucepan, combine the butter, brown sugar, salt, corn syrup, and cream. Bring to a boil over medium heat and cook, stirring occasionally, for 4 minutes. Remove from the heat. Stir in the vanilla and 2¼ cups of the pecans.

Spread the topping evenly over the crust.

Bake in the middle of the oven for 20 to 24 minutes, or until the topping is bubbly, golden brown, and just slightly darker at the edges. Transfer the pan to a wire rack and let stand until cooled to warm. Sprinkle the chocolate morsels evenly over the top. Let stand until the morsels melt, then, using a table knife, spread the melted chocolate over the topping; it will not completely cover the topping. Sprinkle the remaining ¾ cup pecans over the chocolate. Let stand until cooled to barely warm.

Using a large, sharp knife, cut the slab into 32 bars; wipe the knife clean between cuts. Let stand until completely cool.

Store in an airtight container for up to 2 weeks or freeze for up to 2 months. If freezing, leave the slab whole, then cut into bars when partially thawed.

words of kitchen wisdom
"To test the oven without a thermometer, take a piece of white paper. Place in the oven after it has been heated 10 minutes.... If the paper burns black in 5 minutes, the oven is very hot; if it burns a deep brown, it is hot. For the medium oven, the paper should be golden brown in 5 minutes. For a slow oven, it should barely turn the most delicate brown in 5 minutes.

"All of these tests need a little study, and each person will have to work out their own problem."

– Belle DeGraf,
Mrs. DeGraf's Cookbook, 1922

coffee-pecan crunch bars
with coffee icing

The natural sweetness of pecans and bits of almond-crunch candy—as well as a thin, smooth layer of coffee icing—contrast nicely with the slight bitterness of the espresso in these attractive, toothsome bars. The recipe is my interpretation of a bar cookie I sampled at a buffet in Texas. Pecans may have originated in the area that is now Texas, and it is the nation's second-largest producer of these nuts.

2¹/₂ cups all-purpose white flour

1¹/₂ tablespoons very finely ground espresso beans

¹/₂ teaspoon baking powder

¹/₈ teaspoon salt

1 cup (2 sticks) unsalted butter, slightly softened

²/₃ cup packed light or dark brown sugar

2 tablespoons light corn syrup

1 tablespoon plus 1 teaspoon instant coffee powder or granules, dissolved in 1 tablespoon hot water

2 teaspoons vanilla extract

¹/₈ teaspoon almond extract

1¹/₂ cups (6 ounces) chopped pecans

³/₄ cup Bits of Brickle almond-crunch candy pieces, or ¹/₂ cup crushed butterscotch hard candy, pounded in a plastic bag until the pieces are no larger than ¹/₄ inch

COFFEE ICING

1²/₃ cups powdered sugar, sifted after measuring

1 tablespoon unsalted butter, slightly softened

1¹/₄ teaspoons instant coffee powder or granules, dissolved in 2 tablespoons hot water

¹/₂ teaspoon vanilla extract

2–3 drops almond extract

Preheat the oven to 325 degrees F. Generously grease a 9-by-13-inch baking pan or coat with nonstick spray.

In a medium bowl, thoroughly stir together the flour, ground espresso beans, baking powder, and salt; set aside. In a large bowl, with an electric mixer on medium speed, beat together the butter, brown sugar, corn syrup, coffee mixture, vanilla, and almond extract until lightened and fluffy. Stir or beat in the flour mixture, then the pecans and candy, until evenly incorporated. Turn out the mixture into the pan, spreading to the edges. Place a sheet of wax paper over the layer, and press it out until flat and smooth on top. Peel off and discard the paper.

Bake in the middle of the oven for 23 to 27 minutes, or until just barely firm when pressed in the center and faintly darker at the edges; be careful not to overbake. Transfer to a wire rack and let stand until barely warm.

FOR THE ICING

In a small bowl, vigorously stir together the powdered sugar, butter, coffee mixture, vanilla, and almond extract until well blended and smooth. Stir in enough warm water, a little at a time, to yield a slightly runny icing. Using a table knife, immediately spread the icing evenly over the bars; work quickly, as the icing firms rapidly. Let stand until completely cooled and the icing is completely set, about 1 hour.

Using a large, sharp knife, cut the slab into 24 bars; wipe the knife clean between cuts.

Store in an airtight container for up to 1 week or freeze for up to 1 month. If freezing, leave the slab whole, then cut into bars when partially thawed.

Nineteenth-century Java

Although America's gourmet coffee shop craze of the 1990s probably accounts for the current popularity of coffee-flavored cookies, they date back at least to nineteenth-century America. *Mrs. Porter's New Southern Cookery Book,* published in 1871, included a coffee-and-molasses-flavored drop cookie called "Coffee Cakes." And the 1881 *Complete Bread, Cake and Cracker Baker* included professional bakers' recipes for both macaroons and sweet biscuits flavored with "essence of coffee," as well as for a thin coffee icing suitable for glazing the biscuits.

Hazelnut-Honey caramel Bars

makes 32 (2-by-2¼-inch) bars
or 40 (1-by-2½-inch) sticks.

This terrific combination of chewy honey caramel, mellow bits of toasted hazelnuts, and a sprinkling of chocolate is the creation of pastry chef Maureen McCarthy for McMenamin's Edgefield, an upscale hotel and fine dining complex outside Portland, Oregon. A native of Portland, Maureen is the proprietor of her own Portland cake-decorating business called Blooming Cakes and likes to use the region's products, hazelnuts being among the most notable.

The bars keep very well.

1½ cups all-purpose white flour

½ teaspoon baking powder

Generous ¼ teaspoon salt

½ cup plus 1 tablespoon (1 stick plus 1 tablespoon) unsalted butter, slightly softened

½ cup sugar

1 large egg

HAZELNUT–HONEY CARAMEL LAYER

2 cups (10 ounces) hazelnuts

½ cup (1 stick) cold unsalted butter, cut into chunks

½ cup clover honey or other mild honey

¼ cup plus 2 tablespoons packed light brown sugar

3 tablespoons heavy (whipping) cream

2 teaspoons vanilla extract

1½ ounces bittersweet (*not* unsweetened) or semisweet chocolate, finely grated or finely chopped, for topping

Preheat the oven to 400 degrees F. Lightly grease a 9-by-13-inch baking pan or coat with nonstick spray. Line the pan with aluminum foil, letting the foil overhang the two narrow ends by about 2 inches. Grease the foil or coat with nonstick spray.

In a small bowl, thoroughly stir together the flour, baking powder, and salt; set aside. In a large bowl, with an electric mixer on medium speed, beat together the butter, sugar, and egg until lightened and fluffy, about 2 minutes. Beat or stir in the flour mixture until well blended and smooth. Turn out the mixture into the pan, spreading to the edges. Lay a sheet of wax paper over the dough and press it out to the edges until flat and smooth on top. Peel off and discard the paper.

Bake in the middle of the oven for 12 to 16 minutes, or until tinged with brown all over and slightly darker at the edges. Transfer the pan to a wire rack and set aside.

FOR THE HAZELNUT–HONEY CARAMEL LAYER

Reduce the oven temperature to 350 degrees F. Spread the hazelnuts in a medium baking pan and toast in the oven, stirring occasionally, for 15 to 19 minutes, or until the hulls loosen and the nuts are nicely browned; be careful not to burn. Immediately turn out into a medium bowl and let stand until cool enough to handle. Rub the hazelnuts between your hands or in a clean kitchen towel, loosening and discarding as much hull as possible. In a food processor or by hand, chop the nuts moderately fine; set aside.

In a medium, heavy saucepan, melt the butter over medium-high heat. Using a long-handled wooden spoon, stir in the honey, brown sugar, and cream. Bring to a boil; adjust the heat so the mixture boils briskly but not hard. If testing doneness with a candy thermometer, insert it into the mixture, being sure the tip doesn't touch the bottom of the pan; if testing doneness with ice water, set out a small cup of water and add 3 ice cubes. Boil the honey mixture, stirring occasionally and watching carefully to prevent burning, for 4 to 5 minutes, or until it thickens to the consistency of gravy and darkens slightly; it should register 250 degrees F on the thermometer. To check doneness with ice water, drop about ½ teaspoon of the caramel into the water and let stand for about 20 seconds; when squeezed, the caramel should form a soft ball that flattens out upon removal from the water. Immediately remove from the heat. Stir in 1 cup of the hazelnuts and the vanilla.

Spread the caramel evenly over the crust, all the way to the edges. Sprinkle the remaining 1 cup hazelnuts over the top.

Bake in the middle of the oven for 13 to 18 minutes, or until nicely browned and bubbly all over. Transfer the pan to a wire rack and let stand for 15 minutes. Sprinkle the chocolate over the top. Let stand until the chocolate melts. Refrigerate for 1½ hours, or until well chilled and firm.

Using the overhanging foil as handles, transfer the slab to a cutting board. Carefully peel off and discard the foil. Using a large, sharp knife, cut the slab into 32 bars or 40 narrow sticks; wipe the knife clean between cuts.

Store in an airtight container for up to 10 days or freeze for up to 2 months. If freezing, leave the slab whole, then cut into bars or sticks when partially thawed.

TIP
The cookies are sturdy enough to cut into either brownie-shaped bars or narrow sticks (the latter look particularly nice on a cookie tray).

chocoLate-GLazed macadamia-carameL shortbread Bars

makes 36
(1½-by-2-inch) bars.

Yes, these luxurious bars are a bit more trouble than your average cookies. But if you want something to secure your reputation as a dessert maker, this is it! They are almost candy-like and deliver both great texture and taste. Chewy caramel, crunchy macadamia nuts, lush chocolate, and rich shortbread all come together in a sensory extravaganza.

Note that the method for making caramel called for here is different from the one usually employed. It's borrowed from pastry chefs and produces a caramel with exceptionally fine flavor and color.

SHORTBREAD

10½ tablespoons (1 stick plus 2½ tablespoons) unsalted butter, slightly softened

¼ cup plus 2 tablespoons powdered sugar

¼ teaspoon salt

1 teaspoon vanilla extract

1½ cups all-purpose white flour

CARAMEL

¾ cup heavy (whipping) cream

3½ tablespoons unsalted butter

¼ teaspoon salt

1⅓ cups sugar (divided)

3 tablespoons light corn syrup

1½ teaspoons vanilla extract

1¼ cups (about 5¾ ounces) coarsely chopped macadamia nuts

CHOCOLATE GLAZE

2½ tablespoons heavy (whipping) cream

2½ tablespoons light corn syrup

5½ ounces bittersweet (*not* unsweetened) or semisweet chocolate, broken up or coarsely chopped

1 ounce unsweetened chocolate, broken up or coarsely chopped

2 tablespoons (¼ stick) unsalted butter, cut into chunks

1 teaspoon vanilla extract

Preheat the oven to 325 degrees F. Lightly grease a 9-by-13-inch glass baking pan or coat with nonstick spray. Line the pan with aluminum foil, letting the foil overhang the two narrow ends by about 2 inches.

FOR THE SHORTBREAD

In a large bowl, with an electric mixer on low, then medium, speed, beat together the butter, powdered sugar, salt, and vanilla until light and very well blended, about 2 minutes. Beat or stir in the flour until evenly incorporated.

TIP

If salted macadamia nuts are used, wipe off the excess salt with paper towels.

Firmly press the dough into the baking dish. Lay a sheet of wax paper over the dough, then press it out to the edges until flat and smooth on top. Peel off and discard the paper.

Bake in the middle of the oven for 27 to 32 minutes, or until pale golden all over and slightly darker at the edges. Transfer the dish to a wire rack and set aside.

FOR THE CARAMEL

In a small, heavy saucepan, combine the cream, butter, and salt. Bring just to a simmer over medium-high heat; immediately remove from the heat. In a medium, heavy saucepan, combine half of the sugar and the corn syrup over medium heat, stirring constantly. When the sugar is fully incorporated and liquefies, stir in about half of the remaining sugar. When this sugar liquefies, stir in the remaining sugar. Cook, stirring and scraping down the pan sides, for 5 to 7 minutes more, or until all the sugar liquefies, bubbles, and turns a medium tan color. Immediately remove from the heat. *Working carefully to avoid splatters and steam,* pour the hot cream mixture into the caramel, stirring and scraping the pan bottom and sides with a long-handled wooden spoon until the caramel completely dissolves. Rinse all of the sugar crystals from the spoon.

Return the caramel mixture to the burner over medium-high heat. Insert a candy thermometer into the mixture, being sure the tip doesn't touch the bottom of the pan. Continue cooking, stirring gently, until the thermometer registers 246 to 247 degrees F. Immediately remove the pan from the heat. Stir in the vanilla. *Being careful not to scrape any caramel or sugar crystals from the pan sides,* pour the caramel through a fine sieve over the shortbread. Tip the baking dish back and forth to distribute the caramel evenly. Sprinkle the macadamia nuts evenly over the caramel. Let stand until the caramel cools to warm. Using the palm of your hand, press down on the nuts to embed them.

FOR THE GLAZE

In a small, microwave-safe bowl, microwave the cream and corn syrup on 100-percent power for 30 seconds, or until very hot but not boiling; set aside. (Alternatively, heat the cream and corn syrup to very hot in a small saucepan over medium heat.)

In a small, microwave-safe bowl, microwave the chocolates and butter on 100-percent power for 1 minute. Stir well. Continue microwaving on 50-

percent power, stirring at 30-second intervals. Stop microwaving before the chocolates completely melt and let the residual heat finish the job. (Alternatively, in a small, heavy saucepan, melt the chocolates and butter over lowest heat, stirring frequently; be careful not to burn.) Slowly stir the cream mixture into the chocolate mixture until well blended and smooth. Stir in the vanilla. Spread the glaze evenly over the cooled caramel. Let stand until completely cooled. Refrigerate the shortbread until chilled.

Using the overhanging foil as handles, transfer the shortbread to a cutting board. Carefully peel off and discard the foil. Using a large, sharp knife, cut the shortbread into 36 bars; wipe the knife clean between cuts.

Store in an airtight container in a cool place for up to 1 week (if the caramel softens upon standing, store in the refrigerator) or freeze for up to 1 month. If freezing, leave the shortbread whole, then cut into bars when partially thawed.

Brown sugar-pecan sticky Bars

These chewy-crunchy bars combine the flavors of brown sugar, pecans, butter, coconut, and oats with a caramel-pecan topping. They are homey and unassuming, yet very good.

1 cup old-fashioned rolled oats	**TOPPING**
1¼ cups packed light brown sugar	¾ cup (3 ounces) chopped pecans
¾ cup (1½ sticks) unsalted butter, slightly softened	¼ cup (½ stick) unsalted butter, cut into chunks
⅛ teaspoon salt	⅔ cup packed light brown sugar
1 large egg	Pinch of salt
1¼ teaspoons vanilla extract	¼ cup heavy (whipping) cream
1⅓ cups all-purpose white flour	2½ tablespoons light corn syrup
1 cup (about 4 ounces) chopped pecans	1 teaspoon vanilla extract
¾ cup (about 2 ounces) shredded or flaked sweetened coconut	

Preheat the oven to 350 degrees F. Generously grease a 9-by-13-inch baking pan or coat with nonstick spray.

In a small bowl, thoroughly stir together the oats and ¼ cup hot water; set aside. In a large bowl, with an electric mixer on medium speed, beat together the brown sugar, butter, and salt until well blended and fluffy. Add the egg and vanilla and beat until evenly incorporated. Beat or stir in the flour and the oat mixture until well blended. Fold in the pecans and coconut. Turn out the mixture into the baking pan, spreading to the edges.

Bake in the upper third of the oven for 25 to 30 minutes, or until the top is nicely browned and a toothpick inserted in the center comes out clean. Transfer the pan to a wire rack and let stand until cooled to warm, about 5 minutes.

FOR THE TOPPING
Meanwhile, while the crust is cooling, in a 2-quart heavy saucepan, combine the pecans and butter. Bring to a simmer over medium-high heat and cook, stirring constantly, for 3 to 4 minutes, or until the butter is lightly browned; be careful not to burn. Using a long-handled wooden

spoon to avoid any splattering, stir in the brown sugar, salt, cream, and corn syrup until evenly incorporated. Return to a boil, and boil briskly, stirring constantly, for exactly 2 minutes. Remove from the heat. Stir in the vanilla.

Immediately spread the topping evenly over the still-warm crust. Let stand until completely cooled.

Using a large, sharp knife, cut the slab into 24 bars. Before each cut, dip the knife in hot water and dry off.

Store in an airtight container for up to 1 week or freeze for up to 1 month. If freezing, leave the slab whole, then cut into bars when partially thawed.

words of kitchen wisdom
"There can be no positive rules as to the exact time of baking each article.... Much, of course, depends on the state of the fire, and on the size of the things to be baked, and on the thickness of the pans or dishes."

– A Lady of Philadelphia (Eliza Leslie),
Seventy-Five Receipts for Pastry, Cakes and Sweetmeats, 1828

caramel-apple crumb bars

makes 24
(2⅛-by-2¼-inch) bars.

This is an example of traditional American baking at its best: The ingredients are kitchen staples like brown sugar, butter, apples, and oats, imaginatively yet straightforwardly used. The techniques are basic. And the results are at once homespun and sublime.

The caramel involves no more than boiling together cream, brown sugar, corn syrup, and salt. Though I give instructions for checking the caramel's doneness either with a candy thermometer or by testing the mixture in ice water, an exact temperature isn't really critical. Undercook the caramel slightly, and your bars will be on the softer, gooier side; overcook and they'll be on the brittler, chewier side. Either way, you win!

I reconstructed this recipe from some sketchy cook's notes in a hand-me-down file box. The scrawled instructions–"Make crumb mixture. Dice apples. Make caramel. Layer and bake."–were just enough to lead me to the following to-die-for caramel-apple bars.

CRUMB MIXTURE
- 2²/₃ cups all-purpose white flour
- 1²/₃ cups quick-cooking (*not* instant) oats
- Scant ²/₃ cup packed light brown sugar
- ¹/₄ teaspoon salt
- 1 cup (2 sticks) unsalted butter, melted

- 2 cups peeled and chopped Granny Smith or other tart apples (2–3 medium)

CARAMEL
- 1 cup heavy (whipping) cream
- ¹/₄ cup light corn syrup
- ³/₄ cup packed light brown sugar
- ¹/₄ teaspoon salt
- ¹/₄ cup all-purpose white flour
- 1¹/₂ teaspoons vanilla extract

Preheat the oven to 350 degrees F. Generously grease a 9-by-13-inch baking pan or coat with nonstick spray.

FOR THE CRUMB MIXTURE

In a large bowl, thoroughly stir together the flour, oats, sugar, and salt. Add the butter; stir or knead with your hands until the mixture is well blended and crumbly. Firmly press half the crumb mixture evenly into the pan; set aside the remaining crumb mixture.

Bake in the middle of the oven for 10 minutes. Transfer the pan to a wire rack. Evenly spread the apples over the crumb layer; set aside.

FOR THE CARAMEL

In a 3-quart heavy saucepan, thoroughly stir together the cream, corn syrup, brown sugar, and salt. Bring to a boil over high heat, stirring constantly. Adjust the heat so the mixture boils briskly but not hard. If testing doneness with a candy thermometer, insert it into the mixture, being sure the tip doesn't touch the bottom of the pan; if testing doneness with ice water, set out a small cup of water and add 3 ice cubes. Boil the mixture, stirring occasionally, for 6 to 8 minutes, or until it thickens slightly, begins to darken, and registers 243 to 244 degrees F on the thermometer. To check doneness with ice water, drop about ½ teaspoon of the caramel into the water and let stand for about 20 seconds; when squeezed, the caramel should form a slightly firm (but not hard) ball that flattens out upon removal from the water. Immediately remove from the heat. Stir in the flour until evenly incorporated. Stir in the vanilla.

Pour the caramel evenly over the apples. Sprinkle the remaining crumb mixture evenly over the caramel.

Bake in the middle of the oven for 25 to 30 minutes, or until golden on top, browned at the edges, and cooked through in the center. Transfer to a wire rack. Carefully run a table knife around the edges of the pan to loosen the caramel from the sides. Let stand until completely cooled.

Using a large, sharp knife, cut the slab into 24 bars; wipe the knife clean between cuts.

Store in an airtight container for up to 1 week or freeze for up to 1 month. If freezing, leave the slab whole, then cut into bars when partially thawed.

River House Blue Ribbon Apple Butter-cheesecake Bars

Makes 18
(2¼-by-3-inch) bars.

I obtained the recipe for these unusual and very good apple butter–cream cheese bars from Kit Patten and Connie Wilson, proprietors of River House, a bed-and-breakfast in Great Cacapon, West Virginia. Connie created the bars for the local Berkeley Springs Apple Butter Festival cooking contest and earned a blue ribbon. The spicy, slightly piquant apple butter and mild, creamy cheesecake layer are terrific together. These bars are easy to make and keep well. They are sweetened with maple syrup, which Connie prefers to refined sugar.

Held annually to celebrate the area's abundant apple crop, the festival is a throwback to the days when folks needed to "put by" as much of the harvest for winter as possible.

½ cup (1 stick) unsalted butter, slightly softened

¼ cup pure maple syrup

Generous ¼ teaspoon salt

1⅓ cups all-purpose white flour or whole wheat pastry flour

1 cup apple butter

CREAM-CHEESE LAYER

1 8-ounce package plus one 3-ounce package cream cheese, slightly softened and cut into chunks

¼ cup plus 2 tablespoons pure maple syrup

1 large egg

2 teaspoons vanilla extract

½ teaspoon ground cinnamon, for topping

Preheat the oven to 350 degrees F. Grease a 9-by-13-inch baking pan or coat with nonstick spray.

In a large bowl, with an electric mixer on medium speed, beat together the butter, maple syrup, and salt until lightened and fluffy, about 2 minutes. Beat or stir the flour into the butter mixture just until evenly incorporated. Firmly press the dough into the pan. Lay a sheet of wax paper over the dough, then press it out to the edges until flat and smooth on top. Peel off and discard the paper. Using a fork, prick the dough all over.

Bake in the upper third of the oven for 17 to 21 minutes, or until tinged with brown at the edges. Transfer the pan to a wire rack and let cool briefly. Using a table knife, spread the apple butter evenly over the dough.

FOR THE CREAM-CHEESE LAYER

In a food processor, process the cream cheese, maple syrup, egg, and vanilla until well blended and completely smooth, about 30 seconds, stopping and scraping down the bowl sides several times. (Alternatively, in a medium bowl, with an electric mixer on low speed, beat the cream cheese until very smooth. Add the maple syrup, egg, and vanilla and continue beating until well blended.)

Pour the cream-cheese mixture over the apple butter; rap the pan or gently shake it to spread the cream-cheese mixture out to the edges.

Bake in the upper third of the oven for 25 to 30 minutes, or until the cream-cheese layer is beginning to brown and appears barely set when the pan is jiggled. Transfer the pan to a wire rack and let stand until cooled. Sift the cinnamon over the top. Refrigerate until chilled and firm, about 1 hour.

Using a large, sharp knife, cut the slab into 18 bars; wipe the knife clean between cuts.

Store in an airtight container in the refrigerator for up to 1 week or freeze for up to 1 month. If freezing, leave the slab whole, then cut into bars when partially thawed.

Apple-Butter Socials

The custom of socializing while making apple butter is an old one, as revealed in this 1839 *Genessee Farmer* passage quoted in Joseph E. Dabney's fascinating book *Smokehouse Ham, Spoon Bread and Scuppernong Wine*:

"The host should in the autumn invite his neighbors, particularly the young men and maidens, to make up an apple butter party. Being assembled, let three bushels of fair sweet apples be pared, quartered and the cores removed. Meanwhile, let two barrels of new cider be boiled down to one half. When this is done, commit the prepared apples to the cider and henceforth let the boiling go on briskly and systematically. . . . The party must take turns at stirring the contents without cessation, that they do not become attached to the side of the kettle and be burned. Let this stirring go on till the liquid becomes concrete—in other words, till the amalgamated cider and apples become as thick as hasty pudding."

Brownies, Blondies, and Other Bar Cookies

Raspberry-cream cheese swirl Brownies

Today, the word "brownie" is nearly synonymous with "chocolate," but it wasn't always so. Early-twentieth-century brownies didn't always contain chocolate, nor were they necessarily bars. The very first American baked goods called brownies were actually small molasses cakes that appeared in the 1896 *Boston Cooking-School Cook Book.* As late as 1931, when *The Joy of Cooking* was first published, Irma Rombauer did not assume readers would know what brownies were. Her sole brownie entry (among the more than 150 cakes, small cakes, and cookies) was listed as "Brownies or Fudge Squares."

The General Foods test kitchen may have been responsible for the first cream-cheese swirl brownie. As part of a product promotion campaign, the company circulated a "German's Cream Cheese Brownies" recipe in several American magazine ads in the late 1960s. It paved, or should I say swirled, the way for a number of luxurious brownie variations to come.

Since "brownie" now means not only chocolate but maximum decadence per square inch, I've followed the trend with these over-the-top, sweet-tart raspberry–cream cheese treats.

6 tablespoons (¾ stick) unsalted butter

2½ ounces unsweetened chocolate, broken up or coarsely chopped

1½ ounces bittersweet (*not* unsweetened) or semisweet chocolate, broken up or coarsely chopped

¾ cup all-purpose white flour

¼ teaspoon salt

1¼ cups sugar

2 teaspoons vanilla extract

2 large eggs

CREAM-CHEESE SWIRL

1 8-ounce package cream cheese, slightly softened and cut into chunks

⅓ cup sugar

2 tablespoons (¼ stick) unsalted butter, melted

1 large egg

¼ teaspoon finely grated lemon zest (colored part of the skin)

½ teaspoon vanilla extract

⅓ cup seedless raspberry preserves, for swirling

Preheat the oven to 350 degrees F. Lightly grease a 9-inch square baking pan or coat with nonstick spray. Line the pan with aluminum foil, letting the foil overhang two opposing sides of the pan by about 2 inches. Grease the foil or coat with nonstick spray.

In a medium, microwave-safe bowl, microwave the butter and chocolates on 100-percent power for 1 minute. Stir well. Continue microwaving on 50-percent power, stirring at 30-second intervals. Stop microwaving before the chocolates completely melt and let the residual heat finish the job. (Alternatively, in a medium, heavy saucepan, melt the butter and chocolates over lowest heat, stirring frequently; be very careful not to burn. Immediately remove from the heat.) Let cool to warm.

In a small bowl, thoroughly stir together the flour and salt; set aside. Stir the sugar and vanilla into the chocolate mixture until well blended. Beat in the eggs, one at a time. Stir until the sugar dissolves and the mixture is smooth. Stir in the flour mixture until evenly incorporated. Turn out about two-thirds of the batter into the baking pan, spreading to the edges.

FOR THE CREAM-CHEESE SWIRL

In a food processor, process the cream cheese, sugar, butter, egg, lemon zest, and vanilla until well blended and completely smooth. (Alternatively, in a large bowl with an electric mixer on low speed, beat the cream cheese and sugar until completely smooth. Add the butter, egg, lemon zest, and vanilla and continue beating until completely smooth.)

Evenly drop the cream-cheese mixture by tablespoonfuls over the batter. Evenly drop the raspberry preserves by teaspoonfuls over the cream-cheese mixture. Spoon the remaining chocolate batter into 4 or 5 pools over the top. Holding a table knife vertically, run it through the batter to swirl it decoratively.

Bake in the middle of the oven for 42 to 48 minutes, or until the cream-cheese swirls are browned and a toothpick inserted in the center comes out clean except for the bottom ¼ inch, which should still look moist. Transfer the pan to a wire rack and let stand until the brownie is completely cooled. Refrigerate until well chilled.

Using the overhanging foil as handles, transfer the brownie to a cutting board. Carefully peel off and discard the foil. Using a large, sharp knife, cut the brownie into 16 squares; wipe the knife clean between cuts.

Store in an airtight container for up to 4 days or freeze for up to 1 month. If freezing, leave the brownie slab whole, then cut into squares when partially thawed.

apricot-almond bars

A well-flavored dried apricot filling, slightly crispy almond streusel top, and noticeable buttery taste make these rich, tender bars memorable. For ease of preparation, both the bottom crust and the streusel topping are prepared with the same basic crumb mixture.

These bars make a perfect teatime treat.

CRUMB MIXTURE

- 2 cups all-purpose white flour
- ⅔ cup packed light brown sugar
- ¼ teaspoon salt
- 1 cup minus 2 tablespoons (2 sticks minus 2 tablespoons) cold unsalted butter, cut into chunks

APRICOT LAYER

- 1⅔ cups (about 8½ ounces) chopped dried apricots
- Grated zest (colored part of the skin) and juice of 1 large orange
- 2 tablespoons (¼ stick) unsalted butter
- 1¼ cups sugar (divided)
- 2 large eggs
- 1½ teaspoons vanilla extract
- ¼ teaspoon almond extract
- ⅓ cup all-purpose white flour

- ½ cup (1½ ounces) blanched or unblanched sliced almonds, for topping

Preheat the oven to 325 degrees F. Generously grease a 9-by-13-inch baking dish or coat with nonstick spray.

FOR THE CRUMB MIXTURE

In a large bowl, thoroughly stir together the flour, brown sugar, and salt. Using forks, a pastry blender, or your fingertips, cut in the butter until the mixture is well blended and crumbly. Press a generous two-thirds of the crumb mixture evenly into the pan; set aside the remaining crumb mixture.

Bake in the middle of the oven for 17 to 20 minutes, or until lightly browned around the edges. Transfer the pan to a wire rack and let cool slightly.

FOR THE APRICOT LAYER

In a medium, heavy, nonreactive saucepan, combine the apricots, orange zest and juice, butter, and ⅔ cup water. Bring to a simmer over medium-high heat. Cook, stirring occasionally, until the apricots are softened and most of the liquid is absorbed, 7 to 10 minutes. (If all the liquid is ab-

TIP

For a slightly tarter, tangier filling, use American apricots, which are bright orange and flattish. For a milder, smoother one, use Turkish or other imported apricots, which are plump and paler in color.

sorbed and the apricots are still firm, add a little more water and cook a bit longer.) Remove from the heat. Stir in ¼ cup of the sugar until dissolved. Refrigerate the apricot mixture until cooled to warm.

In a large bowl, with an electric mixer on medium, then high, speed (use a whisk-shaped beater, if available), beat together the remaining 1 cup sugar, the eggs, vanilla, and almond extract until the mixture is lightened and smooth, about 4 minutes. Fold in the flour just until evenly incorporated. Fold the apricot mixture into the egg mixture until well blended. Spread the mixture evenly over the crust. Stir together the almonds and reserved crumb mixture and sprinkle evenly over the apricot layer.

Bake in the middle of the oven for 35 to 40 minutes, or until golden on top, browned at the edges, and cooked through in the center. Transfer to a wire rack and let stand until completely cooled.

Using a large, sharp knife, cut the slab into 16 bars; wipe the knife clean between cuts.

Store in an airtight container for up to 10 days or freeze for up to 1 month. If freezing, leave the slab whole, then cut into bars when partially thawed.

strawberry-rhubarb streusel bars

These bars feature a crunchy crumb topping, a zesty fruit filling, and a rich buttery taste that balances the tartness of the rhubarb nicely. They are perfect for serving at a coffee klatch or as dessert after an informal meal.

This soul-satisfying American recipe spotlights an old-fashioned country garden staple, rhubarb—a hardy, unfussy perennial that, like magic, offers up succulent red stalks each spring. (The leaves aren't edible.)

Until fruits and vegetables became widely available year-round in America, rhubarb was considered an important spring restorative because it appeared very early in the season and helped break the monotony of a starchy winter diet. It's probably no coincidence that this recipe pairs the rhubarb with strawberry jam: Not only does its berry flavor complement rhubarb beautifully, but the jam is in the pantry when fresh local berries can't be had. Moreover, the fresh, astringent rhubarb perks up the strawberry jam and makes it taste fresh, too.

It's best to serve these bars promptly—the topping loses its crispness upon standing.

FILLING

- ¼ cup sugar
- 2½ tablespoons cornstarch
- 2½ cups ¾-to-1-inch-long rhubarb pieces (a generous ¾ pound untrimmed), fresh or frozen, thawed and drained
- 1¼ cups strawberry jam or preserves
- ¼ teaspoon ground cinnamon
- ⅛ teaspoon finely grated orange zest (colored part of the skin; optional)

CRUMB MIXTURE

- 1⅔ cups all-purpose white flour
- 1⅔ cups old-fashioned rolled oats
- 1 cup sugar
- ½ teaspoon ground cinnamon
- ¼ teaspoon salt
- ¾ cup (1½ sticks) unsalted butter, very soft but not melted

- 1 large egg, lightly beaten with 1½ teaspoons water

Preheat the oven to 350 degrees F. Generously grease a 9-by-13-inch glass baking pan or coat with nonstick spray.

FOR THE FILLING

In a medium, heavy, nonreactive saucepan, stir together the sugar and cornstarch until well blended. Stir in the rhubarb, jam or preserves, cin-

namon, and orange zest, if using. Bring to a simmer, stirring, over medium-high heat. Cook, stirring, for 3 to 6 minutes, or until the rhubarb softens just slightly (fresh rhubarb will take longer than thawed frozen). Set aside.

FOR THE CRUMB MIXTURE

In a large bowl, thoroughly stir together the flour, oats, sugar, cinnamon, and salt. Add the butter and stir or knead with your hands until the mixture is well blended and crumbly. Firmly press a scant half of the crumb mixture into the baking dish; set aside the remaining crumb mixture.

Bake in the middle of the oven for 13 to 16 minutes, or until firm but not browned. Spread the rhubarb filling evenly over the crumb layer. Stir together the reserved crumb mixture and 2½ tablespoons of the egg mixture until the streusel forms small clumps; add a little more of the egg mixture, if needed. Sprinkle the streusel evenly over the filling, breaking up any large clumps with a fork or your fingertips.

Bake in the middle of the oven for 35 to 40 minutes, or until the streusel is nicely browned and the filling is bubbly. Transfer the pan to a wire rack and let stand until completely cooled.

Using a large, sharp knife, cut into 20 bars; wipe the knife clean between cuts.

Store in an airtight container for up to 2 days. The bars may be frozen for up to 1 month but will lose their crispness. If freezing, leave the slab whole, then cut into bars when partially thawed.

maple-NUT bars

These golden brown bars feature a flaky shortbread crust and an enticing maple-cream layer that can be studded with either walnuts or pecans. Maple bars occasionally turn up in American recipe collections (especially from maple-producing states), though none I've seen are really like mine. I wanted the maple layer to have a slightly gooey consistency, a bit like pecan pie filling but with a distinctly maple rather than corn syrup flavor. After a number of attempts, I hit the mark with these.

Most Americans associate maple sugaring with New England, but it has also long been a custom in states ranging from Virginia, western Maryland, and Ohio to Pennsylvania, New York, Wisconsin, and Minnesota. At one time, many rural families in the Northeast and northern heartland depended on maple syrup and maple sugar as their main sweetener; refined cane sugar was expensive and required hard cash. Even today, when warm spring days alternating with cold nights cause the maple sap to start "running," friends and neighbors still gather to make syrup for their yearly household needs.

1¹/₂ cups all-purpose white flour

Generous ¹/₄ teaspoon salt

¹/₂ cup plus 2 tablespoons (1¹/₄ sticks) cold unsalted butter, cut into chunks

3 tablespoons pure maple syrup

MAPLE LAYER

1 cup pure maple syrup

¹/₃ cup heavy (whipping) cream

2 tablespoons light corn syrup

¹/₄ cup (¹/₂ stick) cold, unsalted butter, cut into chunks

3 tablespoons sugar

2 tablespoons all-purpose white flour

¹/₈ teaspoon salt

2 large eggs, plus 1 large egg yolk

2 teaspoons vanilla extract

1¹/₄ cups (5 ounces) chopped pecans or walnuts, for topping

Lightly grease a 9-by-13-inch baking pan or coat with nonstick spray.

In a large bowl, thoroughly stir together the flour and salt. Using forks, a pastry blender, or your fingertips, cut in the butter until the mixture is the consistency of coarse meal. Sprinkle the maple syrup over the flour mixture and knead until the mixture holds together. (Alternatively, in a food processor, process the dry ingredients and butter in on/off pulses until the mixture is the consistency of coarse meal. Turn out the mixture onto a large sheet of wax paper. Sprinkle the maple syrup over the flour mixture and knead until the mixture holds together.) Firmly press the dough into the baking pan. Lay a sheet of wax paper over the dough, then press it out to the edges until flat and smooth on top. Refrigerate for 20 minutes. Peel off and discard the wax paper.

Preheat the oven to 350 degrees F.

Bake in the middle of the oven for 13 to 16 minutes, or until almost firm when pressed in the center and lightly browned at the edges. Transfer the pan to a wire rack and set aside.

FOR THE MAPLE LAYER

Meanwhile, in a medium, heavy saucepan, combine the maple syrup, cream, and corn syrup. Bring to a boil over high heat, stirring constantly. Boil briskly, stirring occasionally, for 2 minutes. Remove from the heat. Stir in the butter until melted. Let stand until cooled slightly.

In a medium bowl, stir together the sugar, flour, and salt. Using a fork, beat in the eggs and egg yolk and vanilla until well blended and smooth. When the maple mixture has cooled to barely hot, in a thin stream beat it into the egg mixture until evenly incorporated; be sure the maple mixture is not too hot, and add it slowly to avoid curdling the eggs.

Pour the maple mixture evenly over the baked layer. Sprinkle the pecans or walnuts evenly over the top.

Bake in the middle of the oven for 20 to 25 minutes, or until nicely browned and barely firm when pressed in the center. Transfer the pan to a wire rack and let stand until completely cooled.

Using a large, sharp knife, cut the slab into 18 bars; wipe the knife clean between cuts.

Store in an airtight container in the refrigerator for up to 10 days or freeze for up to 2 months. If freezing, leave the slab whole, then cut into bars when partially thawed.

SAP'S RUNNING!

In her book *Home Life in Colonial Days,* Alice Morse Earle quotes the 1706 comments of Virginia's Governor Berkeley on the maple sugaring process:

"The Sugar-Tree yields a kind of Sap or Juice which by boiling is made into Sugar. This Juice is drawn out, by wounding the Trunk of the Tree, and placing a Receiver under the Wound. It is said that the Indians make one Pound of Sugar out of eight Pounds of the Liquor. It is bright and moist with a full large Grain, the Sweetness of it being like that of good Muscovada."
(Muscovada was an unrefined sugar made from cane.)

iced Lemon shortbread Fingers

These bars are flavored with lemon juice, zest, and extract and enhanced with a thin layer of sprightly lemon icing. They are simple in the manner of all traditional shortbreads, yet elegant and sophisticated, too. I like them with a fruit compote or a cup of tea.

1¹/₂ cups all-purpose white flour

¹/₃ cup cornstarch

¹/₂ cup powdered sugar

2¹/₂ tablespoons sugar

2 tablespoons finely grated lemon zest (colored part of the skin)

³/₄ cup (1¹/₂ sticks) unsalted butter, slightly softened

¹/₄ teaspoon salt

2 teaspoons fresh lemon juice

¹/₂ teaspoon lemon extract

LEMON ICING

2 tablespoons sugar

1 teaspoon finely grated lemon zest (colored part of the skin)

1¹/₂ tablespoons fresh lemon juice

1 teaspoon light corn syrup

1 cup powdered sugar

Lightly grease a 9-inch square baking pan or coat with nonstick spray. Line the pan with aluminum foil, letting the foil overhang two opposing sides of the pan by about 2 inches.

In a medium bowl, thoroughly stir together the flour and cornstarch; set aside. In a food processor, process the powdered sugar, sugar, and lemon zest until the sugar is yellow and the zest is finely pulverized, about 3 minutes, stopping and scraping down the bowl sides several times. Add the butter, salt, lemon juice, and lemon extract and process until well blended and fluffy, about 1 minute. Sprinkle the flour mixture over the butter mixture and process in on/off pulses until well blended and smooth, stopping and scraping down the bowl sides several times.

Turn out the dough onto a large sheet of plastic wrap; pat the dough into a 6-inch disk. Fold the wrap around the dough. Refrigerate for 20 to 30 minutes, or until the dough is cool and slightly firmer.

Preheat the oven to 300 degrees F.

Press the dough evenly into the pan. Lay a sheet of wax paper on the dough, then press it out to the edges until the top is flat and smooth. Peel off and discard the paper.

Bake in the middle of the oven for 37 to 45 minutes, or until pale golden all over and just slightly darker at the edges. Transfer the pan to a wire rack and let stand until completely cooled.

Using the overhanging foil as handles, transfer the shortbread to a cutting board. Carefully peel off and discard the foil.

FOR THE ICING

In a food processor, combine the sugar and lemon zest and process until the sugar is lightly colored and the zest is finely pulverized, about 1 minute, stopping and scraping down the bowl sides once or twice. Add the lemon juice and corn syrup and process until the sugar dissolves. Add the powdered sugar and process until evenly incorporated, scraping down the sides of the bowl, if necessary. Add enough water, a few drops at a time, to yield a fluid but not runny icing.

Immediately spread the icing evenly over the shortbread. Let stand for 5 minutes.

Using a large, sharp knife, trim off and discard the uneven edges; work carefully, as the shortbread is slightly crumbly. Wipe the knife clean between cuts. Cut the shortbread into 24 fingers. Using a table knife or spatula, carefully separate and lift out the fingers; let stand, slightly separated, until the icing completely sets, about 1 hour.

Store in a single layer or layered with wax paper in an airtight container for up to 10 days or freeze for up to 1 month.

peanut Butter (or caramel) candy mini Brownie cups

makes 24 (2-inch) mini brownie cups.

The trend toward ever more candy-like cookies continues with the growing popularity of brownie cups in bakeries and coffee bars around the country. Usually, brownie cups feature a rich brownie dough baked in muffin cups, along with an accent of sticky caramel, peanut butter, or fudge.

Here, I've simplified the idea by using either miniature Reese's peanut butter cups or Rolo caramel candies as the brownie cup centers—creating novelty cookies both children and adults enjoy. You can vary the brownie dough by including peanut butter in the peanut-butter-cup version but omitting it from the caramel version. (Of course, you could use the peanut butter brownie dough with Rolo caramel centers, if you wish.) The brownie cups sold in bakeries are usually similar in size to regular muffins, but these are baked in minimuffin tins—just the perfect scale for the 1-inch peanut butter cups or Rolo candies.

5 tablespoons unsalted butter, cut into chunks

2 ounces unsweetened chocolate, broken up or coarsely chopped

1 ounce semisweet chocolate, broken up or coarsely chopped

$2/3$ cup sugar

$2/3$ cup all-purpose white flour

$1/4$ teaspoon baking soda

$1/4$ teaspoon salt

1 large egg

2 tablespoons smooth peanut butter (optional)

1 teaspoon vanilla extract

24 Reese's *miniature* peanut butter cups or Rolo candies, thoroughly chilled and unwrapped

24 roasted peanut halves, for peanut-butter-cup topping (optional)

Preheat the oven to 350 degrees F. Grease two 12-cup minimuffin pans or coat with nonstick spray.

In a medium, microwave-safe bowl, microwave the butter and chocolates on 50-percent power for 1 minute. Stir well. Continue microwaving on 50-percent power, stirring at 30-second intervals. Stop microwaving before the chocolates completely melt and let the residual heat finish the job. (Alternatively, in a medium, heavy saucepan, melt the butter and chocolates over lowest heat, stirring frequently; be very careful not to burn. Immediately remove from the heat.)

Stir the sugar into the chocolate mixture until well blended. Let cool to warm. In a small bowl, thoroughly stir together the flour, baking soda,

TiP
Note that the candies should be chilled in advance and are inserted into the cups immediately *after* the brownies are baked.

and salt; set aside. Beat the egg and peanut butter, if using, into the chocolate mixture. Add the vanilla and stir vigorously until the mixture is completely smooth and shiny. Stir in the flour mixture until evenly incorporated. Spoon the batter equally into the minimuffin cups. Set the muffin pans on a baking sheet.

Bake in the middle of the oven for 10 to 14 minutes, or until almost firm when pressed in the centers. Immediately press 1 peanut butter cup or Rolo candy, smaller end down, into the center of each cup until flush with the surface of the brownie. Place a peanut half, if using, in the center of each peanut butter cup. (There's no need to press down; the peanuts become embedded as the chocolate softens.)

Transfer the muffin pans to a wire rack and let stand until the brownie cups are completely cooled. Gently loosen the brownie cups with the point of a table knife, then remove from the pans.

Store in an airtight container for up to 4 days or freeze for up to 1 month.

BLACK BOTTOM mini Brownie cups

According to John Egerton's *Southern Food,* the catchy, alliterative name "black bottom" was initially applied to food in the early 1940s, when a two-toned chocolate-and-rum custard pie (with the chocolate on the bottom) turned up in a restaurant in Oklahoma City and a black bottom pie recipe was published in a book by Florida author Marjorie Kinnan Rawlings. Later, devil's food and chocolate chip–studded cream-cheese cupcakes (again with the devil's food underneath) called black bottoms started appearing all around the country. As far as I can tell, the first cookbook to include a black bottom cupcake was the 1967 work *America Cooks,* published by the General Federation of Women's Clubs.

Lately, black bottoms featuring brownie and cream-cheese batters baked in muffin pans have also come on the scene. The following black bottom brownie cups are dense and sumptuous. Because they are so rich, I make them in minimuffin pans.

CREAM-CHEESE LAYER

- 1 3-ounce package cream cheese, slightly softened and cut into chunks
- 2¹/₂ tablespoons sugar
- 1 tablespoon unsalted butter, melted
- 1 large egg yolk
- ¹/₂ teaspoon vanilla extract
- ¹/₂ cup (3 ounces) semisweet chocolate minimorsels

CHOCOLATE LAYER

- ¹/₄ cup (¹/₂ stick) unsalted butter, cut into chunks
- 2 ounces unsweetened chocolate, broken up or coarsely chopped
- ³/₄ cup sugar
- ¹/₂ cup minus 1 tablespoon all-purpose white flour
- ¹/₄ teaspoon salt
- ¹/₈ teaspoon baking soda
- 1 large egg
- 1 teaspoon vanilla extract

Preheat the oven to 350 degrees F. Grease two 12-cup minimuffin pans or coat with nonstick spray.

FOR THE CREAM-CHEESE LAYER

In a food processor, process the cream cheese, sugar, butter, egg yolk, and vanilla until well blended and completely smooth. By hand, stir in the chocolate minimorsels; set aside. (Alternatively, in a large bowl with an electric mixer on low speed, beat the cream cheese and sugar until completely smooth. Add the butter, egg yolk, and vanilla, and continue beating until completely smooth. Stir in the minimorsels.)

FOR THE CHOCOLATE LAYER

In a medium, microwave-safe bowl, microwave the butter and chocolate on 50-percent power for 1 minute. Stir well. Continue microwaving on 50-percent power, stirring at 30-second intervals. Stop microwaving before the chocolate completely melts and let the residual heat finish the job. (Alternatively, in a medium, heavy saucepan, melt the butter and chocolate over lowest heat, stirring frequently; be very careful not to burn. Immediately remove from the heat.)

Stir the sugar into the chocolate mixture until well blended. Let cool to warm. In a small bowl, thoroughly stir together the flour, salt, and baking soda; set aside. Beat the egg, 1 tablespoon water, and vanilla into the chocolate mixture until the mixture is well blended and the sugar dissolves. Stir in the flour mixture until evenly incorporated.

Spoon about ½ tablespoon of the chocolate mixture into each minimuffin cup. Spoon about 1 teaspoon of the cream-cheese mixture over the tops, dividing it equally among the cups. Spoon the remaining chocolate mixture equally over the cream-cheese mixture. Set the muffin pans on a baking sheet.

Bake in the middle of the oven for 11 to 14 minutes, or until a toothpick inserted in the center comes out clean except for the bottom ¼ inch, which should still look moist. Transfer the muffin pans to a wire rack and let stand until the brownie cups are completely cooled. Gently loosen the brownie cups with the point of a table knife, then remove from the pans.

Store in an airtight container for up to 4 days or freeze for up to 1 month.

Getting to the Bottom of It

The term "black bottom" was part of early-twentieth-century southern culture well before it was applied to baked goods. A bottom referred (and still does in some localities) to a low-lying area; presumably, a black bottom was one where black families lived. Around the time folks were doing the Charleston, some were dancing the Black Bottom, possibly named for its origination in black culture. There is no real evidence that black bottom desserts had any connection to black cooks, however. Most likely, one of the early makers of the dramatic, two-toned pie cast about for a clever, memorable name and thought "black bottom" worked. Obviously, it did—and still does!

6

Fruit, Pumpkin, and Carrot Cookies

iced Apple softies

Apple cookies don't always taste much like apples, but these do. The secret is the combination of fresh and dried chopped apples, plus apple jelly—which provides concentrated flavor without overmoistening the dough. As the name suggests, these drop cookies have a light, slightly soft texture—as well as an enticing fruit-and-spice aroma. They are topped with a quick drizzle of powdered-sugar icing. These are particularly appealing served in the autumn (with or without apple cider), but they also make nice lunch-box cookies any time of year.

Apples are not native to America, but the English Puritans who established the Plymouth, Massachusetts, colony in 1620 brought and planted apple seeds and cuttings. Nearly all early Americans followed suit, and by the 1700s, both George Washington and Thomas Jefferson maintained orchards on their plantations. By the late eighteenth century, the itinerant nurseryman John Chapman (Johnny Appleseed) was on the move from New York toward Ohio and Indiana, establishing nurseries of apple seedlings as he went. Homesteaders also planted apple orchards as they moved westward and settled the frontier. Today, apples grow in all 50 states and are as American as—well—apple pie!

1¹/₂ cups peeled and finely chopped Golden Delicious apple (about 1 large)

¹/₄ cup finely chopped dried apples

¹/₄ cup apple jelly

1 teaspoon ground cinnamon

¹/₂ teaspoon ground nutmeg

2 cups all-purpose white flour

¹/₂ teaspoon baking soda

¹/₈ teaspoon salt

1 cup (2 sticks) unsalted butter, slightly softened

³/₄ cup packed light brown sugar

1 large egg yolk

ICING

²/₃ cup powdered sugar, sifted after measuring, if lumpy

¹/₂ teaspoon light corn syrup

2–3 drops vanilla extract

Preheat the oven to 350 degrees F. Grease several baking sheets or coat with nonstick spray.

In a large saucepan over medium-high heat, stir together the fresh and dried apples, apple jelly, cinnamon, and nutmeg. Cook, stirring frequently, until the jelly melts and the fresh apples are softened, about 5 minutes; be careful not to burn. Let stand or refrigerate until cooled to room temperature.

In a medium bowl, thoroughly stir together the flour, baking soda, and salt; set aside. In a large bowl, with an electric mixer on medium speed, beat together the butter and brown sugar until well blended and fluffy. Add the egg yolk and beat until evenly incorporated. Gently beat in half of the flour mixture. Add the cooled apple mixture and beat until well blended. Stir in the remaining flour mixture until evenly incorporated. Let the dough stand for 5 minutes, or until firmed up slightly.

Using a ⅛-cup measure or coffee scoop, drop the dough onto the baking sheets, spacing about 2¾ inches apart. With a greased hand, pat down the cookie tops until flat.

Bake the cookies, one sheet at a time, in the middle of the oven for 9 to 12 minutes, or until lightly tinged with brown all over and barely firm when pressed in the centers. Reverse the sheet from front to back halfway through baking to ensure even browning. Transfer the sheet to a wire

words of kitchen wisdom
"Apples in small quantities, may be preserved by the following. First, completely dry a glazed jar, then put a few pebbles at the bottom, fill it with apples, and cover it with a piece of wood exactly fitted, and fill up the interstices with a little fresh mortar. The pebbles attract the moisture of the apples, while the mortar excludes the air from the jar and secures the fruit from pressure."

— Anthony F. M. Willich,
The Domestic Encyclopedia: A Dictionary of Facts and Useful Knowledge, 1803

fruit, pumpkin, and carrot cookies

rack and let stand until the cookies firm up slightly, 1 to 2 minutes. Using a spatula, transfer the cookies to wire racks. Let stand until completely cooled.

FOR THE ICING

In a small bowl, stir together the powdered sugar, corn syrup, vanilla, and enough drops of warm water to yield a thin icing. Spoon the icing into a paper cone or a small pastry bag fitted with a fine writing tip. (Or place in a small, sturdy plastic bag with one bottom corner cut away at the tip.)

Set the wire racks with the cookies over wax paper to catch drips. Drizzle the icing back and forth over the cookies to form thin, decorative lines. Let stand until the icing completely sets, about 30 minutes.

Store in an airtight container for up to 1 week or freeze for up to 2 months.

TIP
For a Halloween theme, drizzle the cookies back and forth vertically with plain white icing. Then tint the remaining icing orange and add the horizontal lines.

mini Apple stack cakes

Known throughout the Ozarks and Appalachia since at least the 1800s, apple stack cakes are testimony to the resourcefulness of mountain cooks faced with limited resources and meager winter larders. The wonderfully succulent cakes most often featured a dried apple puree, an important ingredient because apples were easily grown and then cored and dried, strung on cord, and stashed in the rafters for use when fresh fruits were unavailable. Usually, recipes called for preparing five or six cake-sized cookies, then sandwiching them together with a slow-simmered dried-apple filling to form a "stack cake."

Though tradition calls for making one large cake and forming sandwich cookies only with leftover dough and filling, the individual cookies are so appealing and convenient for serving that I prefer to prepare the entire recipe this way.

Both the cookies and the puree can be readied ahead, but, due to the juiciness of the apple filling, it's best to assemble the sandwiches the same day they'll be eaten. They need to stand for an hour or two, so the cookie and filling can meld together, but no longer than about 12 hours, because they'll get soggy.

Either sorghum or mild molasses may be used in this recipe. Sorghum tastes like molasses but is produced by pressing juice from the stems of sorghum plants rather than sugar cane stalks. Sorghum is popular in rural areas with climates too cold for sugar cane. Sorghum can be obtained in some health food stores.

FILLING

- 1 6-ounce package (2½ cups lightly packed) coarsely chopped dried apples
- ½ teaspoon ground cinnamon
- 1 cup sweet (*not* hard) apple cider or apple juice
- 2–4 tablespoons sugar

DOUGH

- 3⅓ cups all-purpose white flour, plus more if needed
- ¾ teaspoon baking soda
- ¾ teaspoon salt
- 1 cup white vegetable shortening or good-quality lard
- 1 cup plus 2 tablespoons sugar
- 1 large egg
- ½ cup sorghum or light molasses

FOR THE FILLING

In a medium, heavy saucepan, stir together the dried apples, cinnamon, cider or juice, and ¾ cup water. Bring to a simmer over medium heat. Cook, stirring frequently, for 15 minutes, or until the apples are rehydrated and the liquid is absorbed; be careful not to burn. If the mixture dries out during cooking, stir in 1 to 2 tablespoons more water to prevent sticking, but be careful not to overmoisten. Transfer the mixture to a food processor. Add 2 tablespoons sugar and process until the mixture is the consistency of very stiff, chunky applesauce, 3 to 4 minutes. Taste and add more sugar if the filling seems too tart. Cover and refrigerate until cooled, at least 1 hour. (The filling may be refrigerated for up to 4 days; warm to room temperature and stir before using.)

FOR THE DOUGH

In a medium bowl, thoroughly stir together the flour, baking soda, and salt; set aside. In a large bowl, with an electric mixer on medium speed, beat together the shortening or lard and sugar until light and well blended. Beat in the egg until evenly incorporated and fluffy. Beat in the sorghum or molasses. Stir or beat in the flour mixture until evenly incorporated. If the dough seems too soft, mix in 3 to 4 tablespoons more flour.

Divide the dough in half. Place each portion between large sheets of wax paper. Roll out each portion a scant ¼ inch thick; check the underside of the dough and smooth out any wrinkles that form. Stack the rolled portions (paper still attached) on a baking sheet. Refrigerate for 1½ hours, or until chilled and firm, or freeze for 45 minutes to speed chilling. (The dough may be held for up to 24 hours; if frozen, let it warm up slightly before using.)

Preheat the oven to 375 degrees F. Grease several baking sheets or coat with nonstick spray.

Working with one portion at a time and leaving the remaining dough chilled, gently peel away, then pat one sheet of wax paper back into place. Flip the dough over, then peel off and discard the second sheet. Using a 2½-inch plain or scalloped round cutter, cut out enough cookies to fill one baking sheet. (If at any point the dough softens too much to handle easily, transfer the paper and cookies to a baking sheet and refrigerate or freeze until firm again.) Using a spatula, carefully transfer the cookies to the baking sheet, spacing about 2 inches apart. These cookies must be baked while still cold, as they will spread too much if allowed to warm up first. Reroll any dough scraps. Continue cutting out the cookies until all the dough is used.

Bake the cookies, one sheet at a time, in the middle of the oven for 5 to 8 minutes, or until faintly tinged with brown all over, slightly darker at the edges, and firm when pressed in the centers. Reverse the sheet from front to back halfway through baking to ensure even browning. Transfer the sheet to a wire rack and let stand until the cookies firm up slightly, 1 to 2 minutes. Using a spatula, transfer the cookies to wire racks. Let stand until completely cooled.

At least 1 hour before serving time, spread a scant 2 tablespoons of the filling almost to the edges of the undersides of half the cookies. Top each cookie with a second cookie about the same size. Press the two together just slightly. Let stand for at least 1 hour or up to 12 hours before serving.

Store the unassembled cookie rounds in an airtight container for up to 1 week. Store the filling in an airtight container in the refrigerator for up to 4 days. Or freeze both for up to 1 month. Once the stack cakes have been assembled, they should be stored for no more than 12 hours.

Lemon sweetie pies

I was about ten when I first tasted this thumbprint cookie at a country store near my cousin's childhood home. My cousin and I used to make the mile-long trek there in the summer to buy ourselves a Nehi soda or a grape Popsicle. One day Mrs. Jenkins, the store's owner, gave us each a cookie she had baked; I thought it was even better than my favorite dessert, lemon pie. Round and handsome, it tasted buttery and had an intensely lemony circle of filling in the center. Both the store and Mrs. Jenkins were long gone by the time I wanted the recipe, but I have successfully recreated it from memory.

Both the dough and the lemon curd are easy, though the lemon curd needs to be made ahead and cooled. (For convenience, prepare it several days in advance and refrigerate.) The cookies are best when fresh, since they gradually soften upon standing.

LEMON CURD

- 2 large eggs, plus 2 large egg yolks
- Finely grated zest (colored part of the skin) of 2 very large lemons
- ½ cup fresh lemon juice
- 1 cup sugar
- ¼ cup (½ stick) unsalted butter, cut into chunks

DOUGH

- 2⅔ cups all-purpose white flour
- ¼ teaspoon baking powder
- ¼ teaspoon baking soda
- ¼ teaspoon salt
- 1 cup (2 sticks) unsalted butter, slightly softened
- ⅔ cup sugar
- 1½ teaspoons finely grated lemon zest (colored part of the skin)
- 1 large egg
- 2½ teaspoons vanilla extract
- Generous 2 teaspoons fresh lemon juice

FOR THE LEMON CURD

In a medium, heavy, nonreactive saucepan, combine the eggs and egg yolks, lemon zest, lemon juice, sugar, and butter. Bring to a full boil, whisking constantly, over medium-high heat. Boil for 1 minute, whisking constantly; it will be fairly thin. Remove from the heat; whisk for 30 seconds more. Let stand until cooled to warm. Strain the lemon curd through a fine sieve into a medium bowl. Cover tightly and refrigerate until chilled and thickened, at least 1½ hours. (The lemon curd may be refrigerated for up to 4 days.)

FOR THE DOUGH

Preheat the oven to 350 degrees F. Grease several baking sheets or coat with nonstick spray.

In a medium bowl, thoroughly stir together the flour, baking powder, baking soda, and salt; set aside. In a large bowl, with an electric mixer on medium speed, beat together the butter, sugar, and lemon zest until very light and fluffy. Add the egg, 1 tablespoon water, the vanilla, and lemon juice and beat until thoroughly incorporated. Reduce the speed to low and beat in half of the flour mixture. Gradually beat or stir in the remaining flour mixture until well blended.

Shape portions of the dough into generous 1¼-inch balls with lightly greased hands. Place on the baking sheets, spacing about 2½ inches apart. Using your thumb or knuckle, press a deep well into the center of each ball; take care not to break through the dough, or the lemon curd will leak out during baking. Place about ¾ teaspoon lemon curd in each well, mounding it slightly.

Bake the cookies, one sheet at a time, in the middle of the oven for 10 to 13 minutes, or until the lemon curd is bubbly and the cookies are lightly browned at the edges. Reverse the sheet from front to back halfway through baking to ensure even browning. Transfer the sheet to a wire rack and let stand until the cookies firm up slightly, 1 to 2 minutes. Using a spatula, transfer the cookies to wire racks. Let stand until completely cooled.

Store in an airtight container for up to 2 days. The cookies may be frozen for up to 1 month but will be soft rather than crisp.

words of kitchen wisdom

"None of your new-fangled lemon squeezers for me. Anything, especially acid — squeezed through metal, such as many of the improved ones are, is very bad. . . . There is but one way to squeeze a lemon, and that is the simple, old-fashioned way, between your fingers. Plenty of power can be brought to bear, particularly if the lemon is well-rolled first."

– A Philadelphia housewife, quoted in *The Ladies' Home Journal*, September 1889

lemon cheesecake tassies

These are dainty, bite-sized lemon cheesecakes presented in an easy-to-serve, easy-to-eat cookie form. They're a nice dessert choice when guests will be eating standing up. Like regular cheesecake, they can be baked ahead and refrigerated or even frozen for later use. This recipe requires a food processor.

DOUGH

- ³/₄ cup plus 2 tablespoons all-purpose white flour
- 5 tablespoons cold unsalted butter, cut into chunks
- 1 large egg yolk
- ¹/₂ teaspoon vanilla extract
- 2¹/₂ tablespoons sugar
- ¹/₂ teaspoon finely grated lemon zest (colored part of the skin)
- Pinch of salt

FILLING

- 1 8-ounce package cream cheese, slightly softened and cut into chunks
- Generous ¹/₃ cup sugar
- 1 large egg
- 1¹/₄ teaspoons finely grated lemon zest (colored part of the skin)
- 2 teaspoons fresh lemon juice
- ¹/₂ teaspoon vanilla extract

- About 2 tablespoons seedless blackberry or raspberry jam or cherry preserves, for topping

Preheat the oven to 350 degrees F. Grease two 12-cup minimuffin pans or coat with nonstick spray.

FOR THE DOUGH

In a food processor, combine the flour and butter. Process in on/off pulses until the mixture is the consistency of fine crumbs. In a small bowl, beat together the egg yolk, vanilla, sugar, lemon zest, and salt until well blended. Pour the egg-yolk mixture over the flour mixture and process in on/off pulses until just evenly incorporated and smooth; do not overprocess.

Divide the dough into quarters. Divide each quarter into 6 equal portions. Shape the portions into balls with lightly greased hands. Flatten each ball just slightly. Place each ball in a muffin cup; press down in the center so the dough fits the cup snugly and is slightly concave. Set the muffin pans on a baking sheet.

Bake in the upper third of the oven for 16 to 19 minutes, or until lightly browned all over and slightly darker at the edges. Transfer the baking sheet with the muffin pans to wire racks.

FOR THE FILLING

In a food processor, process the cream cheese, sugar, egg, lemon zest, lemon juice, and vanilla until blended and completely smooth. Transfer the filling to a 2-cup measure with a spout. Pour the filling over the baked dough rounds, dividing it evenly among the muffin cups.

Bake in the upper third of the oven for 10 to 12 minutes, or until the filling is set and just beginning to color at the edges. Add about ¼ teaspoon jam or preserves to the center of each tassie and continue baking until the filling is puffed and slightly tinged with color, 4 to 5 minutes more. Transfer the muffin pans to wire racks. Let stand until completely cooled.

Refrigerate in an airtight container for up to 1 week or freeze for up to 1 month.

key Lime frosties

I set out to capture the bracing tartness and fresh, tingly lime flavor of a good Florida key lime pie in these cookies. Topped with the glossy lime glaze, they say "fresh limes" in every bite. They are lovely served with a summer fruit bowl or a tropical fruit sorbet.

Despite the recipe name, it isn't necessary to use key limes in this recipe; regular supermarket limes work very well, although they are a bit less acidic and have a slightly different taste. Nowadays, key limes are actually rare in the Florida Keys, as hurricanes and development have decimated the groves.

2½ cups all-purpose white flour

¼ teaspoon baking powder

¼ teaspoon baking soda

¼ teaspoon salt

1 cup (2 sticks) unsalted butter, slightly softened

¼ cup corn oil or other flavorless vegetable oil

1 cup powdered sugar

1 large egg

1 tablespoon finely grated lime zest (colored part of the skin)

2 teaspoons finely grated lemon zest (colored part of the skin)

2 tablespoons fresh lime juice

2 teaspoons vanilla extract

½ teaspoon lemon extract

LIME GLAZE

1⅓ cups powdered sugar

1½ teaspoons finely grated lime zest (colored part of the skin)

1½ tablespoons fresh lime juice

¾ teaspoon light corn syrup

1 tiny drop green liquid food coloring, or as desired

1 drop yellow liquid food coloring, or as desired

In a medium bowl, thoroughly stir together the flour, baking powder, baking soda, and salt; set aside. In a large bowl, with an electric mixer on low speed, beat together the butter, oil, and powdered sugar until blended. Increase the speed to high and beat until very well blended. Add the egg, lime and lemon zests, lime juice, vanilla, and lemon extract and beat until lightened and smooth. Beat or stir in the flour mixture until evenly incorporated. Refrigerate the dough for 1½ hours, or until firm enough to handle.

Preheat the oven to 350 degrees F. Grease several baking sheets or coat with nonstick spray.

Shape portions of the dough into generous 1-inch balls with lightly greased hands. Place on the baking sheets, spacing about 1½ inches apart.

Bake the cookies, one sheet at a time, in the upper third of the oven for 13 to 16 minutes, or until lightly tinged with brown at the edges. Reverse the sheet from front to back halfway through baking to ensure even browning. Transfer the sheet to a wire rack and let stand until the cookies firm up slightly. Using a spatula, transfer the cookies to wire racks. Let stand until completely cooled.

FOR THE GLAZE

In a medium bowl, stir together the powdered sugar, lime zest, lime juice, corn syrup, and food coloring. Add a few drops of hot water if necessary to blend the ingredients together. Stir until completely smooth. Thin with enough warm water to produce a fluid but not runny glaze.

Set the wire racks with the cookies over wax paper to catch drips. Working gently, since the cookies are fragile, swirl a layer of glaze over each, using a table knife. Return the cookies to the racks. Let stand until the glaze completely sets, at least 1 hour.

Store in a single layer or layered with wax paper in an airtight container for up to 1 week or freeze for up to 1 month.

Florida orange melts

Florida's answer to Kentucky's bourbon balls, these quick, no-bake cookies showcase the flavor of the state's most important fruit, along with another southern favorite, pecans. Jeanne A. Voltz, coauthor of *The Florida Cookbook,* says she thinks orange melts originated in the Coconut Grove area. They are best if allowed to mellow overnight.

1²/₃ cups coarsely crushed or broken-up vanilla wafers

1¹/₃ cups (about 5¹/₂ ounces) chopped pecans (divided)

²/₃ cup powdered sugar

¹/₄ teaspoon finely grated orange zest (colored part of the skin)

3 tablespoons thawed orange juice concentrate (do not dilute)

2 tablespoons orange liqueur, such as Grand Marnier, Cointreau, or Triple Sec

2 teaspoons light corn syrup

In a food processor, process the vanilla wafers and 1 cup of the pecans until finely ground. Add the powdered sugar and orange zest and process until evenly incorporated. With the motor running, add the orange juice concentrate, orange liqueur, and corn syrup through the feed tube and process just until well blended. If the mixture seems too soft to handle, let it stand for a few minutes until firm; if it seems dry and crumbly, sprinkle in a little water and process briefly to incorporate.

Finely chop the remaining ⅓ cup pecans. Spread them in a shallow bowl. Shape portions of the mixture into scant 1-inch balls with lightly greased hands. Press the balls into the pecans, turning until coated lightly all over. (If the pecans don't stick well, moisten the balls by rolling them in slightly damp hands.) Let the cookies mellow in an airtight container for at least 4 hours and preferably overnight before serving.

Store in an airtight container for up to 4 days, refrigerate for up to 2 weeks, or freeze for up to 1 month.

orange-tangerine coolers

These citrusy, melt-in-your-mouth cookies are finished with a generous coating of powdered sugar. The ground coriander and tangerine zest give the cookies a slightly exotic aroma and complement their fresh orange flavor.

2¼ cups all-purpose white flour

½ teaspoon ground coriander

¼ teaspoon baking soda

¼ teaspoon salt

¾ cup (1½ sticks) unsalted butter, slightly softened

2 tablespoons corn oil or other flavorless vegetable oil

1 cup powdered sugar, plus ½ cup for topping

1 large egg

1 tablespoon plus 2 teaspoons fresh lemon juice

Generous ¼ teaspoon lemon extract

1 tablespoon finely grated orange zest (colored part of the skin)

½–1 teaspoon finely grated tangerine zest (colored part of the skin)

Preheat the oven to 325 degrees F. Grease several baking sheets or coat with nonstick spray.

In a medium bowl, thoroughly stir together the flour, coriander, baking soda, and salt; set aside. In a large bowl, with an electric mixer on low speed, beat together the butter, oil, and 1 cup powdered sugar until blended. Increase the speed to medium and beat until very well blended. Add the egg, lemon juice, lemon extract, and orange and tangerine zests and beat until lightened and smooth. Beat or stir in the flour mixture until evenly incorporated. Let the dough stand for 5 minutes, or until firmed up slightly.

Shape portions of the dough into generous 1-inch balls with lightly greased hands. Place on the baking sheets, spacing about 1 inch apart. Using your hand, press down the balls just until their tops are flat.

Bake the cookies, one sheet at a time, in the upper third of the oven for 14 to 18 minutes, or until the bottoms are nicely browned; lift up a cookie to check. Reverse the sheet from front to back halfway through baking to ensure even browning. Transfer the sheet to a wire rack and let stand until the cookies firm up slightly, 1 to 2 minutes. Using a spatula, transfer the cookies to wire racks. Let stand until cooled to barely warm.

tip
Some varieties of tangerines have very pungent, slightly bitter skins. If the zest smells strong as you're grating it, use only ½ teaspoon. Otherwise, use 1 teaspoon.

In a large, shallow bowl, place the remaining ½ cup powdered sugar. Place the cookies in the bowl, three or four at a time, and turn them in the sugar until well coated.

Store the cookies in an airtight container, sifting additional powdered sugar over each layer. Store in a cool place, but not refrigerated, for up to 2 weeks or freeze for up to 1 month. In the case of freezing, the powdered-sugar coating should not be added until after the cookies are completely thawed.

pineapple-coconut-macadamia Thumbprints

I relied on some of Hawaii's favorite flavors to give the traditional thumbprint cookie a tropical twist. The balls of dough are rolled in coconut and chopped macadamia nuts before the indentations are formed and filled with pineapple preserves or marmalade. This gives the cookies a distinctive texture and attractive look.

2¹/₂ cups all-purpose white flour

Generous ¹/₄ teaspoon salt

¹/₄ teaspoon baking soda

1 cup (2 sticks) unsalted butter, slightly softened

³/₄ cup sugar

1 large egg, plus 1 large egg yolk

1 tablespoon finely grated lemon zest (colored part of the skin)

1¹/₄ teaspoons finely grated orange zest (colored part of the skin)

1 tablespoon fresh lemon juice

2 teaspoons vanilla extract

¹/₂ teaspoon coconut extract (optional)

1²/₃ cups (about 4³/₄ ounces) shredded or flaked sweetened coconut (divided)

1¹/₂ cups (about 8¹/₂ ounces) finely chopped dried sweetened pineapple

³/₄ cup (about 3¹/₂ ounces) macadamia nuts, finely chopped

About 1 cup pineapple preserves or marmalade

Preheat the oven to 350 degrees F. Grease several baking sheets or coat with nonstick spray.

In a medium bowl, thoroughly stir together the flour, salt, and baking soda; set aside. In a large bowl, with an electric mixer on medium speed, beat the butter until lightened and smooth. Add the sugar and egg and egg yolk and beat until fluffy and well blended. Add the lemon and orange zests, lemon juice, vanilla, and coconut extract, if using, and beat for 30 seconds more. Beat in half of the flour mixture. Stir or beat in the remaining flour mixture, 1 cup of the coconut, and the dried pineapple until evenly incorporated.

In a medium, shallow bowl, stir together the macadamia nuts and the remaining ²/₃ cup coconut. Shape portions of the dough into scant 1-inch balls with lightly greased hands. Place the balls, three or four at a time, in the bowl and dredge them in the nut-coconut mixture until well coated. Lift them out with a slotted spoon. Place on the baking sheets, spacing about 1½ inches apart. Using your thumb or knuckle, press a deep well into the center of each ball. Place about ½ teaspoon preserves or marmalade in each well.

Tips

- Be sure to use dried, sweetened pineapple, not candied or glacéed pineapple, in this recipe. Dried pineapple rings or bits are usually available in the dried-fruit section of supermarkets, as well as in many health food stores.
- If salted macadamia nuts are used, wipe off the excess salt with paper towels.

Bake the cookies, one sheet at a time, in the middle of the oven for 10 to 12 minutes, or until lightly tinged with brown. Reverse the sheet from front to back halfway through baking to ensure even browning. Transfer the sheet to a wire rack and let stand until the cookies firm up slightly, 3 to 4 minutes. Using a spatula, transfer the cookies to wire racks. Let stand until completely cooled. (Wipe off and regrease the sheets before reusing.)

Store in an airtight container for up to 10 days or freeze for up to 2 months.

words of kitchen wisdom
"Do not beat the butter, sugar and eggs in a tin basin; it scours the basin, but discolors the ingredients. Use a wooden spoon and a white enameled bowl."

– Sarah Tyson Rorer, *Mrs. Rorer's New Cook Book,* 1898

Fruit, Pumpkin, and Carrot Cookies

ambrosia cookies

Makes 35 to 40
(2¾-to-3-inch)
cookies.

These nutty, fruity goodies have become popular in many Florida communities over the past twenty years. They are packed into lunch boxes, offered at bake sales, and toted to picnics, PTA meetings, and all sorts of other gatherings. I first learned of them from the author of *The Florida Cookbook,* former *Miami Herald* staffer Jeanne A. Voltz.

No one seems to know who created ambrosia cookies, but in true Florida fashion, they are loaded with fruit—especially pineapple and raisins—as well as coconut and pecans. I like to add a pinch of orange zest; I think it brings out the taste of both the fruit and the nuts.

1 cup (5 ounces) golden raisins

¹/₃ cup (about 2 ounces) diced dried apricots (optional)

2³/₄ cups all-purpose white flour

¹/₂ teaspoon baking powder

¹/₂ teaspoon salt

1 cup (2 sticks) unsalted butter, slightly softened

Scant ²/₃ cup corn oil or other flavorless vegetable oil

2 cups packed light brown sugar

1 large egg

2¹/₂ teaspoons vanilla extract

Pinch of finely grated orange zest (colored part of the skin; optional)

1¹/₂ cups (about 4¹/₄ ounces) shredded or flaked sweetened coconut

1¹/₃ cups corn flakes, crushed

1¹/₄ cups (about 7 ounces) diced dried sweetened pineapple or candied pineapple

1 cup (4 ounces) chopped pecans

²/₃ cup old-fashioned rolled oats

Preheat the oven to 375 degrees F. Grease several baking sheets or coat with nonstick spray.

In a colander, rinse the raisins and apricots, if using, well under hot water; let stand until well drained; set aside.

In a medium bowl, thoroughly stir together the flour, baking powder, and salt; set aside. In a large bowl, with an electric mixer on low speed, beat together the butter, oil, and brown sugar until blended. Increase the speed to medium and beat until well blended and smooth. Beat in the egg, vanilla, and orange zest, if using. Beat or stir in the flour mixture until evenly incorporated. Stir in the coconut, corn flakes, pineapple, pecans, oats, and drained fruit until evenly incorporated. Let the dough stand for 10 minutes, or until firmed up; if the room is very warm, re-frigerate the dough.

TIP
To crush the corn flakes, place them in a plastic bag and squeeze several times.

Shape portions of the dough into 1½-inch balls with lightly greased hands. Place on the baking sheets, spacing about 2½ inches apart. Using your hand, press down the balls until they are about ⅓ inch thick.

Bake the cookies, one sheet at a time, in the upper third of the oven for 10 to 13 minutes, or until tinged with brown all over and just beginning to firm up in the centers; be careful not to overbake. Reverse the sheet from front to back halfway through baking to ensure even browning. Transfer the sheet to a wire rack and let stand until the cookies firm up slightly, 1 to 2 minutes. Using a spatula, transfer the cookies to wire racks. Let stand until completely cooled.

Store in an airtight container for up to 1 week or freeze for up to 1 month.

sourcherry (or apricot) hamantaschen

MAKES ABOUT 35 (3-inch) cookies.

These days, several very different sweets are called hamantaschen in America. At one end of the spectrum are the small, tricornered prune or poppy-seed cookies sold by old-fashioned Jewish bakeries for Purim. At the other end are the humongous, triangular, Danish-style pastries stuffed with gluey pie fillings and sold by nondenominational pastry shops year-round. Somewhere in the middle (and my preference) are hamantaschen in the spirit of traditional European recipes but updated with a more flavorful dough and lighter, livelier, dried-fruit fillings.

This recipe—one of my favorites—definitely falls into the middle category. The dough is tasty and the filling is succulent, colorful, and boldly flavored with dried cherries and sour cherry jam or preserves. I also like apricot hamantaschen; see the variation.

This recipe requires a food processor.

SOUR CHERRY FILLING

1¹/₂ cups (7¹/₂ ounces) dried sweetened sour cherries
²/₃ cup sour cherry jam or preserves
¹/₈ teaspoon ground cinnamon

DOUGH

3 cups all-purpose white flour
¹/₂ teaspoon salt
Scant ¹/₂ teaspoon baking soda
¹/₂ cup (1 stick) cold unsalted butter, cut into chunks

¹/₄ cup corn oil or other flavorless vegetable oil
³/₄ cup sugar
1 large egg, plus 1 large egg white
2 teaspoons finely grated lemon zest (colored part of the skin)
1¹/₂ teaspoons fresh lemon juice
1¹/₂ teaspoons vanilla extract

1 large egg yolk, lightly beaten with 1 tablespoon water (optional)

FOR THE FILLING

In a medium, heavy, nonreactive saucepan, combine the dried cherries and ¹/₃ cup water. Bring to a simmer over medium-high heat; immediately remove from the heat. Let stand for 5 minutes to rehydrate the cherries. Transfer the mixture to a food processor. Process until the cherries are coarsely chopped. Add the jam or preserves and cinnamon and process in on/off pulses just until evenly incorporated. Cover and refrigerate the filling until chilled, about 1 hour. (The filling may be refrigerated for up to 4 days; let come to room temperature and stir before using.)

TIP

Prepare the cherry filling (or apricot filling variation, if preferred) far enough ahead that it can cool at least to room temperature before using.

203

fruit, pumpkin, and carrot cookies

FOR THE DOUGH

In a food processor, combine the flour, salt, and baking soda. Process in on/off pulses until well blended. Sprinkle the butter and oil over the flour mixture and process in on/off pulses until the mixture is the consistency of coarse meal. In a small bowl, beat together the sugar, egg and egg white, lemon zest, lemon juice, and vanilla until very well blended. Drizzle the egg mixture over the flour mixture and process in on/off pulses just until evenly incorporated; scrape down the sides as necessary and do not overprocess.

Divide the dough into thirds. Place each portion between large sheets of wax paper. Roll out each portion ⅛ inch thick; check the underside of the dough and smooth out any wrinkles that form. Stack the rolled portions (paper still attached) on a baking sheet. Refrigerate for 45 minutes, or until chilled and firm, or freeze for 25 minutes to speed chilling. Chill a second baking sheet so it can be used as a work surface to keep the dough cool and manageable as the cookies are cut out.

Preheat the oven to 375 degrees F. Grease several baking sheets or coat with nonstick spray.

Working with one portion at a time and leaving the remaining dough chilled, gently peel away one sheet of wax paper, then pat back into place. Flip the dough over, place on the chilled baking sheet, then peel off and discard the second sheet. Using a 2¾-to-3-inch fluted or plain round cutter, cut out the cookies. Using a spatula, carefully transfer the rounds to the baking sheets, spacing about 2 inches apart. If desired, create guides for forming tricornered pockets by marking the perimeter of each round into thirds with nicks from a paring knife. (If you are experienced at making hamantaschen, omit the guides and form the pockets as you normally would.) Place about 1 teaspoon filling in the center of each round.

TO FORM A TRICORNERED POCKET

Lift up one side of a round at one mark. Very firmly pinch it together to form one corner. Using both hands, lift up the dough at the two remaining marks and very firmly pinch each one together to form the second and third corners. If necessary, add enough more filling so that it mounds just slightly in the center of each cookie, but avoid overfilling, or the cookies may break apart as they bake. (If at any point the dough softens too much to handle easily, transfer it along with the wax paper and baking sheet to the refrigerator or freezer until firm again.) Using a pastry brush or a paper towel, very lightly brush the hamantaschen with the egg-yolk wash, if using; use only a minimum of wash and blot up any drips from the baking pan. Reroll any dough scraps. Continue cutting out the cookies until all the dough is used.

Bake the cookies, one sheet at a time, in the upper third of the oven for 10 to 15 minutes, or until the cookies are lightly tinged with brown. Reverse the sheet from front to back halfway through baking to ensure even browning. Using a spatula, immediately transfer the cookies to wire racks. Let stand until completely cooled.

Store in an airtight container for up to 2 weeks or freeze for up to 2 months.

VARIATION ## Apricot Filling

1½ cups (about 7½ ounces) coarsely chopped dried
    apricots, preferably American
⅓ cup (about 1¾ ounces) golden raisins
½ cup clover or other mild honey, plus more if needed
¼ cup orange marmalade
½ teaspoon ground cinnamon

In a medium, heavy, nonreactive saucepan, stir together the dried apricots, raisins, honey, marmalade, cinnamon, and ½ cup water. Bring to a simmer over medium heat. Cook, stirring occasionally, until the dried fruit is soft and almost all the liquid is absorbed, about 10 minutes. If the filling dries out during cooking, add a little more water. Remove from the heat. Let stand until cooled slightly. Transfer the mixture to a food processor. Process until coarsely pureed. Taste the filling; if it is too tart, add 1 to 2 tablespoons more honey and process just until evenly incorporated. Cover and refrigerate the filling until chilled, about 1 hour. (The filling may be refrigerated for up to 4 days; let come to room temperature and stir before using.)

TIP
Dried apricot packages are usually labeled as either "Turkish" or "American," but the two types also look different: the Turkish are plump, slightly pale, and almost translucent. The American are fairly flat and bright orange. Turkish (or other imported) apricots tend to be more tender and less tart than American apricots and are a better choice in these cookies.

Nana's Date ROCKS

Every time I bake these wonderful, homespun cookies, the distinctive aroma of cinnamon and cloves takes me back to the pleasant times I spent with my grandmother in her kitchen. The taste of Nana's rocks is memorable, too—mellow and spicy and richly fruity from an abundance of dates. The name comes from the fact that the cookies look like little boulders; they are not hard, however, but enticingly chewy and moist. (Lumpy cookies were often called rocks in late-nineteenth- and early-twentieth-century America, and prior to that, similarly shaped candies and small cakes were known as rocks in Britain.)

As a child, I took little notice of the fact, but these cookies are formed in an unusual way. After being rolled into balls between the palms, the portions of dough are then very lightly coated with flour. This key step keeps the cookies compact during baking, contributing to their moistness and rock-like appearance. They are best if allowed to mellow overnight.

2 cups minus 2 tablespoons all-purpose white flour
Generous 1 teaspoon ground cinnamon
Generous 1 teaspoon ground cloves
³/4 teaspoon baking soda
¹/4 teaspoon salt
1 cup sugar

³/4 cup (1¹/2 sticks) unsalted butter, slightly softened
2 large eggs
2 teaspoons vanilla extract
3 cups (about 15 ounces) coarsely chopped pitted dates

About 3 tablespoons all-purpose white flour, for coating

Preheat the oven to 350 degrees F. Grease several baking sheets or coat with nonstick spray.

In a medium bowl, thoroughly stir together the flour, cinnamon, cloves, baking soda, and salt; set aside. In a large bowl, with an electric mixer on medium speed, beat together the sugar and butter until very well blended and fluffy. Add the eggs, one at a time, then the vanilla, and beat until very well blended. Beat or stir in the flour mixture until evenly incorporated. Fold in the dates until evenly incorporated. Let the dough stand for 5 to 10 minutes, or until firmed up slightly.

Shape portions of the dough into 1¼-inch balls with lightly greased hands. Dust your hands with flour and roll each ball in your hands until lightly coated with flour. Place on the baking sheets, spacing about 2½ inches apart.

Bake the cookies, one sheet at a time, in the upper third of the oven for 10 to 14 minutes, or until tinged with brown all over and just barely firm when pressed in the centers. Reverse the sheet from front to back halfway through baking to ensure even browning. Transfer the sheet to a wire rack and let stand until the cookies firm up slightly, 1 to 2 minutes. Using a spatula, transfer the cookies to wire racks. Let stand until completely cooled. Let the cookies mellow in an airtight container for at least 6 hours and preferably overnight before serving.

Store in an airtight container for up to 2 weeks or freeze for up to 2 months.

St. Joseph's Day Fig Cookies

These unusual fig-filled cookies are a fond tradition in the local Catholic community of New Orleans and are a variation on traditional Sicilian fig-stuffed cookies called *cucidati.* The New Orleans versions, including at least one commercial brand, are always fancifully decorated with drizzles of pink, white, and green icing to symbolize the Italian flag, as well as a shower of confetti-colored sprinkles. The cookies are served during the Feast of St. Joseph, an annual celebration held on March 19. Metsy Hingle, a popular romance novelist and New Orleans native who shared this recipe with me, says the cookies are part of a huge array of dishes heaped upon the church altar and blessed by the priest. Afterward, the congregation invites the whole neighborhood into the church to join the feasting.

I have modified the original recipe so that both the dough and the filling can be conveniently prepared in a food processor.

FILLING

- 2 cups (12 ounces) trimmed and coarsely chopped dried figs
- 1 cup (5 ounces) coarsely chopped pitted dates
- Generous ½ cup orange marmalade
- 1 teaspoon grated orange zest (colored part of the skin)
- 3 tablespoons orange juice, plus more if needed
- 2 tablespoons (¼ stick) unsalted butter, melted
- 1½ teaspoons ground cinnamon

DOUGH

- 3 cups all-purpose white flour
- Generous ¼ cup sugar
- ½ teaspoon baking powder
- ¼ teaspoon salt
- 1 cup white vegetable shortening, cut into chunks

ICING

- 1¼ cups powdered sugar, sifted after measuring, if lumpy
- 3 tablespoons milk, plus more if needed
- ¼ teaspoon anise extract *or* ½ teaspoon vanilla extract
- 1 drop green liquid food coloring
- 1 drop red liquid food coloring

  Multicolored nonpareils, for topping

FOR THE FILLING

In a food processor, combine the figs, dates, marmalade, orange zest, 3 tablespoons orange juice, butter, and cinnamon. Process until coarsely pureed, about 1 minute; if the mixture begins to clump, stop and redistribute the contents as necessary. If the mixture seems dry, add about 1 tablespoon more orange juice. (The filling may be refrigerated for up to 4 days; let come to room temperature and stir before using.)

FOR THE DOUGH

In a food processor, combine the flour, sugar, baking powder, and salt. Process in on/off pulses until well blended. Drop spoonfuls of the shortening over the flour and process in on/off pulses until the mixture is the consistency of coarse meal. Sprinkle ⅓ cup plus 1½ tablespoons ice water over the mixture and process in on/off pulses just until evenly incorporated; do not overprocess. Working on a sheet of wax paper, knead until a smooth, slightly moist but not wet dough forms. If the dough is too dry or crumbly to hold together easily, sprinkle on a little more water, 1 to 2 teaspoons at a time, and continue kneading.

Divide the dough in half. Place each portion between large sheets of wax paper. Roll out each portion into a 12-inch square; check the underside of the dough and smooth out any wrinkles that form. Cut and patch the dough as necessary to even the dough sides. Stack the rolled portions (paper still attached) on a baking sheet. Refrigerate for 20 to 30 minutes, or until chilled and firm.

Preheat the oven to 375 degrees F. Set out several baking sheets.

Working with one portion at a time and leaving the remaining dough chilled, gently peel away, then lightly pat one sheet of wax paper back into place. Flip the dough over, then peel off and discard the second sheet. Using a large, sharp knife, cut the dough crosswise into four 3-by-12-inch strips. Spoon about ¼ cup filling down the length of each strip, keeping the filling in the middle third of the strip. Fold the sides of each strip over the filling so they overlap slightly. Moisten the edges where the folded-over portions meet, then press down on the seam to seal. Trim off and discard the uneven ends of each strip. Cut each strip crosswise at 2-inch intervals to form the cookies. Using a spatula, transfer the cookies to the baking sheets, seam side down, spacing about 2 inches apart. If desired, cut two parallel 1-inch slits down the length of each cookie top so the filling shows through. Slightly bend each cookie into a crescent shape. Repeat with the remaining dough and filling.

Bake the cookies, one sheet at a time, in the upper third of the oven for 14 to 19 minutes, or until browned on the bottoms and slightly darker at the edges. Reverse the sheet from front to back halfway through baking to ensure even browning. Transfer the sheet to a wire rack and let stand until the cookies firm up slightly, 1 to 2 minutes. Using a spatula, transfer the cookies to wire racks. Let stand until completely cooled.

fig uses

Fig trees grow abundantly in Louisiana, and cookbook author Jude Theriot, who grew up there, says that most of the fruit is put to use in fig cake. But he also reports a novel use for the surplus fruit: local cooks use it to make "strawberry" jam, by cooking the fresh figs with a package of strawberry Jell-O. "It's surprising how much the figs actually taste like strawberry jam," he says.

FOR THE ICING

In a medium bowl, stir together the powdered sugar, milk, and anise or vanilla extract to form a fluid icing; if necessary, thin it with a little more milk. Transfer one-third of the icing to a small bowl and stir in the green food coloring. Transfer another one-third to a separate small bowl and stir in the red food coloring.

Set the wire racks with the cookies over wax paper to catch drips. Using a spoon, drizzle a line of the pink icing crosswise over the cookies. Immediately top with some nonpareils before the icing sets. Keeping the colors separated so they don't run together, neatly drizzle lines of the green and white icing over the cookies, and sprinkle with more nonpareils. Let stand until the icing completely sets, at least 1 hour.

Store in an airtight container for up to 1 week or freeze for up to 1 month.

orange-glazed fruit chews

These cookies get their great fruit flavor and succulence from a secret ingredient: prunes. This is a case in which the whole really is more than the sum of its parts.

1½ teaspoons finely grated orange zest (colored part of the skin)

⅔ cup orange juice

1½ cups (about 8 ounces) chopped pitted prunes

½ cup (2½ ounces) golden raisins

3½ cups all-purpose white flour

1½ teaspoons ground cinnamon

1 teaspoon baking soda

½ teaspoon salt

Generous ¼ teaspoon ground cloves

1 cup (2 sticks) unsalted butter, at room temperature, cut into chunks

1⅔ cups packed dark brown sugar

1 large egg

1 teaspoon vanilla extract

1 cup (4 ounces) chopped walnuts (optional)

ORANGE GLAZE

3 cups powdered sugar, sifted after measuring, if lumpy

½ teaspoon finely grated orange zest (colored part of the skin)

3½ tablespoons orange juice, plus more if needed

2 teaspoons fresh lemon juice

¼ teaspoon vanilla extract

Preheat the oven to 350 degrees F. Grease several baking sheets or coat with nonstick spray.

In a large saucepan, combine the orange zest, orange juice, prunes, and raisins. Bring to a simmer over medium-high heat. Cook, stirring frequently, until the fruit rehydrates and the juice is absorbed, about 5 minutes. Remove from the heat. Let stand until cooled to warm.

In a medium bowl, thoroughly stir together the flour, cinnamon, baking soda, salt, and cloves; set aside. Add the butter and brown sugar to the fruit mixture and stir until the butter melts and the ingredients are well blended. Add the egg and vanilla and stir until evenly incorporated. Stir in the flour mixture and walnuts, if using, until evenly incorporated.

Drop the dough by golf-ball-sized mounds onto the baking sheets, spacing about 2½ inches apart.

Bake the cookies, one sheet at a time, in the upper third of the oven for 10 to 13 minutes, or until tinged with brown and just barely firm in the centers. Reverse the sheet from back to front halfway through baking to ensure even browning. Transfer the sheet to a wire rack and let stand until the cookies firm up slightly, about 2 minutes. Using a spatula, transfer the cookies to wire racks. Let stand until cooled to warm.

FOR THE GLAZE

In a medium bowl, stir together the powdered sugar, orange zest, orange juice, lemon juice, and vanilla to form a fluid icing; if necessary, thin it with a little more orange juice or water.

Set the wire racks with the cookies over wax paper to catch drips. Dip the tops of the warm cookies into the glaze until coated; shake off the excess. Return the cookies to the racks. Let stand until the glaze completely sets, at least 1½ hours.

Store in an airtight container for up to 1 week or freeze for up to 1 month.

Kentucky Bourbon
fruitcake cookies

Kentucky fruitcake cookies—which some locals call Christmas rocks—are fragrant with spices, spiked with bourbon, and chockablock with colorful fruit. Since they contain no molasses and include pecans rather than walnuts, they are milder and mellower than most classic fruitcakes. The cookies are nice for the holidays and are good keepers. The idea of baking fruitcake cookies instead of full-sized fruitcake loaves at Christmas may seem modern, but, in fact, bite-sized fruited cakes, known as Roxbury cakes, were introduced to America by early British settlers. Fruitcake itself is English, widely baked in this country since colonial days.

Bourbon, on the other hand, is wholly American. Distilled from corn, it dates back to the early 1800s. The name comes from Bourbon County, originally part of Virginia but now in Kentucky. The whiskey didn't start turning up in cookbooks until after Prohibition.

FRUIT-NUT MIXTURE

1½ cups (7½ ounces) golden raisins or dark raisins, or a combination

1 cup (4 ounces) chopped pecans

½ cup (2¾ ounces) chopped dried apricots

½ cup (3 ounces) diced dried sweetened pineapple or candied pineapple

½ cup (2½ ounces) chopped mixed red and green candied cherries

½ cup good-quality bourbon

⅓ cup orange marmalade, combined with 3 tablespoons hot water

DOUGH

¾ cup all-purpose white flour

1¼ teaspoons ground cinnamon

¾ teaspoon ground ginger

½ teaspoon ground nutmeg

¼ teaspoon baking soda

⅛ teaspoon salt

½ cup packed light brown sugar

⅓ cup (5⅓ tablespoons) unsalted butter, slightly softened

2 large eggs

1 teaspoon finely grated orange zest (colored part of the skin)

Red and green candied-cherry halves or pecan halves, for topping

FOR THE FRUIT-NUT MIXTURE

In a large, nonreactive bowl, thoroughly stir together the raisins, pecans, apricots, pineapple, cherries, bourbon, and marmalade mixture. Cover and let stand for at least 8 hours or up to 24 hours, stirring several times.

FOR THE DOUGH

In a medium bowl, thoroughly stir together the flour, cinnamon, ginger, nutmeg, baking soda, and salt; set aside. In a large bowl, with an electric mixer on medium speed, beat together the brown sugar and butter until well blended. Add the eggs and orange zest and beat until well blended; the mixture may look curdled. Stir in the flour mixture and fruit-nut mixture until evenly incorporated. Cover and freeze the dough for at least 2 hours, or until firm enough to shape into balls. (The dough may be frozen for up to 2 weeks; if frozen, let it warm up slightly before using.)

Preheat the oven to 350 degrees F. Grease several baking sheets or coat with nonstick cooking spray.

Shape portions of the dough into 1-inch balls with lightly greased hands. Place on the baking sheets, spacing about 1½ inches apart. Press a candied-cherry half or pecan half into the center of each cookie.

Bake the cookies, one sheet at a time, in the upper third of the oven for 11 to 16 minutes, or until tinged with brown and slightly darker at the edges. Reverse the sheet from front to back halfway through baking to ensure even browning. Transfer the sheet to a wire rack and let stand until the cookies firm up slightly, 1 to 2 minutes. Using a spatula, transfer the cookies to wire racks. Let stand until completely cooled. Let the cookies mellow in an airtight container for at least 24 hours before serving.

Store in an airtight container for up to 3 weeks or freeze for up to 2½ months.

Four-Fruit Trolls

A generous blend of fruit and spices adds appealing flavor and chewiness to this whole-some drop cookie. Apple butter (which in fact contains no butter) contributes extra fruitiness and sweetness and helps keep the cookies moist. These fairly sturdy cookies make guilt-free lunch-box treats and also are good "trail" cookies. I often prepare them for family snacks.

My inspiration was a recipe for a lunch-box cookie published in the early 1980s by the consumer affairs department of Giant Food, a regional supermarket chain. Accord-ing to staff member Janet Tenney, the idea was to provide an easy, tasty cookie with in-creased fiber and reduced fat and sugar, in response to consumers' strong interest in feeding their children healthful fare. She says the staff came up with the name "trolls" because the cookies were a takeoff on old-fashioned hermits.

Other dried fruits, such as dark raisins, diced pitted prunes, or dried, sweetened cherries, can be substituted, depending on what you have on hand. Like golden raisins and dried cranberries, these should be soaked and drained before using.

²/₃ cup (about 3¹/₂ ounces) golden raisins

²/₃ cup (2³/₄ ounces) dried sweetened cranberries

1 cup finely diced unpeeled Golden Delicious apple (about 1 medium)

²/₃ cup (about 3¹/₂ ounces) chopped pitted dates

1 cup all-purpose white flour

1 cup whole wheat flour

1¹/₄ teaspoons ground cinnamon

¹/₂ teaspoon ground nutmeg

¹/₂ teaspoon ground cloves

1 teaspoon baking soda

Generous ¹/₄ teaspoon salt

1¹/₃ cups packed light brown sugar

¹/₄ cup corn oil or canola oil

3 tablespoons unsalted butter or stick margarine, slightly softened

2 large eggs

¹/₄ cup apple butter, thinned with 1 tablespoon water

Preheat the oven to 350 degrees F. Grease several baking sheets or coat with nonstick spray.

In a medium bowl, cover the raisins and cranberries with hot water. Let soak for about 10 minutes; drain well. Stir in the apple and dates; set aside.

In a medium bowl, thoroughly stir together the white and whole wheat flours, cinnamon, nutmeg, cloves, baking soda, and salt; set aside. In a large bowl, with an electric mixer on medium speed, beat together the brown sugar, oil, and butter until very well blended. Add the eggs and apple butter and beat until fluffy and evenly incorporated. Reduce the speed to low, add one-third of the flour mixture, and beat until the dough stiffens. Stir in the remaining flour mixture until evenly incorporated. Fold in the fruit mixture until evenly incorporated.

Drop the dough onto the baking sheets in generous golf-ball-sized mounds, spacing about 2½ inches apart.

Bake the cookies, one sheet at a time, in the middle of the oven for 9 to 12 minutes, or until browned and barely firm when touched in the centers. Reverse the sheet from front to back halfway through baking to ensure even browning. Transfer the sheet to a wire rack and let stand until the cookies firm up, 1 to 2 minutes. Using a spatula, transfer the cookies to wire racks. Let stand until completely cooled.

Store in an airtight container for up to 1 week or freeze for up to 1 month.

pumpkin ROCKS
with cream-cheese frosting

The real pumpkin-pie flavor of these plump, fragrant drop cookies always wins fans. They are topped with a smooth cream-cheese frosting that goes nicely with the pumpkin and spice. While you might be tempted to think of them strictly as autumn cookies, they are appealing at any time of the year.

The pumpkin is one of numerous winter squashes that Native Americans introduced to the colonists. Before pumpkin pies as we now know them were created, various pumpkin-pudding dishes were prepared. Some early settlers cut off pumpkin tops, scraped out the seeds, then added milk, honey, and spices to the cavities. The pumpkins were set into the embers and roasted. Finally, their contents were scraped out and eaten.

1 cup (5 ounces) raisins
3 cups all-purpose white flour
1½ teaspoons ground cinnamon
1 teaspoon baking soda
¾ teaspoon ground cloves
¾ teaspoon ground nutmeg
Scant ½ teaspoon salt
1⅓ cups sugar
⅔ cup (1 stick plus 2⅔ tablespoons) unsalted butter, slightly softened

½ cup corn oil or other flavorless vegetable oil
¼ cup light molasses
1½ teaspoons vanilla extract
1 cup canned pumpkin (*not* seasoned pumpkin-pie filling)

CREAM-CHEESE FROSTING

2½ cups powdered sugar
1 3-ounce package cream cheese, slightly softened and cut into chunks
¼ teaspoon vanilla extract
1 tablespoon orange juice

Preheat the oven to 350 degrees F. Grease several baking sheets or coat with nonstick spray.

In a small bowl, cover the raisins with hot water. Let stand for 10 minutes. Drain well and set aside.

In a medium bowl, thoroughly stir together the flour, cinnamon, baking soda, cloves, nutmeg, and salt; set aside. In a large bowl, with an electric mixer on medium speed, beat together the sugar and butter until very well blended and fluffy. Reduce the speed to low and beat in the oil, molasses, vanilla, and pumpkin until evenly incorporated. Beat or stir in the flour mixture, then the raisins, until evenly incorporated.

Drop the dough onto the baking sheets in golf-ball-sized mounds, spacing about 2 inches apart.

Bake the cookies, one sheet at a time, in the upper third of the oven for 12 to 15 minutes, or until lightly browned all over and slightly darker at the edges. Reverse the sheet from front to back halfway through baking to ensure even browning. Transfer the sheet to a wire rack and let stand until the cookies firm up slightly, 1 to 2 minutes. Using a spatula, transfer the cookies to wire racks. Let stand until completely cooled.

FOR THE FROSTING

In a large bowl, with an electric mixer on low, then medium, speed, beat together the powdered sugar, cream cheese, and vanilla until well blended and very smooth. Add the orange juice and beat until evenly incorporated. If the frosting is very stiff, add enough water to thin it to a spreadable but still firm consistency.

Set the wire racks with the cookies over wax paper to catch drips. Using a table knife, swirl about 1 teaspoon frosting over the center of each cookie top. Let stand until the frosting completely sets, at least 1 hour.

Store in a single layer or layered with wax paper in an airtight container for up to 1 week or freeze for up to 1 month.

pumpkin keepers

Before modern canning and freezing methods became available, cooks preserved many favorite products, including pumpkin, by drying. In her 1833 cookbook, *The American Frugal Housewife*, Lydia Child noted that "some people cut pumpkin, string it, and dry it like apples." However, Child herself preferred another method: "It is a much better way to boil and sift the pumpkin, then spread it out in tin plates and dry hard in a warm oven. It will keep good all year round."

spiced carrot
lunch-box cookies

These healthful cookies have an enticing spice flavor, a pleasant moistness, and not a hint of "healthy" taste. For convenience, the ingredients are mixed together in a saucepan.

The idea of adding carrots to baked goods is hardly new. In 1783, George Washington is said to have eaten carrot cake in Manhattan. But carrot cookies didn't make their entrance until the 1960s, when health food was all the rage. Modern carrot cakes and cookies may have evolved from the same recipe, since both generally call for vegetable oil rather than the usual butter or margarine, as well as spices, nuts, and dried fruit.

1 cup (5 ounces) golden raisins or dark raisins, or a combination

¾ cup peeled and finely grated or finely chopped carrots (about 2 medium)

¼ cup plus 2 tablespoons orange juice

½ cup chopped dried, sweetened pineapple or ⅓ cup chopped candied pineapple (optional)

2 cups all-purpose white flour

1½ teaspoons ground cinnamon

1 teaspoon ground allspice

¾ teaspoon baking soda

½ teaspoon ground nutmeg

¼ teaspoon ground cloves

Generous ¼ teaspoon salt

¾ cup plus 2 tablespoons packed light brown sugar

⅔ cup corn oil or other flavorless vegetable oil

1 large egg

1 teaspoon finely grated orange zest (colored part of the skin)

1½ teaspoons vanilla extract

1 cup (4 ounces) chopped walnuts (optional)

Preheat the oven to 350 degrees F. Grease several baking sheets or coat with nonstick spray.

In a large saucepan, stir together the raisins, carrots, and orange juice. Bring to a simmer over medium-high heat. Cook, stirring occasionally, for 5 minutes; if the mixture becomes dry, add 1 to 2 tablespoons water. Remove from the heat. Stir in the pineapple, if using. Let stand until cooled to warm.

In a medium bowl, thoroughly stir together the flour, cinnamon, allspice, baking soda, nutmeg, cloves, and salt; set aside. Stir the brown sugar and oil into the carrot mixture until well blended. Add the egg, orange zest, and vanilla and stir until evenly incorporated. Beat or stir in the flour mixture, then the walnuts, if using, until evenly incorporated.

Drop the dough onto the baking sheets by heaping measuring table-spoonfuls, spacing about 2½ inches apart.

Bake the cookies, one sheet at a time, in the middle of the oven for 9 to 12 minutes, or until lightly tinged with brown all over and firm when pressed in the centers. Reverse the sheet from front to back halfway through baking to ensure even browning. Transfer the sheet to a wire rack and let stand until the cookies firm up slightly, 1 to 2 minutes. Using a spatula, transfer the cookies to wire racks. Let stand until completely cooled.

Store in an airtight container for up to 1 week or freeze for up to 1½ months.

raisinpockets

These fine, old-fashioned cookies have been enjoyed in America at least since the late 1800s. They routinely appear in Pennsylvania Dutch recipe collections, as well as in old community cookbooks from Maryland, Virginia, and other areas where Amish, Moravian, and Mennonite groups settled.

The cookies feature a cooked raisin filling mounded on a round of tender, pastrylike dough, then topped with a second dough round. The edges of the pockets are pressed together and sealed with the tines of a fork. Homey and unpretentious, these just seem to belong in an antique crock or cookie jar. They won't stay there long, though–they're too good!

FILLING

- 1²/₃ cups (about 8½ ounces) raisins
- ½ cup packed light or dark brown sugar
- 1 tablespoon all-purpose white flour
- 1½ teaspoons finely grated lemon zest (colored part of the skin)
- ¾ teaspoon ground cinnamon

DOUGH

- 2²/₃ cups all-purpose white flour
- 1¼ teaspoons baking powder
- ½ teaspoon baking soda
- ½ teaspoon ground cinnamon
- ½ teaspoon salt
- 1 cup sugar
- ¾ cup (1½ sticks) unsalted butter, slightly softened
- 1 large egg
- 2 tablespoons buttermilk
- 2 teaspoons vanilla extract
- ½ teaspoon finely grated lemon zest (colored part of the skin)

FOR THE FILLING

In a medium, heavy saucepan, stir together the raisins, brown sugar, flour, lemon zest, cinnamon, and ½ cup water. Bring to a simmer over medium heat. Cook, stirring frequently, for 5 to 8 minutes, or until the raisins are rehydrated and most of the liquid is absorbed. If the mixture looks dry during cooking, stir in 1 to 2 tablespoons more water. Transfer the mixture to a food processor. Process until the raisins are coarsely ground. Cover and refrigerate the filling until cool and thickened slightly, at least 1 hour. (The filling may be refrigerated for up to 4 days; let come to room temperature and stir before using.)

FOR THE DOUGH

In a medium bowl, thoroughly stir together the flour, baking powder,

TIP

If you don't have buttermilk, add ½ teaspoon lemon juice to a scant 2 tablespoons milk and use in place of the buttermilk.

baking soda, cinnamon, and salt; set aside. In a large bowl, with an electric mixer on medium speed, beat together the sugar and butter until well blended and lightened. Add the egg, buttermilk, vanilla, and lemon zest and beat until well blended and smooth. Beat in half of the flour mixture just until evenly incorporated. Stir in the remaining flour mixture until evenly incorporated.

Divide the dough into thirds. Place each portion between large sheets of wax paper. Roll out each portion a generous ⅛ inch thick; check the underside of the dough and smooth out any wrinkles that form. Stack the rolled portions (paper still attached) on a baking sheet. Refrigerate for 1 hour, or until chilled and firm, or freeze for 30 minutes to speed chilling. (The dough may be held for up to 24 hours; if frozen, let it warm up slightly before using.)

Preheat the oven to 375 degrees F. Grease several baking sheets or coat with nonstick spray.

Working with one portion at a time and leaving the remaining dough chilled, gently peel away, then pat back into place one sheet of wax paper. Flip the dough over, then peel off and discard the second sheet. Using a 2½-to-2¾-inch plain round cutter, cut out enough cookies to fill one baking sheet. (If at any point the dough softens too much to handle easily, transfer the dough and paper to a baking sheet and refrigerate or freeze until firm again.) Place on the baking sheet, spacing about 2 inches apart. Place a heaping measuring teaspoonful of the filling in the center of each round, spreading it out just slightly. Cut out enough cookies to top the ones on the baking sheet and immediately place them over the filled rounds. As the cookie tops soften enough to be pliable, using the tines of a fork, decoratively press the pocket edges together. (Dip the tines in flour occasionally to prevent sticking.) Reroll any dough scraps. Continue cutting out and filling cookies until all the dough is used.

Bake the cookies, one sheet at a time, in the upper third of the oven for 6 to 9 minutes, or until lightly browned all over and slightly darker at the edges. Reverse the sheet from front to back halfway through baking to ensure even browning. Transfer the sheet to a wire rack and let stand until the cookies firm up slightly, 1 to 2 minutes. Using a spatula, transfer the cookies to wire racks. Let stand until completely cooled.

Store in an airtight container for up to 1 week or freeze for up to 1 month.

The Labor-intensive Raisin

Originally, preparing raisins for baking was labor intensive, because most raisins had seeds. A nineteenth-century cookbook gives us a glimpse of the difficulty:

"To remove the stems and extraneous matter, place your raisins in a coarse towel and rub them in this until as clean as rubbing will make them; then pick over carefully, remove any stems or other defects which may be left. . . . To seed, clip with the scissors, or cut with a sharp knife."

– Estelle Woods Wilcox (ed.), *Buckeye Cookery and Practical Housekeeping*, 1880

spiced cranberry-apricot icebox cookies

makes about 70 to 80 (2½-inch) cookies.

These lightly spiced, fruit-studded cookies are aromatic, festive, and flavorful, with a crispy-chewy texture. Make the dough up to two months ahead, shape it into logs, and freeze it. Then, for fresh cookies during the hectic holidays (or anytime), simply slice and bake. They are particularly appealing dressed up with a quick drizzle of icing, but if you're in a hurry, it's fine to skip this step. (If you are baking only one dough log at a time, the icing recipe may be halved.)

1½ cups (about 6 ounces) dried sweetened cranberries, chopped

¾ cup (about 3¾ ounces) dried Turkish apricots, chopped (see tip, page 205)

¼ cup plus 2 tablespoons orange juice

2¼ cups all-purpose white flour

¾ teaspoon baking powder

¼ teaspoon baking soda

1½ teaspoons ground cinnamon

½ teaspoon ground cardamom

½ teaspoon ground nutmeg

Scant ½ teaspoon salt

⅔ cup (1 stick plus 2⅔ tablespoons) unsalted butter, slightly softened

¼ cup corn oil or other flavorless vegetable oil

2 cups plus 2 tablespoons powdered sugar

1 large egg

Generous 2½ teaspoons finely grated orange zest (colored part of the skin)

2½ teaspoons vanilla extract

½ cup (2 ounces) finely chopped unsalted (and undyed) pistachios

ICING (OPTIONAL)

1 cup powdered sugar, sifted after measuring, if lumpy

About 1 tablespoon orange juice

In a medium bowl, stir together the cranberries, apricots, and orange juice. Let stand for 30 minutes, or until the dried fruit is rehydrated.

In a large bowl, thoroughly stir together the flour, baking powder, baking soda, cinnamon, cardamom, nutmeg, and salt; set aside. In another large bowl, with an electric mixer on low speed, beat together the butter, oil, and powdered sugar until well blended. Increase the speed to medium and beat until very fluffy and smooth. Add the egg, orange zest, and vanilla and beat until very smooth. Beat or stir in the flour mixture just until evenly incorporated. Fold in the dried-fruit mixture and pistachios. Refrigerate the dough for 1 hour, or until firmed up slightly.

Spoon half of the dough onto a sheet of wax paper, forming a rough log about 8 inches long. Repeat with the second dough portion. Smooth the wax paper around the dough to help form the logs. Roll the logs up in

225

sheets of plastic wrap, twisting the ends to keep the logs from unrolling. Freeze the logs until completely frozen, at least 3 hours. Bake immediately, or transfer to an airtight plastic bag and freeze for up to 2 months.

Preheat the oven to 350 degrees F. Grease several baking sheets or coat with nonstick spray.

Carefully peel the wrap from a dough log. Using a large, serrated knife, cut the log in half lengthwise. Then, with the cut side down, cut each half crosswise into generous ¾-inch-thick slices. (If the log is too hard to slice easily, let stand for a few minutes; don't let it thaw too much, or the dough will be more difficult to slice cleanly.) Using a spatula, carefully transfer the slices to the baking sheets, spacing about 2 inches apart. If desired, repeat with the second log, or save it to bake another time.

Bake the cookies, one sheet at a time, in the upper third of the oven for 8 to 11 minutes, or until just slightly darker around the edges. Reverse the sheet from front to back halfway through baking to ensure even browning. Transfer the sheet to a wire rack and let stand until the cookies firm up slightly, 1 to 2 minutes. Using a spatula, transfer the cookies to wire racks. Let stand until cooled completely.

FOR THE ICING, IF USING

In a small bowl, stir together the powdered sugar and enough orange juice to yield a thin icing. Spoon the icing into a paper cone or a small pastry bag fitted with a fine writing tip. (Or use a kitchen spoon for decorating, if necessary.) Set the wire racks with the cookies over wax paper to catch drips. Drizzle the icing back and forth across the cookies several times to produce decorative squiggles; the cookies should be only lightly iced. Let stand until the icing completely sets, about 45 minutes.

Store in an airtight container for up to 2 weeks or freeze for up to 1½ months.

Iced cranberry-
white chocolate drop cookies

Cranberries and white chocolate may at first seem an unexpected combination, but the interplay of boldly flavored fresh cranberries, chewy dried cranberries, and creamy white chocolate is quite enticing. These are great served at Thanksgiving and Christmastime, but I keep cranberries in the freezer and make them all winter long.

1²/₃ cups all-purpose white flour

1 teaspoon ground cinnamon

1 teaspoon baking powder

¼ teaspoon baking soda

¼ teaspoon salt

1 cup (2 sticks) unsalted butter, slightly softened

1 cup packed light brown sugar

1¼ teaspoons finely grated orange zest (colored part of the skin)

1 large egg

2½ teaspoons vanilla extract

1½ cups (6 ounces) chopped pecans

1½ cups (6 ounces) dried sweetened cranberries

1¹/₃ cups (about 8 ounces) top-quality white chocolate morsels

½ cup cranberries, fresh or frozen, thawed, chopped

ICING (OPTIONAL)

1 cup powdered sugar, sifted after measuring, if lumpy

1 tablespoon fresh lemon juice

⅛ teaspoon vanilla extract

Preheat the oven to 350 degrees F. Grease several baking sheets or coat with nonstick spray.

In a medium bowl, thoroughly stir together the flour, cinnamon, baking powder, baking soda, and salt; set aside. In a large bowl, with an electric mixer on medium speed, beat the butter until lightened. Add the brown sugar and orange zest and beat until well blended, about 2 minutes more. Add the egg and vanilla and beat until very light and fluffy, about 1½ minutes more. Beat or stir in the flour mixture until evenly incorporated. Stir in the pecans, dried cranberries, white chocolate morsels, and chopped cranberries until evenly incorporated.

Drop the dough onto the baking sheets by heaping measuring tablespoonfuls, spacing about 2¾ inches apart.

Bake the cookies, one sheet at a time, in the upper third of the oven for 8 to 11 minutes, or until lightly tinged with brown all over and just firm when pressed in the centers. Reverse the sheet from front to back halfway through baking to ensure even browning. Transfer the sheet to a wire rack and let stand until the cookies firm up slightly, 1 to 2 minutes. Using a spatula, transfer the cookies to wire racks.

FOR THE ICING, IF USING

In a small bowl, stir together the powdered sugar, lemon juice, vanilla, and 2 to 4 teaspoons water to yield a slightly runny icing.

Set the wire racks with the cookies over wax paper to catch drips. Using a spoon, immediately drizzle the icing back and forth over the warm cookies until lightly decorated. Let stand until completely cooled and the icing completely sets, at least 1 hour.

Store in an airtight container for up to 2 weeks or freeze for up to 1½ months.

words of kitchen wisdom

"Too much care cannot be given to the preparation of the oven.... A good plan is to fill the stove with hard wood (ash is best for baking), let it burn until there is a good body of heat, and then turn the damper so as to throw the heat to the bottom of the oven for fully ten minutes before [baking]."

– Estelle Woods Wilcox (ed.), *Buckeye Cookery and Practical Housekeeping,* 1880

cranberry-cherry icebox ribbons

Native to the American North and grown commercially in Massachusetts, New Jersey, Wisconsin, Washington, and Oregon, the cranberry was part of the cooking tradition of some Native American tribes and quickly became popular with the early colonists.

These convenient icebox cookies, which I created for a holiday menu several years ago, contain cranberries and sour cherry jam or preserves. The recipe involves placing alternating layers of cranberry-cherry filling and vanilla dough in a loaf pan and freezing the stack until firm. The frozen loaf is cut crosswise into three long blocks, which can be cut lengthwise into pretty red-and-white-striped ribbons and baked. These cookies have a great chewy-crispy texture and an exceptional fruit flavor. They keep very well.

CRANBERRY-CHERRY FILLING

Generous ³/₄ cup (about 3 ounces) dried sweetened cranberries
Generous ¹/₃ cup sour cherry jam or preserves
1¹/₂ tablespoons sugar
¹/₈ teaspoon almond extract

DOUGH

2 cups plus 2 tablespoons all-purpose white flour
¹/₄ teaspoon baking powder
¹/₄ teaspoon salt
³/₄ cup sugar
²/₃ cup (1 stick plus 2²/₃ tablespoons) unsalted butter, slightly softened
1 large egg
2¹/₄ teaspoons vanilla extract
¹/₂ teaspoon almond extract

FOR THE FILLING

In a food processor, process the cranberries, jam or preserves, and sugar until coarsely pureed. Transfer the mixture to a small, heavy saucepan. Cook over medium-high heat, stirring occasionally, until it just comes to a boil; immediately remove from the heat. Let stand until cooled slightly. Stir in the almond extract. Cover and refrigerate for at least 1 hour, or until well chilled, or freeze for 30 minutes to speed chilling. (The filling may be refrigerated for up to 4 days; return to room temperature and stir before using.)

FOR THE DOUGH

In a medium bowl, thoroughly stir together the flour, baking powder, and salt; set aside. In a large bowl, with an electric mixer on medium speed, beat together the sugar and butter until well blended and smooth.

TIP

The cranberry-cherry filling can be made ahead and refrigerated up to 4 days.

Add the egg, vanilla, and almond extract and beat until well blended. Beat or stir in the flour mixture just until evenly incorporated. Let the dough stand for 10 minutes, or until firmed up slightly.

Line a 4½-by-8½-inch loaf pan with aluminum foil, letting the foil overhang the long sides by about 3 inches; this will keep the plastic wrap surrounding the dough from sticking to the pan. On top of the foil, line the pan with two long sheets of plastic wrap laid crosswise, overlapping in the middle and overhanging the longer sides by about 4 inches.

Divide the dough into quarters. Working on a large sheet of wax paper, roughly pat each portion into the shape of the loaf pan. Pat one dough portion firmly into the pan bottom, forming a smooth, even layer. Using a rubber spatula, spread one-third of the filling over the dough in the pan; the filling may seem stiff, but spread it as evenly as possible. Repeat the layers, using all four dough portions and all the filling. Fold the plastic wrap over the dough. Freeze until the loaf is cold and very firm, at least 1½ hours and preferably longer. (The dough can be transferred to an airtight plastic bag and frozen for up to 1 month.)

Preheat the oven to 350 degrees F. Grease several baking sheets or coat with nonstick spray.

Carefully peel the plastic wrap from the loaf. Using a large, sharp knife, trim off and discard the excess dough so the sides of the loaf are straight up and down rather than flared; wipe the knife clean between cuts. (If the loaf is too hard to cut easily, let stand for a few minutes; don't let it thaw too much, or it will be more difficult to slice cleanly.) Carefully cut the loaf crosswise into thirds, forming three 2¾-by-4-inch blocks. Working with one block at a time (keep the others refrigerated), cut each third into ¼-inch-thick slices to produce 2¾-inch-long ribbons; wipe the knife clean between cuts. Using a spatula, carefully transfer the slices to the baking sheets, placing them cut side up about 2 inches apart.

Bake the cookies, one sheet at a time, in the upper third of the oven for 9 to 14 minutes, or until just slightly darker at the edges. Reverse the sheet from front to back halfway through baking to ensure even browning. Using a spatula, immediately transfer the cookies to wire racks. Let stand until completely cooled.

Store in an airtight container for up to 1 week or freeze for up to 1 month.

The cranberry connection

It was probably inevitable that cranberries would be linked with Thanksgiving, since they're harvested in fall. They keep well, an especially important consideration in the days before refrigeration.

Because the cranberry has nodding blooms with stamens that look remarkably like long, thin bird beaks, Dutch settlers dubbed it *kranbeere* ("crane berry" in English), a name that stuck. The Pilgrims, who may have been introduced to cranberries by Native Americans, prized these berries so highly that they instituted strict rules protecting the bogs near their settlements.

Early New England cookbook authors used cranberries in a variety of ways. Amelia Simmons recommended serving cranberry sauce with roast stuffed turkey in her 1796 book, *American Cookery*. Lydia Child included a baked cranberry pudding and a cranberry pie in her 1833 work, *The American Frugal Housewife*. And Sarah Josepha Hale's 1841 cookbook, *The Good Housekeeper*, contained a boiled cranberry-rice pudding. Apparently, however, no one thought to add cranberries to cookies until the twentieth century.

7

Nut and Peanut Cookies

crunchy Peanut Drop cookies

Initially, I was surprised that the first peanut cookies I found appeared in northern cookbooks: the 1896 *Boston Cooking-School Cook Book* contains drop "Peanut Cookies," and a 1898 Philadelphia work, *Mrs. Rorer's New Cook Book,* gives a recipe for simple meringue "Peanut Kisses." That may be because there was never a strong stigma against eating peanuts in the North, as there was in the South, where they were dismissed as hog feed.

Their ignominious beginning as porker fare means that peanuts may never turn up in fancy tea cakes, but they have a robust taste that's perfect in homey cookies like these. They are slightly crunchy and full-flavored from a little molasses and an abundance of chopped peanuts, both folded into the dough and sprinkled on top—very good eating!

2¼ cups all-purpose white flour
Scant ¾ teaspoon salt
½ teaspoon baking soda
1¼ cups sugar
1 cup (2 sticks) unsalted butter, slightly softened

2 large eggs
3 tablespoons light molasses
2 teaspoons vanilla extract
2 cups (9 ounces) finely chopped unsalted peanuts (divided)

Preheat the oven to 350 degrees F. Grease several baking sheets or coat with nonstick spray.

In a medium bowl, thoroughly stir together the flour, salt, and baking soda; set aside. In a large bowl, with an electric mixer on medium speed, beat together the sugar and butter until very well blended and fluffy, about 2 minutes. Add the eggs, molasses, and vanilla and beat until well blended. Beat or stir in the flour mixture, then 1¾ cups of the peanuts, until evenly incorporated.

Drop the dough onto the baking sheets by heaping measuring tablespoonfuls, spacing about 2½ inches apart. With a lightly greased hand, pat down the mounds until flattened just slightly. Sprinkle some of the remaining peanuts over the cookies.

Bake the cookies, one sheet at a time, in the upper third of the oven for 8 to 10 minutes, or until lightly browned all over and slightly darker at the edges. Reverse the sheet from front to back halfway through baking to ensure even browning. Transfer the sheet to a wire rack and let stand until the cookies firm up slightly, 1 to 2 minutes. Using a spatula, transfer the cookies to wire racks. Let stand until completely cooled.

The cookies are best when fresh but can be stored in an airtight container for up to 4 days or frozen for up to 1 month.

NOT JUST PEANUTS

Peanuts have never gotten much respect in America. Their reputation is better than it once was, but if something is "worth peanuts," we know it's trifling. Perhaps the root of the problem —so to speak—was that peanuts were first introduced to America by African slaves. During the Civil War, when food supplies were scarce, both Union and Confederate troops started eating these legumes out of necessity, and goobers gradually caught on. By 1870, P. T. Barnum's vendors were hawking peanuts at his circus. Soon, they were also sold in theaters, where the cheap seats became known as "peanut galleries." Today, we eat about 600 million pounds of peanuts annually and consume 700 million more pounds in the form of peanut butter. American peanut farmers produce between $45 million and $50 million in revenues each year.

classic peanut butter crisscross cookies

Today, the standard American peanut butter cookie is thick yet crispy, rich with peanut butter and brown sugar, and distinctively marked with the tines of a fork. But early peanut butter cookies were an entirely different sort. Among the first I've come across were those that appeared in 1898 in *Mrs. Rorer's New Cook Book;* they were very thin, rolled squares called "Peanut Wafers." The recipe called for homemade peanut butter (it was not yet available commercially) and finely ground peanuts, or peanut meal.

The earliest peanut butter cookies I've found that seem at all similar to today's classics were the "Peanut Butter Drop Cookies" in the 1929 *International Cookbook* compiled by Margaret Weimer Heywood. This version called for dropping the dough rather than rolling it and included a larger proportion of peanut butter than previous recipes had. In 1936, *Ruth Wakefield's Toll House Tried and True Recipes* included a peanut butter cookie recipe that not only contained a good deal of peanut butter but called for shaping the dough into balls and flattening them with a fork.

My cookies are firm at the edges, slightly chewy in the middle, amply flavored with peanut butter, and—of course—flattened with a fork.

2¼ cups all-purpose white flour

½ teaspoon baking soda

Scant ½ teaspoon salt

1 cup packed light brown sugar

¾ cup sugar

¾ cup (1½ sticks) unsalted butter, slightly softened

3 tablespoons toasted peanut oil, peanut oil, or corn oil

2 large eggs

2½ teaspoons vanilla extract

1¼ cups smooth or crunchy peanut butter

About 2 tablespoons sugar, for topping

Preheat the oven to 350 degrees F. Grease several baking sheets or coat with nonstick spray.

In a large bowl, thoroughly stir together the flour, baking soda, and salt; set aside. In another large bowl, with an electric mixer on medium speed, beat together the brown sugar, sugar, butter, and oil until light and fluffy. Add the eggs and vanilla and beat until evenly incorporated. Beat in the peanut butter. Gradually beat or stir in the flour mixture until evenly incorporated. Refrigerate the dough for 15 minutes, or until firmed up slightly.

Shape portions of the dough into generous golf-ball-sized balls with lightly greased hands. Place on the baking sheets, spacing about 3 inches apart. Place the 2 tablespoons sugar in a small, shallow bowl. Lightly oil the tines of a fork. Dip the tines into the sugar. Using the fork tines, firmly press down each ball horizontally and then vertically until the ball is about ½ inch thick; dip the fork into the sugar before pressing down each cookie.

Bake the cookies, one sheet at a time, in the upper third of the oven for 9 to 12 minutes, or until tinged with brown at the edges and just beginning

to firm up in the centers; be careful not to overbake. Reverse the sheet from front to back halfway through baking to ensure even browning. Transfer the sheet to a wire rack and let stand until the cookies firm up slightly, 3 to 4 minutes. Using a spatula, transfer the cookies to wire racks. Let stand until completely cooled.

Store in an airtight container for up to 1 week or freeze for up to 2 months.

crossover appeal

Nobody knows whether Mrs. Wakefield invented the classic peanut butter cookie and the crisscross idea, or simply borrowed it from another cook. As a college graduate and former home economics teacher, she would have been ably suited to develop recipes. And as her enormously successful career as an innkeeper, restaurateur, and cookbook author proved, she had a great marketing flair.

In any case, due to the celebrity gained from her endeavors, all of Mrs. Wakefield's published recipes were widely circulated in the 1930s and 1940s, and she greatly influenced millions of American homemakers, as well as cookbook authors and publishers. Without even being aware of it, the chocolate chip cookie maven may have also set the standard for our favorite peanut butter cookie.

peanut brittle cookies

Peanut brittle has been a popular candy in America for more than a hundred years. It turns up among the confections in a number of late-nineteenth- and early-twentieth-century cookbooks, about the same time that peanut cookies began appearing.

About 8 ounces peanut brittle
1½ cups all-purpose white flour
1¼ teaspoons baking powder
¼ teaspoon baking soda
¼ teaspoon salt

¾ cup plus 2 tablespoons packed light brown sugar
½ cup (1 stick) unsalted butter, slightly softened
1 large egg
2½ teaspoons vanilla extract

Preheat the oven to 375 degrees F. Grease several baking sheets or coat with nonstick spray.

Put the peanut brittle in a heavy plastic bag. With a mallet, heavy rolling pin, or the back of a heavy spoon, crack enough brittle into ¼-inch pieces to yield 1½ cups; set aside.

In a medium bowl, thoroughly stir together the flour, baking powder, baking soda, and salt; set aside. In a large bowl, with an electric mixer on medium speed, beat together the brown sugar and butter until fluffy and well blended. Add the egg and vanilla and beat until evenly incorporated. Beat in the flour mixture, then the peanut brittle, until evenly incorporated.

Shape portions of the dough into generous 1-inch balls with lightly greased hands. Place on the baking sheets, spacing about 2½ inches apart. Using your hand, pat down the cookies until they are ½ inch thick.

Bake the cookies, one sheet at a time, in the upper third of the oven for 8 to 12 minutes, or until just barely tinged with brown; be careful not to overbake. Reverse the sheet from front to back halfway through baking to ensure even browning. Transfer the sheet to a wire rack and let stand until the cookies firm up slightly, about 1 minute. Using a spatula, transfer the cookies to wire racks. Let stand until completely cooled.

Store in an airtight container for up to 2 weeks or freeze for up to 1½ months.

peanut butter-
Molasses chews

The combination of peanut butter and molasses might not sound appealing initially—unless your childhood included the cheery, yellow-wrapped penny candies called Mary Janes. Fortunately, my childhood did, and I am the better for it. Thursday was Mary Jane day for me, because the house where I took Thursday-afternoon piano lessons was a short walk from a country store with a big candy case. In that era, a nickel would still buy five candies—enough of the gratifyingly chewable peanut butter and molasses taffies to provide more than a half hour of eating pleasure. These homey cookies have a robust peanut butter and molasses flavor and slightly chewy texture that takes me back.

2²/₃ cups all-purpose white flour

1 teaspoon baking powder

¹/₂ teaspoon baking soda

¹/₄ teaspoon salt

1³/₄ cups packed dark brown sugar

³/₄ cup (1¹/₂ sticks) unsalted butter, slightly softened

²/₃ cup smooth or crunchy peanut butter

¹/₄ cup white vegetable shortening

¹/₄ cup dark (*not* blackstrap) molasses

2 large eggs

About ¹/₂ cup (2¹/₄ ounces) finely chopped unsalted peanuts, for topping

In a medium bowl, thoroughly stir together the flour, baking powder, baking soda, and salt; set aside. In a large bowl, with an electric mixer on medium speed, beat together the brown sugar, butter, peanut butter, shortening, and molasses until well blended and fluffy, about 2 minutes. Add the eggs and beat until very well blended and smooth. Beat in half of the flour mixture until evenly incorporated. Stir or beat in the rest of the flour mixture until evenly incorporated. Refrigerate the dough for at least 1½ hours or up to 12 hours, or until firmed up.

Preheat the oven to 375 degrees F. Grease several baking sheets or coat with nonstick spray.

Shape portions of the dough into generous 1¼-inch balls with lightly greased hands. Place the peanuts in a small bowl. Dip one half of each ball into the peanuts until some are embedded. Place the balls, peanut side up, on the baking sheets, spacing about 2¾ inches apart. Using your palm, press down on the balls until the tops are just flattened.

Bake the cookies, one sheet at a time, in the upper third of the oven for 8 to 10 minutes, or until tinged with brown and just barely set when pressed in the centers. Reverse the sheet from front to back halfway through baking to ensure even browning. Transfer the sheet to a wire rack and let stand until the cookies firm up slightly, 1 to 2 minutes. Using a spatula, transfer the cookies to wire racks. Let stand until completely cooled.

Store in an airtight container for up to 10 days or freeze for up to 2 months.

words of kitchen wisdom

Mrs. Rorer supplied these directions for making peanut butter:

"Roast the nuts, [then] shell and blow off the brown skins. When making [peanut butter] in large quantities, it will pay to have a bellows for this purpose, or put the peanuts on a coarse towel, cover them with another towel, rub them gently, then blow off the skins. If you use salt dust them lightly with it and grind at once. Pack the butter into glass jars or tumblers, cover them and keep in a cool place. This may be used plain or diluted with water."

– Sarah Tyson Rorer, *Mrs. Rorer's New Cook Book,* 1898

peanut butter- Fudge cookies

makes 32
(3-inch) cookies.

The all-American combination of peanut butter and chocolate is such a natural that they turned up together in cookies not long after peanut butter came on the market. One of the first recipes to pair the two was called "Peanut Brownies" and appeared in the 1924 *Modern Priscilla Cookbook.* Despite the name, these were drop cookies and not brownies as we now know them; brown-colored cookies of various sorts were occasionally called brownies at that time.

My own favorite peanut butter–chocolate cookie is this chocolate-enriched variation of the classic crisscrossed peanut butter cookie. The peanut butter and chocolate are nicely balanced, so the flavors mingle and blend instead of drawing attention to themselves. The cookies have a slightly soft, fudgy texture and, like the classic that inspired them, are marked with a fork.

2 ounces unsweetened chocolate, broken up or coarsely chopped
2¹/₂ cups all-purpose white flour
¹/₂ teaspoon baking soda
¹/₄ teaspoon salt
1 cup plus 2 tablespoons smooth peanut butter
1¹/₂ cups packed light brown sugar

¹/₃ cup sugar
¹/₃ cup unsweetened American-style cocoa powder
1 cup (2 sticks) unsalted butter, slightly softened
2 large eggs
2 teaspoons vanilla extract
1 cup (6 ounces) milk chocolate morsels, finely chopped

Preheat the oven to 350 degrees F. Grease several baking sheets or coat with nonstick spray.

In a small, microwave-safe bowl, microwave the unsweetened chocolate on 50-percent power for 1 minute. Stir well. Continue microwaving on 50-percent power, stirring at 30-second intervals. Stop microwaving before the chocolate completely melts and let the residual heat finish the job. (Alternatively, in a small, heavy saucepan, melt the chocolate over lowest heat, stirring frequently; be very careful not to burn. Immediately remove from the heat.)

In a medium bowl, thoroughly stir together the flour, baking soda, and salt; set aside. In a large bowl, with an electric mixer on low, then medium, speed, beat together the melted chocolate, peanut butter, brown sugar, sugar, and cocoa powder until very well blended. Add the butter and beat until very well blended and smooth. Add the eggs and vanilla and beat until fluffy and well blended, about 2 minutes. Beat or stir in the flour mixture, then the chocolate morsels, just until evenly incorporated. Refrigerate the dough for 15 minutes, or until it firms up slightly.

Divide the dough into quarters, forming each into a flat disk. Divide each portion into quarters, then eighths. Shape the portions into balls with lightly greased hands. Place on the baking sheets, spacing about 2½ inches apart. Lightly oil the tines of a fork. Using the fork tines, firmly press down each ball horizontally and then vertically until the ball is about ½ inch thick.

Bake the cookies, one sheet at a time, in the upper third of the oven for 8 to 11 minutes, or until not quite firm when pressed in the centers; be careful not to overbake. Transfer the sheet to a wire rack and let stand until the cookies firm up slightly, 1 to 2 minutes. Using a spatula, transfer the cookies to wire racks. Let stand until completely cooled.

Store in an airtight container for up to 1 week or freeze for up to 1½ months.

words of kitchen wisdom
"Shall we stir only one way? No; stir any way you please, so long as you blend or mix the ingredients. But after *beating* in air bubbles, don't break them by *stirring*, unless you want to keep up the game of cross purposes indefinitely."

– Mrs. D. A. Lincoln, *The Boston Cooking-School Cook Book*, 1883

nut and peanut cookies

peanut butter-chocolatechunkers

I can't imagine any child or grown-up who likes peanut butter not loving these big, crispy, tender cookies generously studded with chocolate chunks and peanuts.

2½ cups all-purpose white flour

1 teaspoon baking soda

¼ teaspoon salt

1¼ cups smooth or crunchy peanut butter

1 cup (2 sticks) unsalted butter, slightly softened

1½ cups packed light brown sugar

⅔ cup sugar

2 large eggs

1 tablespoon light corn syrup

2 teaspoons vanilla extract

10 ounces bittersweet (*not* unsweetened) or semisweet chocolate, chopped (divided)

About ½ cup (2¼ ounces) chopped unsalted peanuts, for topping

Preheat the oven to 350 degrees F. Grease several baking sheets or coat with nonstick spray.

In a medium bowl, thoroughly stir together the flour, baking soda, and salt; set aside. In a large bowl, with an electric mixer on medium speed, beat together the peanut butter, butter, brown sugar, and sugar until very well blended and fluffy, about 2 minutes. Add the eggs, corn syrup, and vanilla and beat until well blended. Beat or stir in the flour mixture until evenly incorporated. Stir in 1 cup of the chopped chocolate. Let the dough stand for 5 minutes, or until firmed up slightly.

Shape portions of the dough into 1¾-inch balls with lightly greased hands. In a small bowl, stir together the remaining chocolate and the peanuts. Dip one half of each ball into the chocolate-peanut mixture until some bits are embedded. Place the balls, coated side up, on the baking sheets, spacing about 2¾ inches apart. Pat down the tops of the balls just slightly.

Bake the cookies, one sheet at a time, in the upper third of the oven for 13 to 16 minutes, or until lightly browned all over, slightly darker at the edges, and slightly soft when pressed in the centers. Reverse the sheet from front to back halfway through baking to ensure even browning.

Transfer the sheet to a wire rack and let stand until the cookies firm up slightly, 1 to 2 minutes. Using a spatula, transfer the cookies to wire racks. Let stand until completely cooled.

Store in an airtight container for up to 1 week or freeze for up to 1½ months.

An Inauspicious Start

An unknown St. Louis physician who hoped to use peanut meal as a protein source for people with poor teeth may have come up with some approximation of peanut butter around 1890. Shortly thereafter, Battle Creek, Michigan, physician Dr. John Harvey Kellogg tried to create a high-protein, ground-peanut dietary supplement. However, he got off on the wrong foot by steaming instead of roasting the peanuts. As his 1895 "Nut Meal" patent ominously noted, this yielded "a pasty adhesive substance," and Dr. Kellogg and his brother W.K. eventually turned their attention from peanut sludge to cereals.

Others pressed on, though, and soon the product now considered as American as apple pie was born. The first firm to sell peanut butter may have been the Krema Products Company, which began marketing its product in 1908 and still operates. To indicate that his peanut butter was always fresh, the owner's slogan was "I refuse to sell outside of Ohio." This may help explain why Krema is not a household name today.

Almond sweethearts

makes about 30
(2½-inch) cookies.

This charming and unusual almond macaroon cookie comes from *The Kentucky House-wife,* written by Lettice Bryan in 1839. It was an ambitious cookbook (1,300 recipes) and, for its time, a remarkably sophisticated one.

Both the cookie's name and appearance reveal Mrs. Bryan's flair. Though macaroons are usually drop cookies, these are rolled and formed with heart-shaped cutters so that they look more refined.

Although you'll find these chewy-crispy cookies relatively easy to make, they were a considerable undertaking in the 1830s, when the first step involved blanching the almonds and pounding them to a paste using a mortar and pestle. Here, I approximate Mrs. Bryan's homemade almond paste, which is rougher-textured and drier than modern commercial versions, by quickly grinding blanched almonds in a food processor, then adding some commercial almond paste. The procedure takes only a minute or two. Instead of the lemon extract Mrs. Bryan called for, I prefer lemon zest, but if you wish to follow her instructions, you can certainly use lemon extract.

2 cups (about 8½ ounces) blanched slivered almonds

7 ounces almond paste, cut into chunks

1 teaspoon finely grated lemon zest (colored part of the skin) *or* ⅛ teaspoon lemon extract

Scant ⅓ cup egg whites (2–3 large egg whites), free of yolk and at room temperature

1½–2 cups powdered sugar, plus more for shaping and topping

Preheat the oven to 325 degrees F. Line several baking sheets with parchment paper or aluminum foil.

In a food processor, finely grind the almonds. Add the almond paste and lemon zest or extract and process until the mixture is very well blended and crumbly. In a large bowl, with an electric mixer on medium speed (use a whisk-shaped beater, if available), beat the egg whites to very soft peaks. Gradually add 1½ cups of the powdered sugar to the egg whites. Increase the speed to high and beat the egg-white mixture to stiff, glossy peaks. Fold in the almond mixture until evenly incorporated. Let the dough stand for 5 minutes, or until firmed up. If the dough is too soft and sticky to handle, stir or knead in up to ½ cup more powdered sugar.

Generously sprinkle a large sheet of wax paper with powdered sugar. Center the dough on the paper. Sprinkle the top of the dough with more powdered sugar. Cover with a second sheet of wax paper. Roll out the dough a scant ¼ inch thick; check the underside of the dough and smooth out any wrinkles that form. Gently peel away, then pat one sheet of wax paper back into place. Flip the dough over, then peel off and discard the second sheet. Put about ¼ cup powdered sugar in a saucer. Using a 2-to-2¼-inch heart-shaped cutter, cut out the cookies; if the cutter sticks, dip it into the powdered sugar, tapping off the excess. Using a spatula, carefully transfer the cookies to the baking sheets, spacing about 1¼ inches apart. (Mrs. Bryan said to place the hearts "so far apart that they cannot unite with one another.") Reroll any dough scraps. Continue cutting out the cookies until all the dough is used. Generously sift powdered sugar over the cookie tops.

Bake the cookies, one sheet at a time, in the middle of the oven for 14 to 17 minutes, or until just tinged with brown at the edges. Reverse the sheet from front to back halfway through baking to ensure even browning. Slide the cookies, still attached to the parchment or foil, onto a wire rack. Let stand until completely cooled. Carefully peel the cookies from the parchment or foil.

Store in an airtight container for up to 4 days or freeze for up to 1 month.

BEFORE MARTHA STEWART . . .

Lettice Bryan not only clearly understood the intricacies of baking, but she had a much greater flair for presentation than most of her contemporaries. For example, she provided details on creating a "Pyramid of Cakes," which she suggested could be "iced very white" and given a "decorament [*sic*] of devices and borders in white sugar or a very delicate garland or festoon." She even suggested adding a small bunch of flowers to the cake top, a touch many modern pastry chefs may think they devised! Mrs. Bryan also included a chapter on how to create various colored icings, using cochineal for pink and saffron or turmeric for yellow. A green shade could be produced using spinach, she noted, but wouldn't be appropriate for much besides pickles.

Butter-pecan sandies

makes about 35 (2½-inch) cookies.

There is a fine array of pecan recipes in the modern American cookie repertoire, but none shows off the sweet, toasty taste of these native nuts better than Butter-Pecan Sandies. The secret to the following recipe lies in browning the pecans in butter, which simultaneously brings out their flavor and infuses the butter with it. The cookies are also noteworthy for their texture, being—incongruous as it sounds—both sandy-crisp and meltingly smooth.

1¹/₂ cups (6 ounces) chopped pecans

³/₄ cup plus 2 tablespoons (1³/₄ sticks) unsalted butter, cut into chunks

¹/₂ cup corn oil or other flavorless vegetable oil

2²/₃ cups all-purpose white flour

1 cup powdered sugar

³/₄ cup packed light brown sugar

1 large egg, plus 1 large egg yolk

1¹/₂ teaspoons vanilla extract

¹/₈ teaspoon salt

About 35 perfect pecan halves, for topping

In a medium, heavy saucepan, combine the chopped pecans and butter. Bring to a simmer over medium-high heat. Cook, stirring frequently, for 4 to 5 minutes, or until the pecans and butter are nicely browned; be very careful not to burn. Turn out the mixture into a sieve set over a medium, metal bowl. Let stand until the butter drains into the bowl. Freeze the butter mixture, stirring once or twice, until firmed up but not hard, about 10 minutes. Set the pecans aside.

In a food processor, combine the chilled browned butter, oil, flour, and powdered sugar. Process in on/off pulses until well blended, stopping and stirring to redistribute the bowl contents several times. Turn out the butter-flour mixture into a large bowl. Stir ¾ cup of the pecans into the flour mixture. In the food processor, combine the remaining ¾ cup pecans and the brown sugar. Process until the pecans are finely ground and the mixture is crumbly, stopping and scraping down the bowl sides once or twice. Add the egg and egg yolk, 1½ tablespoons water, the vanilla, and salt and process until very well blended, about 1 minute. Stir the egg mixture into the flour mixture until just blended. Knead with your hands until well blended and smooth. (If necessary, add a few drops of water to moisten.)

Divide the dough in half. Place each portion between large sheets of wax paper. Roll out each portion a generous ¼ inch thick; check the underside of the dough and smooth out any wrinkles that form. Stack the rolled portions (paper still attached) on a baking sheet. Freeze for 15 minutes, or until chilled and slightly firmed up but not hard.

Preheat the oven to 350 degrees F. Grease several baking sheets or coat with nonstick spray.

Working with one portion at a time, gently peel away, then pat one sheet of wax paper back into place. Flip the dough over, then peel off and discard the second sheet. Using a fluted or plain round 2¼-inch cutter, cut out the cookies. (If at any point the dough softens too much to handle easily, transfer the paper and cookies to a baking sheet and refrigerate or freeze until firm again.) Using a spatula, carefully transfer the cookies to the baking sheets, spacing about 1 inch apart. Let the cookies stand for a few minutes to soften slightly. Firmly press a pecan half into the center of each cookie. Reroll any dough scraps. Continue cutting out the cookies until all the dough is used.

Bake the cookies, one sheet at a time, in the upper third of the oven for 10 to 14 minutes, or until barely colored on top and just slightly darker at the edges. Reverse the sheet from front to back halfway through baking to ensure even browning. Transfer the sheet to a wire rack and let stand until the cookies firm up slightly, 1 to 2 minutes. Using a spatula, transfer the cookies to wire racks. Let stand until completely cooled.

Store in an airtight container for up to 2 weeks or freeze for up to 1 month.

Pecan Pasts, Pecan Futures

Pecans have long been associated with southern baking, but in fact they were important in the region centuries before the first colonists arrived. Particularly in the area now comprising Texas, New Mexico, and northern Mexico, where pecans first grew, Native Americans relied on the wild pecan trees flourishing along rivers and streams for a key portion of their winter diet. The word "pecan" likely derives from the Cree word *pakan,* meaning "hard-shelled nut."

The large-scale cultivation and marketing of pecans across the nation began only in the early twentieth century. The American horticulturist Luther Burbank reportedly told Texas farmers in 1908: "If I were a young man, I would go to Texas, knowing as I do the possibilities of the pecan industry, and devote my life in propagating new species of the pecan. . . . Your pecan is superior to our walnut and you are standing in your own light—why not develop it?"

However, it was apparently Georgia that ultimately benefited from Burbank's suggestion. With more than two million trees, it now leads the nation in the production of hybrid pecans. Texas, however, continues to be the largest producer of native pecans. The Texas legislature officially designated the pecan its state tree in 1919.

pecan praline wafers

Rich with toasted pecans, caramelized brown sugar, and butter, these brittle, golden brown wafers are about as southern as you can get. I've seen them in a number of southern community cookbooks, particularly from the Lower Cape Fear and the South Carolina coast. The recipe calls for what might seem like a lot of brown sugar, but the generous quantity of pecans keeps the cookies from being too sweet. The following version, which I created after a considerable amount of testing, is one of the best I've tried.

1 cup (4 ounces) chopped pecans
½ cup plus 1 tablespoon all-purpose white flour
¼ teaspoon baking soda
¼ teaspoon salt
1¼ cups packed light brown sugar

3 tablespoons plus 2 teaspoons unsalted butter, melted
1 large egg
1¼ teaspoons vanilla extract

Preheat the oven to 350 degrees F. Line several baking sheets with aluminum foil. Grease the foil or coat with nonstick spray.

Spread the pecans in a small baking pan and toast in the oven, stirring occasionally, for 5 to 8 minutes, or until lightly browned; be careful not to burn. Immediately turn out into a small bowl; set aside.

In a small bowl, thoroughly stir together the flour, baking soda, and salt; set aside. In a medium bowl, vigorously stir together the brown sugar and butter until very well blended. Stir or whisk in the egg and vanilla until evenly incorporated. Stir in the flour mixture, then the pecans, until evenly incorporated.

Drop the dough onto the baking sheets by heaping measuring teaspoonfuls, spacing about 3½ inches apart to allow for expansion.

Bake the cookies, one sheet at a time, in the upper third of the oven for 7 to 9 minutes, or until golden brown all over. Reverse the sheet from front to back halfway through baking to ensure even browning. Slide the cookies, still attached to the foil, onto a wire rack. Let stand until completely cooled. Carefully peel the wafers from the foil. If the cooled wafers are not crisp or do not readily peel off the foil, they are underbaked. Return them to the oven and bake for a few minutes more.

Store in an airtight container for up to 1 week or freeze for up to 1 month.

praLine meringue Puffs

makes about 24 (2½-to-2¾-inch) cookies.

These crispy-chewy, puffy meringue cookies showcase the same flavors as the famous New Orleans candies called pralines. My cookies are modern, but the candies that inspired them date back to at least the 1850s, when, according to James Trager's *The Food Chronology,* a French Quarter shop began offering them for sale. Named for a classic French confection of almonds and cooked sugar, pralines may actually be even older; *The Picayune Creole Cookbook,* published in 1901, notes that for nearly 150 years, the confections "have delighted the younger generations, and the older ones, too."

The airiness and abundance of pecans in these cookies offset the sweetness nicely. The cookies have a lovely brown-sugar flavor, pale caramel color, and appealing sheen.

2 tablespoons all-purpose white flour	¹/₈ teaspoon cream of tartar
²/₃ cup packed light brown sugar (divided)	¹/₃ cup plus 1 tablespoon sugar
¹/₈ teaspoon salt	³/₄ teaspoon vanilla extract
¹/₄ cup egg whites (2 large egg whites), free of yolk and at room temperature	1³/₄ cups (7 ounces) coarsely chopped pecans

Preheat the oven to 325 degrees F. Line two large baking sheets with aluminum foil.

In a small bowl, thoroughly stir together the flour, a generous ⅓ cup brown sugar, and the salt; set aside. In a large bowl, with an electric mixer on low speed, beat the egg whites and cream of tartar until frothy and opaque. Increase the speed to medium and beat until the whites just begin to form soft peaks. Gradually beat in the sugar until the whites form glossy peaks. Gradually beat in the remaining brown sugar and the vanilla. Continue beating until the meringue is stiff and smooth when rubbed between the fingers. Lightly fold the flour mixture and pecans into the egg-white mixture just until evenly incorporated; be careful not to deflate.

Drop the mixture onto the two baking sheets by heaping measuring tablespoonfuls, spacing about 1½ inches apart.

Bake the cookies, with the two sheets on separate racks in the center third of the oven, for 9 minutes; switch the position of the sheets and bake for 8 to 10 minutes more, or until the cookies are lightly colored all over. Slide the cookies, still attached to the foil, onto wire racks. Let stand until completely cooled. Carefully peel the cookies from the foil.

Store in an airtight container for up to 1 week or freeze for up to 1 month.

TIP

To keep these as airy as possible, use two large cookie sheets and bake both sheets at once, rather than letting one pan stand while the other is baked. It's also best not to bake them on a rainy day.

pecanRugeLach

This delicious pecan rugelach is an example of how recipes can be passed from one culture to another and adapted with spectacular results. The traditional rugelach recipes brought to America by central European Jewish immigrants usually contained dried fruit or fruit preserves, spices, and walnuts—not pecans, which were neither available nor known in Europe. At some point, an inventive cook decided to try using pecans, and a brand-new American-style rugelach was born.

This filling has a delicate, sophisticated flavor, which complements the mild cream-cheese pastry better than the bolder-tasting walnut mixture. Tinkering with tradition can sometimes be a very good thing.

2¹/₃ cups all-purpose white flour

¹/₄ teaspoon salt

1 cup (2 sticks) unsalted butter, slightly softened

1 8-ounce package cream cheese, slightly softened and cut into chunks

¹/₂ teaspoon finely grated lemon zest (colored part of the skin)

1¹/₂ teaspoons vanilla extract

FILLING

2¹/₄ cups (9 ounces) chopped pecans

³/₄ cup apricot preserves

1¹/₂ tablespoons clover honey or other mild honey

¹/₄ teaspoon ground cinnamon

1–1¹/₄ cups powdered sugar, for rolling and topping

In a large bowl, thoroughly stir together the flour and salt; set aside. In another large bowl, with an electric mixer on medium speed, beat together the butter, cream cheese, lemon zest, and vanilla until very fluffy and well blended. Beat or stir in the flour mixture until evenly incorporated.

Divide the dough in half. Shape each portion into a 6-inch disk. Wrap each portion in plastic wrap. Refrigerate for at least 1½ hours, or until firm but not hard. (The dough may be refrigerated for up to 2 days; remove the dough from the refrigerator and let stand for 45 minutes, or until just soft enough to roll, before using.)

Preheat the oven to 350 degrees F. Grease several baking sheets or coat with nonstick spray.

FOR THE FILLING
Spread the pecans in a medium baking pan and toast in the oven, stirring occasionally, for 6 to 9 minutes, or until lightly browned; be careful

not to burn. Immediately turn out into a medium bowl. Let stand until cooled; set aside.

In a food processor, combine the apricot preserves, honey, and cinnamon. Process in on/off pulses just until blended. Add the pecans and process until the pecans are coarsely ground. (The filling may be covered and refrigerated for up to 4 days; let come to room temperature and stir before using.)

Sprinkle a clean work surface heavily with powdered sugar. Working with one portion at a time and leaving the remaining dough chilled, roll the dough out into a 12-inch circle of even thickness; it doesn't have to be perfectly round. (If the dough is too stiff to roll, knead it briefly until just soft enough to work with.) Frequently dust the dough surface and rolling pin with powdered sugar and occasionally lift the dough from the work surface to make sure it doesn't stick. Spread half the filling evenly over the dough to within ¼ inch of the edge. Using a large, sharp knife, cut the circle into quarters, then cut each quarter into 6 equal wedges. Working from the wide end, firmly roll up each wedge. Place the rugelach, point side down (to prevent them from unrolling), on the baking sheets, spacing about 1½ inches apart. Using your hand, pat them down just slightly. Repeat the procedure with the remaining dough and filling. Generously dust the rugelach with powdered sugar.

Bake the rugelach, one sheet at a time, in the upper third of the oven for 14 to 18 minutes, or until tinged with brown on top and darker at the edges. Reverse the sheet from front to back halfway through baking to ensure even browning. Dust the cookies with more powdered sugar. Using a spatula, immediately transfer the rugelach to wire racks. Let stand until completely cooled.

Store in an airtight container for up to 10 days or freeze for up to 1 month. If frozen, dust with more powdered sugar before serving.

bourbon balls

Bourbon balls started turning up in the late 1930s and continue to have ardent fans today, especially in the South. Perhaps these pleasingly boozy, no-bake cookies came about in response to the 1933 lifting of Prohibition and the reemergence of bourbon distilling after so many dark years.

The earliest bourbon ball recipes usually included cocoa powder, but no chocolate morsels; Nestlé didn't start making chocolate morsels until 1939. However, I think the chocolate helps round out and enrich the pecan and bourbon flavors, so I have provided a slightly more modern version here. This updated recipe also calls for grinding the vanilla wafers, pecans, and chocolate morsels in a food processor, which means the cookies are a snap to make. They will probably seem too potent when first prepared but will mellow nicely if left overnight.

1¹/₂ cups coarsely crushed vanilla wafers

1¹/₃ cups (about 5¹/₂ ounces) chopped pecans

¹/₃ cup (2 ounces) semisweet chocolate morsels

1¹/₄ cups powdered sugar (divided)

2¹/₂ tablespoons unsweetened cocoa powder, Dutch-process or American-style

2¹/₂ tablespoons light or dark corn syrup

¹/₃ cup bourbon

In a food processor, process the vanilla wafers, pecans, and chocolate morsels until ground to a powder. Add ¾ cup of the powdered sugar and the cocoa powder and process until evenly incorporated. With the motor running, add the corn syrup and bourbon through the feed tube and process just until well blended. If necessary, let the mixture stand for 5 to 10 minutes to firm slightly, or if the mixture is dry, add up to 1 tablespoon water, processing until smoothly incorporated.

Shape the mixture into 1-inch balls with lightly greased hands. Spread the remaining ½ cup powdered sugar in a shallow bowl. Roll the balls in the powdered sugar until thoroughly coated. Let the cookies mellow in an airtight container at least overnight before serving.

Store in an airtight container for up to 4 days, refrigerate for up to 2 weeks, or freeze for up to 1 month.

maple-pecan
sandwich cookies

Maple and pecans both have a sweet, rich, faintly woodsy flavor that becomes even more sumptuous and full-bodied when the two are paired. In this recipe, I combine pecans and a bit of maple syrup in the dough and sandwich the cookies together with a maple buttercream. Cut out with a fluted or scalloped cookie cutter and topped with chopped pecans, these are dressy enough to serve at a party.

1 cup (4 ounces) chopped pecans
2¼ cups all-purpose white flour
½ teaspoon baking soda
   Generous ¼ teaspoon salt
¼ cup packed light brown sugar
¾ cup (1½ sticks) unsalted butter, slightly softened
⅔ cup powdered sugar
3½ tablespoons pure maple syrup
1 large egg yolk
2 teaspoons vanilla extract

MAPLE BUTTERCREAM
⅓ cup pure maple syrup
1 cup powdered sugar
6½ tablespoons cold unsalted butter, cut into chunks
⅛ teaspoon vanilla extract

2 tablespoons finely chopped pecans, for topping

Preheat the oven to 350 degrees F.

Spread the 1 cup pecans in a small baking pan and toast in the oven, stirring frequently, for 6 to 9 minutes, or until lightly browned; be careful not to burn. Immediately turn out into a small bowl. Let stand until completely cooled; set aside.

In a medium bowl, thoroughly stir together the flour, baking soda, and salt; set aside. In a food processor, process the pecans and brown sugar continuously until the pecans are completely pureed and form a paste, 3 to 4 minutes, scraping down the processor sides and bottom several times. Add the butter and process until well blended. Add the powdered sugar, maple syrup, egg yolk, and vanilla and process until very well blended and smooth. Add the flour mixture and process in on/off pulses just until evenly incorporated.

Divide the dough into thirds. Place each portion between large sheets of wax paper. Roll out each portion a generous ⅛ inch thick; check the underside of the dough and smooth out any wrinkles that form. Stack the rolled portions (paper still attached) on a baking sheet. Freeze for 30 minutes, or until chilled and firm. (The dough may be frozen for up to 24 hours; let thaw before using.)

Preheat the oven to 350 degrees F. Grease several baking sheets or coat with nonstick spray.

Working with one portion at a time and leaving the remaining dough chilled, gently peel away, then pat one sheet of wax paper back into place. Flip the dough over, then peel off and discard the second sheet. Using a 1½-to-1¾-inch round or oval, scalloped or fluted cookie cutter, cut out the cookies. (If at any point the dough softens too much to handle easily, transfer the paper and cookies to a baking sheet and refrigerate or freeze until firm again.) Using a spatula, carefully transfer the cookies to the baking sheets, spacing about 1½ inches apart. Reroll any dough scraps. Continue cutting out the cookies until all the dough is used. Lightly sprinkle half the cookies with the finely chopped pecans, patting down to embed them slightly; these rounds will be the sandwich tops.

Bake the cookies, one sheet at a time, in the upper third of the oven for 6 to 8 minutes, or until just tinged with brown and slightly darker around the edges. Reverse the sheet from front to back halfway through baking to ensure even browning. Transfer the sheet to a wire rack and let stand until the cookies firm up slightly, 2 to 3 minutes. Using a spatula, transfer the cookies to wire racks. Let stand until completely cooled.

FOR THE BUTTERCREAM
In a small, heavy saucepan, bring the maple syrup to a simmer over medium-high heat. Simmer briskly for 2 minutes. Remove from the heat. Let cool slightly. Pour the syrup into the food processor. Let stand until barely warm. Add the powdered sugar, butter, and vanilla and process just until well blended and smooth.

Spread a generous measuring teaspoon of buttercream over the underside of each untopped round. Cover each with a pecan-topped round. Gently press down and then adjust the top if necessary.

Store in an airtight container for up to 1 week or freeze for up to 1 month.

TIP
Keep these cookies small and use a fluted or scalloped cutter for a fancy presentation. A plain round cutter yields a homey look.

Black walnut wafers

I am always excited to see chopped, ready-to-use black walnuts on modern supermarket shelves. Normally, they appear only briefly in fall, and I buy and freeze extra bags so I can have them any time of the year. They can also be purchased by mail order from King Arthur Flour, P.O. Box 876, Norwich, VT 05055 (800-827-6836). Don't be tempted to substitute regular (English) walnuts for black walnuts, which have an intense, very distinctive flavor that can't be duplicated.

Although black walnut trees are native to North America and grow freely in many states, commercial production occurs in only a few. Missouri calls itself the "black walnut capital of the world," and the following Missouri Ozark recipe that I obtained from a friend of a friend puts the Show Me State's prized product to fine use. These plain-looking drop wafers are very thin and crisp, and richly flavored with black walnuts. Like many Ozark baked goods, they also take great advantage of the flavor of brown sugar. They smell quite enticing as they bake.

½ cup all-purpose white flour	2 large eggs
¼ teaspoon baking soda	1 teaspoon vanilla extract
⅛ teaspoon salt	2 tablespoons (¼ stick) unsalted butter, melted
Scant 1 cup packed light brown sugar	⅔ cup (about 3 ounces) finely chopped black walnuts

Preheat the oven to 350 degrees F. Line several baking sheets with aluminum foil. Grease the foil or coat with nonstick spray.

In a small bowl, thoroughly stir together the flour, baking soda, and salt; set aside. In a medium bowl, using a fork, beat together the brown sugar, eggs, and vanilla until very well blended. Stir in the melted butter and the flour mixture, then the black walnuts, until evenly incorporated.

Drop the dough onto the baking sheets by heaping measuring teaspoonfuls, spacing about 2½ inches apart.

Bake the cookies, one sheet at a time, in the upper third of the oven for 7 to 9 minutes, or until well browned all over and slightly darker at the edges. Reverse the sheet from front to back halfway through baking to ensure even browning. Slide the cookies, still attached to the foil, onto a wire rack. Let stand until completely cooled. Carefully peel the cookies from the foil. If the cooled cookies stick, they are underbaked; return them to the oven and bake for a few minutes more.

Store in a single layer or layered with wax paper in an airtight container for up to 10 days or freeze for up to 1½ months.

A Tough Nut

When I was growing up, black walnuts were a faithful harbinger of autumn. Without fail, golf-ball-sized orbs from overhanging black walnut trees would start thumping onto the tin roof of our screened porch. Eventually, more of the heavy, green-hulled nuts would plop to the ground than anybody — human or squirrel — could eat. (The squirrels did their best, though, then busily buried the rest for winter.)

The idea of getting something for nothing always enticed me to pick up the nuts, too. Unfortunately, with black walnuts, gathering is the only easy part. Getting to the nut meats requires peeling or rubbing off the thick, acrid-smelling hulls (blackening your hands in the process); setting out the nuts to dry for weeks; pounding their ridged, rock-like shells open with a hammer; and finally, prying out the narrow veins of meat with a pick. Not something for nothing after all!

macadamia-chocolate meltaways

Macadamia nuts, one of Hawaii's premium products, inspired these rich, elegant cookies. They are melt-in-the-mouth tender, subtly flavored with macadamia nut butter, and accented with an ultra-fine ribbon of chocolate down the center. Nevertheless, the chocolate isn't merely ornamental; it provides a lovely counterpoint to the mild, nutty flavor.

Hawaii produces not only macadamias but also a limited amount of cocoa beans, which the Hawaiian Vintage Chocolate Company turns into fine but pricey chocolate. You can use Hawaiian Vintage chocolate in this recipe with excellent results, but other top-quality brands, such as Lindt, Valhrona, or Callebaut, work equally well.

1³/₄ cups (about 8 ounces) macadamia nuts (divided)

2¹/₂ tablespoons sugar

¹/₂ cup (1 stick) cold unsalted butter, cut into chunks

2¹/₂ tablespoons corn oil or other flavorless vegetable oil (divided)

1 large egg yolk

1¹/₂ teaspoons vanilla extract

1¹/₂ cups all-purpose white flour

¹/₂ cup powdered sugar

¹/₄ teaspoon salt (omit if salted macadamia nuts are used)

¹/₂ ounce bittersweet (*not* unsweetened) or semisweet chocolate, broken up or coarsely chopped

In a food processor, process 1½ cups of the macadamia nuts and the sugar until ground to a fairly smooth paste, about 1½ minutes, scraping down the bowl several times. Add the butter, 2 tablespoons of the oil, the egg yolk, and vanilla and process in on/off pulses just until well blended, stopping and stirring to redistribute the contents several times. Add the remaining ¼ cup macadamia nuts, the flour, powdered sugar, and salt, if using, and process in on/off pulses just until the macadamia nuts are chopped moderately fine.

In a small, microwave-safe bowl, microwave the remaining ½ tablespoon oil and the chocolate on 50-percent power, stirring at 30-second intervals, until just melted. (Alternatively, melt the oil and chocolate in a double boiler set over gently simmering water, stirring occasionally. Remove from the heat.) Let stand until cooled.

Line a 4½-by-8½-inch loaf pan with two long sheets of plastic wrap laid crosswise, overlapping in the middle and overhanging the longer sides by about 3 inches.

TIP
If you use salted macadamia nuts, wipe off the excess salt with paper towels before using.

Divide the dough in half. Spoon half of the dough into the pan. Lay a sheet of wax paper over the top, then press down and smooth to even the surface; peel off and discard the paper. Using a pastry brush or a rubber spatula, spread the chocolate mixture thinly over the dough. Immediately place in the freezer until the chocolate completely sets, about 10 minutes. Spoon the remaining dough over the chocolate. Lay a sheet of wax paper over the top and very firmly press down on the dough and smooth its surface; peel off and discard the paper. Fold the plastic wrap over the dough. Freeze until the loaf is cold and very firm, at least 3 to 4 hours or up to 24 hours. Bake immediately, or remove from the pan, transfer to an airtight plastic bag, and freeze for up to 1 month.

Preheat the oven to 325 degrees F. Grease several baking sheets or coat with nonstick spray.

Carefully peel the plastic wrap from the loaf. Using a large, sharp knife, trim off and discard the excess dough so the sides of the loaf are straight up and down rather than flared; wipe the knife clean between cuts. (If the dough is too hard to cut easily, let stand for a few minutes; don't let it thaw too much, or the dough will be more difficult to slice cleanly.) Carefully cut the loaf in half crosswise, then in half lengthwise, to form 4 logs for baking. Cut each log crosswise into ¼-inch-thick slices; wipe the knife clean between cuts. Using a spatula, carefully transfer the slices to the baking sheets, spacing about 2 inches apart.

Bake the cookies, one sheet at a time, in the upper third of the oven for 11 to 15 minutes, or until just tinged with brown and slightly darker around the edges. Reverse the sheet from front to back halfway through baking to ensure even browning. Transfer the sheet to a wire rack and let stand until the cookies firm up slightly, 3 to 4 minutes. Using a spatula, transfer the cookies to wire racks. Let stand until completely cooled.

Store in an airtight container for up to 1 week or freeze for up to 1 month. Handle gently, because the cookies are fragile.

Hazelnut-chocolate sandwich cookies

The inspiration for these thin, sophisticated hazelnut-chocolate sandwich cookies came from an Oregon hostess who was reluctant to share her recipe—but had no objection to my trying to duplicate it.

According to Dr. Shawn A. Mehlenbacher, a hazelnut expert at Oregon State University, the state's commercial crop was developed from imported European varieties. Early on, growers called the nuts filberts to distinguish them from the small, inferior wild hazelnuts already growing in the region. The designation proved confusing to American consumers, however, so the name was recently officially dropped by Oregon growers.

These are fine cookies to serve with afternoon tea or coffee. They feature tender little rectangles of buttery hazelnut shortbread sandwiched around bittersweet chocolate and topped with finely chopped hazelnuts—a great combination if ever there was one. My version is very close to the original—and maybe even better!

1 cup (about 5 ounces) hazelnuts

1⅓ cups all-purpose white flour

⅛ teaspoon salt

½ cup minus 1 tablespoon sugar

½ cup (1 stick) unsalted butter, slightly softened

1 large egg yolk

1 teaspoon vanilla extract

3½ ounces bittersweet (*not* unsweetened) or semisweet chocolate, broken up or coarsely chopped (divided)

1½ teaspoons corn oil or other flavorless vegetable oil

Preheat the oven to 350 degrees F. Grease several baking sheets or coat with nonstick spray.

Spread the hazelnuts in a small baking pan and toast in the oven, stirring occasionally, for 15 to 19 minutes, or until the hulls loosen and the nuts are lightly browned; be careful not to burn. Immediately turn out into a small bowl and let stand until cool enough to handle. Rub the hazelnuts between your hands or in a clean kitchen towel, loosening and discarding as much hull as possible. Finely chop ¼ cup of the hazelnuts; set aside.

In a medium bowl, thoroughly stir together the flour and salt; set aside. In a food processor, combine the ¾ cup whole hazelnuts and sugar. Process until the hazelnuts are completely pureed and form a coarse paste, 3 to 4 minutes, stopping and scraping down the bowl sides once or twice. Add the butter, egg yolk, and vanilla and process until very well blended, about 1 minute. Add the flour mixture and process just until evenly incorporated; do not overprocess. Turn out the dough onto a sheet of wax paper and press it together into a ball. If it is too crumbly to hold together, sprinkle 1 to 2 teaspoons cold water over it and lightly knead until it holds together.

Divide the dough in half. Place each portion between large sheets of wax paper. Roll out each portion a scant ⅛ inch thick into an approximately 11-inch square, cutting and patching at the edges, if necessary; check the underside of the dough and smooth out any wrinkles that form. Stack the rolled portions (paper still attached) on a baking sheet. Refrigerate for 30 minutes, or until chilled and firm.

Working with one portion at a time and leaving the remaining dough chilled, gently peel away, then pat one sheet of wax paper back into place. Flip the dough over, then peel off and discard the second sheet. Measure, mark, and then, using a large, sharp knife, cut the dough into as many 1¼-by-2-inch rectangles as possible. (If at any point the dough softens too much to handle easily, transfer the paper and cookies to a baking sheet and refrigerate or freeze until firm again.) Using a spatula, carefully transfer the rectangles to the baking sheets, spacing about 1½ inches apart. Reroll any dough scraps. Continue cutting the cookies until all the dough is used. Top half of the rectangles with the remaining ¼ cup chopped hazelnuts, patting down to embed them slightly; these rectangles will be the sandwich tops. Using a fork, prick the remaining rectangles several times.

Bake the cookies, one sheet at a time, in the upper third of the oven for 5 to 8 minutes, or until lightly browned at the edges. Reverse the sheet from front to back halfway through baking to ensure even browning. Transfer the sheet to a wire rack and let stand until the cookies firm up slightly, 1 to 2 minutes. Using a spatula, transfer the cookies to wire racks. Let stand until completely cooled.

In a small, microwave-safe bowl, microwave 2½ ounces of the chocolate and the oil on 50-percent power for 1 minute. Stir well. Continue microwaving, stirring at 30-second intervals, until just barely melted. (Alternatively, melt the chocolate and oil in a double boiler set over gently simmering water, stirring occasionally. Transfer the mixture to a small bowl.) Stir in the remaining 1 ounce chocolate until it melts and cools down the rest of the mixture.

Place the cookie bottoms, underside up, on a wax-paper-lined rimmed baking sheet. Spoon a generous ½ teaspoon chocolate mixture onto each cookie bottom. Cover each with a cookie top. Gently press down to spread out the chocolate, being careful not to squeeze it out the sides or break the cookies. (If the chocolate mixture begins to set, microwave it on 50-percent power for about 30 seconds, or until just slightly warm; stir well before using.) Transfer the baking sheet to the refrigerator and chill the cookies until the chocolate completely sets, about 30 minutes. Let the cookies return to room temperature.

Store in an airtight container in a cool (not refrigerated) place for up to 2 weeks or freeze for up to 2 months.

8

Oat, Coconut, and Sesame Seed Cookies

soft raisin-oatmeal drop cookies

Most oatmeal cookies fall into the homey category, but these rise to the level of complete comfort food. They have a mild yet mellow oat flavor, a chewy-soft texture, and, due to the abundance of plumped raisins, a pleasing succulence that keeps drawing you back to the cookie jar. The recipe is also easy enough for beginning bakers; I started making a version of this cookie when I was nine.

1½ cups (7½ ounces) raisins
 2 cups all-purpose white flour
½ teaspoon baking soda
    Generous ¼ teaspoon salt
 1 cup (2 sticks) unsalted butter, slightly softened
 1 cup packed light brown sugar

½ cup sugar
 1 large egg, plus 1 large egg yolk
2½ tablespoons light or dark corn syrup
2½ teaspoons vanilla extract
1½ cups old-fashioned rolled oats

Preheat the oven to 325 degrees F. Grease several baking sheets or coat with nonstick spray.

In a medium bowl, combine the raisins and enough hot water to cover; set aside.

In a medium bowl, thoroughly stir together the flour, baking soda, and salt; set aside. In a large bowl, with an electric mixer on medium speed, beat together the butter, brown sugar, and sugar until light and smooth, about 1 minute. Add the egg and egg yolk, corn syrup, and vanilla and beat until well blended and fluffy, about 2 minutes. Beat in the flour mixture until well blended. Thoroughly drain the raisins. Add the raisins and oats to the dough and stir until evenly incorporated.

Drop the dough onto the baking sheets by heaping measuring tablespoonfuls, spacing about 2½ inches apart.

Bake the cookies, one sheet at a time, in the middle of the oven for 12 to 15 minutes, or until lightly tinged with brown and almost firm when pressed in the centers. Reverse the sheet from front to back halfway through baking to ensure even browning.

Transfer the sheet to a wire rack and let stand until the cookies firm up slightly, about 2 minutes. Using a spatula, transfer the cookies to wire racks. Let stand until completely cooled.

Store in an airtight container for up to 2 weeks or freeze for up to 1 month.

oat cuisine

When an innovative and enterprising immigrant Ohio miller named Ferdinand Schumacher began promoting his new steel-cut oats as a nutritious cereal in the 1860s, editorial writers and cartoonists of the day scoffed, insinuating that oat-eaters robbed horses and would develop the whinnies. The Scots, whose taste for oats was already known, were dismissed as being too cheap or too poor to consume anything else.

Nevertheless, Schumacher's steel-cut oats and, later, his even more convenient rolled oats began catching on as breakfast fare, probably because they were economical and satisfying as well as relatively easy to prepare. (Schumacher eventually became one of the founders of what is now the Quaker Oats Company.) By 1881, oats had also made their way into baked goods: a book of recipes for commercial bakers called *The Complete Bread, Cake and Cracker Baker* contained recipes for oatmeal muffins, puffs, and rolls and a rolled oatmeal-molasses cookie called "Oatmeal Snaps" or "Scotch Perkins." Presumably Scottish in origin—gingerbread cookies called "parkins" do turn up in old British cookbooks—these snaps may well have been the first oatmeal cookies baked in America.

Only eight years later, rolled oatmeal cookies called "Oatmeal Biscuits" debuted in a work for home cooks, *Mrs. Clarke's Cookery Book*. The earliest oatmeal-raisin drop cookie I've come across appeared in the *Capital City Cook Book,* a Madison, Wisconsin, church cookbook published in 1906. Sometime after 1910, oatmeal cookies edged further into the American mainstream when Quaker Oats first put an oatmeal cookie recipe on its box. While no one paid particular attention then, the public did notice—and vigorously complained—when the company stopped putting oatmeal cookie recipes on its containers in the early 1950s. The recipes immediately were reinstated, and various oatmeal cookies have been featured on Quaker Oats boxes ever since. Today, the oatmeal cookie is second in popularity in America only to the chocolate chip.

oat, coconut, and sesame seed cookies

Dairy Hollow House oatmeal-raisin cookies

These delicious oatmeal-raisin cookies were a specialty of the now-closed Dairy Hollow House, a popular Eureka Springs, Arkansas, bed-and-breakfast establishment of cookbook and children's book author Crescent Dragonwagon. At checkout, guests were always presented with a neatly bagged giant oatmeal cookie to nibble during the trip home—the inn's way of saving the best for last. Happily, a yearning for these crispy-chewy treats can always be satisfied, even if the chance to get them from the Dairy Hollow House has passed.

In the following slightly adapted version, I have cut down the recipe yield and reduced the cookies to normal size. You could make them bigger (and bake them longer), if desired.

1 cup (5 ounces) raisins

3 cups old-fashioned rolled oats

2 cups all-purpose white flour

1 teaspoon ground cinnamon

½ teaspoon baking powder

½ teaspoon baking soda

½ teaspoon salt

⅔ cup (1 stick plus 2⅔ tablespoons) unsalted butter, slightly softened

½ cup white vegetable shortening

1 cup packed light brown sugar

1 cup sugar

2 large eggs

1 teaspoon vanilla extract

1 cup (4 ounces) chopped walnuts or pecans

Preheat the oven to 375 degrees F. Grease several baking sheets or coat with nonstick spray.

In a small bowl, combine the raisins and enough hot water to cover; set aside.

In a large bowl, thoroughly stir together the oats, flour, cinnamon, baking powder, baking soda, and salt; set aside. In another large bowl, with an electric mixer on medium speed, beat together the butter and shortening until light and fluffy. Add the brown sugar and sugar and beat until fluffy and smooth. Add the eggs and vanilla and beat until evenly incorporated. Stir or beat in all but 1 cup of the oat mixture until evenly incorporated. Thoroughly drain the raisins. In a medium bowl, stir together the remaining oat mixture, the raisins, and walnuts or pecans. Fold into the dough until evenly incorporated.

Shape the dough into generous golf-ball-sized balls with lightly greased hands. Place on the baking sheets, spacing about 2 inches apart. Pat down the balls until just flattened on top.

Bake the cookies, one sheet at a time, in the center of the oven for 8 to 11 minutes, or until lightly tinged with brown all over and still slightly soft in the centers; be careful not to overbake. Reverse the sheet from front to back halfway through baking to ensure even browning. Transfer the sheet to a wire rack and let stand until the cookies firm up slightly, 1 to 2 minutes. Using a spatula, transfer the cookies to wire racks. Let stand until completely cooled.

Store in an airtight container for up to 1 week or freeze for up to 1 month.

"old-Timey" oatmeal sandwich cookies

I put the "Old-Timey" in quotes when I named these large sandwich cookies because, while they seem old-fashioned, they're in fact a late-twentieth-century invention. They boast a pleasing nutty oat flavor, crispy-chewy texture, and billowy marshmallow creme filling.

COOKIES

- 2²/₃ cups all-purpose white flour
- 2 teaspoons ground cinnamon
- 1 teaspoon baking powder
- ³/₄ teaspoon baking soda
- Generous ¹/₂ teaspoon salt
- Generous 1³/₄ cups packed light brown sugar
- 1 cup (2 sticks) unsalted butter, slightly softened
- ²/₃ cup white vegetable shortening
- 1¹/₂ tablespoons light or dark corn syrup
- 3 large eggs
- 2¹/₂ teaspoons vanilla extract
- 1¹/₂ cups old-fashioned rolled oats

FILLING

- ³/₄ cup powdered sugar
- ²/₃ cup (1 stick plus 2²/₃ tablespoons) unsalted butter, slightly softened
- ¹/₂ cup white vegetable shortening
- 1¹/₂ tablespoons light corn syrup
- 2 teaspoons vanilla extract
- ¹/₈ teaspoon salt
- 1 7-ounce jar (1¹/₃ cups) marshmallow creme

Preheat the oven to 350 degrees F. Grease several baking sheets or coat with nonstick spray.

FOR THE COOKIES

In a medium bowl, thoroughly stir together the flour, cinnamon, baking powder, baking soda, and salt; set aside. In a large bowl, with an electric mixer on medium speed, beat together the brown sugar, butter, shortening, and corn syrup until well blended and lightened, about 1½ minutes. Add the eggs, one at a time, then the vanilla, and beat until very light and fluffy, about 2 minutes. Beat in half of the flour mixture. Beat or stir in the remaining flour mixture and the oats until evenly incorporated.

Drop the dough onto the baking sheets using a ⅛-cup measure or coffee scoop, spacing about 3 inches apart. Using a lightly greased hand, pat down the cookies just slightly.

Bake the cookies, one sheet at a time, in the middle of the oven for 9 to 12 minutes, or until lightly browned and barely firm when lightly pressed in the centers. Reverse the sheet from front to back halfway through baking to ensure even browning. Transfer the sheet to a wire rack and let stand until the cookies firm up slightly, about 2 minutes. Using a spatula, transfer the cookies to wire racks. Let stand until completely cooled.

FOR THE FILLING

In a large bowl, with an electric mixer on medium speed, beat together the powdered sugar, butter, shortening, corn syrup, vanilla, and salt until well blended and fluffy. Add the marshmallow creme and beat until well blended and smooth.

Place half of the cookies underside up. Spoon a generous 2 tablespoons filling in the center of each cookie. Spread the filling to within ½ inch of the edge. Cover each with a second cookie of about the same size. Gently press down so the filling almost extends to the edges.

Store in individual plastic bags in the refrigerator for up to 1 week or freeze for up to 1 month; let come to room temperature before serving.

TIP

Dough that is too warm may yield cookies that spread too much. If the baked cookies on your first sheet are more than about 3¼ inches across, refrigerate the remaining dough for a few minutes before continuing. This will produce slightly sturdier, more compact rounds, which are better suited for sandwiches.

cranberry-walnut oatmeal cookies

Zingy from cranberries, orange zest, and spices, these flavorful oatmeal drop cookies are nice for lunch boxes, autumn picnics, satisfying snacks, or even simple holiday treats. They have a good deal of fiber and a chewy, nubby texture due to the walnuts, berries, and oats.

Crystallized ginger makes a pleasant addition to the cookies, but they are good without it, too.

1¹/₃ cups (about 4¹/₂ ounces) cranberries, fresh or frozen, thawed

1¹/₄ cups plus 3 tablespoons packed light brown sugar (divided)

1³/₄ cups all-purpose white flour

1¹/₂ teaspoons ground cinnamon

³/₄ teaspoon ground coriander

³/₄ teaspoon baking soda

Generous ¹/₄ teaspoon ground cloves

Generous ¹/₄ teaspoon salt

²/₃ cup (1 stick plus 2²/₃ tablespoons) unsalted butter, slightly softened

¹/₃ cup white vegetable shortening

2 large eggs

1¹/₂ tablespoons light corn syrup

1¹/₂ teaspoons vanilla extract

1¹/₂ tablespoons finely chopped crystallized ginger (optional)

1¹/₂ teaspoons finely grated orange zest (colored part of the skin)

1²/₃ cups old-fashioned rolled oats

1¹/₄ cups (5 ounces) chopped walnuts

Preheat the oven to 350 degrees F. Grease several baking sheets or coat with nonstick spray.

In a food processor, process the cranberries in on/off pulses until coarsely chopped. Sprinkle 3 tablespoons of the brown sugar over the berries and pulse several times to incorporate. (Alternatively, chop the cranberries by hand. In a small bowl, toss together the chopped cranberries and 3 tablespoons brown sugar.) Set aside.

In a medium bowl, thoroughly stir together the flour, cinnamon, coriander, baking soda, cloves, and salt; set aside. In a large bowl, with an electric mixer on medium speed, beat together the butter, shortening, and remaining 1¼ cups brown sugar until well blended and lightened, about 1½ minutes. Beat in the eggs, one at a time, then the corn syrup, vanilla, crystallized ginger (if using), and orange zest until very light and fluffy, about 2 minutes. Beat in half of the flour mixture. Beat or stir in the remaining flour mixture. Fold in the cranberry mixture, oats, and walnuts until evenly incorporated.

Drop the dough onto the baking sheets using a ⅛-cup measure or coffee scoop, spacing about 3 inches apart.

Bake the cookies, one sheet at a time, in the upper third of the oven for 11 to 14 minutes, or until lightly browned on top and almost firm when lightly pressed in the centers. Reverse the sheet from front to back halfway through baking to ensure even browning. Transfer the sheet to a wire rack and let stand until the cookies firm up slightly, about 3 minutes. Using a spatula, transfer the cookies to wire racks. Let stand until cooled completely.

Store in an airtight container for up to 1 week or freeze for up to 1 month.

words of kitchen wisdom
"In breaking eggs, do not break them over the vessels in which they are to be beaten. Break them, one by one, over a saucer, so that if you come across a defective one, you will not spoil the rest by mixing it with them."

— Marion Cabell Tyree,
Housekeeping in Old Virginia, 1879

ultimate oatmeal chocolate chippers

Immodest or not, I'm declaring these chocolate chip-oatmeal cookies first-rate. I experimented with the recipe during the years my son was growing up, and while the resulting cookies always disappeared rapidly, they never reached the pinnacle of golden, crisp perfection I sought. But finally I achieved my goal: mellow oat, butter, and brown sugar flavor, chewy-crispness, and a rough-textured, chocolate-studded look. These seem made for the cookie jar but probably won't stay there long.

2 cups all-purpose white flour

1 teaspoon baking powder

1/2 teaspoon baking soda

Generous 1/4 teaspoon salt

1 cup (2 sticks) unsalted butter, slightly softened

1/4 cup white vegetable shortening

1 cup packed light brown sugar

3/4 cup sugar

1 large egg

3 tablespoon light or dark corn syrup

2 teaspoons vanilla extract

2 1/3 cups old-fashioned rolled oats

2 cups (12 ounces) semisweet chocolate morsels

1 cup (about 3 ounces) shredded or flaked sweetened coconut (optional)

Preheat the oven to 350 degrees F. Grease several baking sheets or coat with nonstick spray.

In a medium bowl, thoroughly stir together the flour, baking powder, baking soda, and salt; set aside. In a large bowl, with an electric mixer on medium speed, beat together the butter and shortening until light and smooth, about 1 minute. Add the brown sugar and sugar and beat until well blended, about 2 minutes. Add the egg, corn syrup, and vanilla and beat until very light and fluffy, about 1½ minutes. Beat in the flour mixture until evenly incorporated. Stir in the oats, chocolate morsels, and coconut, if using, until evenly incorporated. Let the dough stand for 5 to 10 minutes, or until firmed up slightly.

Divide the dough into quarters. Divide each quarter into 8 equal portions. Shape the portions into balls with lightly greased hands. Place on the baking sheets, spacing about 3 inches apart. Using your hand, pat down the balls to about ½ inch thick.

Bake the cookies, one sheet at a time, in the middle of the oven for 11 to 14 minutes, or until tinged with brown, slightly darker at the edges, and almost firm when pressed in the centers; be careful not to overbake. Reverse the sheet from front to back halfway through baking to ensure even browning. Transfer the sheet to a wire rack and let stand until the cookies firm up slightly, about 4 minutes. Using a spatula, transfer the cookies to wire racks. Let stand until completely cooled.

Store in an airtight container for up to 2 weeks or freeze for up to 1½ months.

Honey-currant oatmeal cookies

Honey has a great affinity for both oats and currants, bringing out the toasty goodness of the former and taming the slight bitterness in the latter. Besides contributing its own faintly floral aroma and flavor, honey also encourages browning, so these chewy rounds come out of the oven not only wonderfully fragrant but possessing a rich, golden hue. And thanks to the honey, these cookies stay moist and keep well.

1 cup (4½ ounces) dried currants	1 cup (2 sticks) unsalted butter, slightly softened
1¼ cups all-purpose white flour	¾ cup sugar
¾ teaspoon baking soda	¼ cup clover honey or other mild honey
½ teaspoon ground cinnamon	2½ teaspoons vanilla extract
Generous ¼ teaspoon salt	2⅓ cups old-fashioned rolled oats

Preheat the oven to 350 degrees F. Grease several baking sheets or coat with nonstick spray.

In a small bowl, combine the currants and enough hot water to cover; let stand for 5 minutes.

In a medium bowl, thoroughly stir together the flour, baking soda, cinnamon, and salt; set aside. In a large bowl, with an electric mixer on medium speed, beat together the butter and sugar until lightened and fluffy, about 1 minute. Add the honey and vanilla and beat until well blended. Beat in the flour mixture until evenly incorporated. Thoroughly drain the currants. Stir the currants and oats into the dough until evenly incorporated. Let the dough stand for 5 minutes, or until firmed up slightly.

Shape portions of the dough into 1½-inch balls with lightly greased hands. Place on the baking sheets, spacing about 2½ inches apart. Using your hand, pat down the cookie tops just slightly.

Bake the cookies, one sheet at a time, in the middle of the oven for 9 to 13 minutes, or until lightly browned and almost firm when pressed in the centers. Reverse the sheet from front to back halfway through baking to ensure even browning. Transfer the sheet to a wire rack and let stand until the cookies firm up slightly, about 2 minutes. Using a spatula, transfer the cookies to wire racks. Let stand until completely cooled.

Store in an airtight container for up to 2 weeks or freeze for up to 1 month.

words of kitchen wisdom
"It will be found a good plan after purchasing currants, to wash in three waters, pick and dry in a cloth. Then look them carefully over, discarding any stone, stalk, or grit. Lay before the fire or in the sun to dry. Put by in a jar, and they will always be ready for use."

– Mrs. Clarke, *Mrs. Clarke's Cookery Book*, 1889

oat, coconut, and sesame seed cookies

cane syrup oatmeal-raisin cookies

• makes 40 to 45
• (2½-inch) cookies.

Though not widely known in other regions, cane-sugar table syrup is a commonplace product in parts of the South. Much milder and sweeter than molasses but with a hint of molasses flavor, it is used for everything from basting ham to topping hotcakes to "sopping" biscuits.

Vivian and Royce Lowery of Georgiana, Alabama, who created this recipe, make and sell a pure cane-sugar table syrup called Carson Ann syrup. The cane syrup not only adds a mellow sugar taste but helps keep these chewy, nicely spiced cookies exceptionally moist.

Mrs. Lowery recalls that in the past, rural Alabamians often grew sugar cane and made their own syrup each autumn. The process involved stripping the leaves and cutting down the canes, then extracting their juice with a mule- or tractor-powered roller mill. Next, the juice was boiled down in huge metal pots. In about four hours, 100 gallons could be reduced to about 8 gallons of cane syrup. "It was a lot of work," Mrs. Lowery says.

Considering the amount of labor required for the yield, it's not surprising that most households today buy their syrup at local stores. Outside the South, it can easily be ordered by phone or via the Internet from sources such as Lowrey's, P.O. Box 129, Georgiana, AL 36033 (800-611-3337).

1¼ cups (6¼ ounces) raisins
2 cups all-purpose white flour
1 teaspoon baking soda
1 teaspoon ground cinnamon
½ teaspoon ground cloves
½ teaspoon salt
1 cup (2 sticks) unsalted butter, slightly softened

¾ cup sugar
⅔ cup pure southern cane-sugar syrup (see tip)
1 large egg
2½ teaspoons vanilla extract
2 cups old-fashioned rolled oats
1¼ cups (5 ounces) chopped pecans

Preheat the oven to 350 degrees F. Grease several baking sheets or coat with nonstick spray.

In a small bowl, combine the raisins and enough hot water to cover; set aside. In a medium bowl, thoroughly stir together the flour, baking soda, cinnamon, cloves, and salt; set aside. In a large bowl, with an electric mixer on medium speed, beat together the butter and sugar until light and smooth, about 1 minute. Add the cane syrup, egg, and vanilla and beat until well blended and fluffy, about 2 minutes. Beat in the flour mixture until well blended. Thoroughly drain the raisins. Stir in the raisins, oats, and pecans until evenly incorporated. Let the dough stand for 5 to 10 minutes, or until firmed up slightly.

Shape portions of the dough into generous 1¼-inch balls with lightly greased hands. Place on the baking sheets, spacing about 2½ inches apart. Using your hands, pat down the balls slightly.

Bake the cookies, one sheet at a time, in the middle of the oven for 9 to 11 minutes, or until lightly tinged with brown and almost firm when pressed in the centers. Reverse the sheet from front to back halfway through baking to ensure even browning. Transfer the sheet to a wire rack and let stand until the cookies firm up slightly, about 2 minutes. Using a spatula, transfer the cookies to wire racks. Let stand until completely cooled.

Store in an airtight container for up to 2 weeks or freeze for up to 2 months.

TIP
Though the results will not be exactly the same, the recipe will work with Lyle's Golden Syrup (a British cane-sugar syrup often sold in gourmet grocery sections in the United States) mixed with a little molasses. Replace the ⅔ cup southern cane-sugar syrup with ½ cup Lyle's Golden Syrup and 2 generous tablespoons molasses. Don't substitute corn syrup or maple syrup in this recipe; check product labels to be sure you're getting pure cane-sugar syrup.

Ranger cookies

These large, hearty cookies are a fairly recent addition to the American repertoire, appearing sometime in the latter half of the twentieth century. Most ranger cookies contain rolled oats and coconut, and some also include pecans and crushed corn flakes. Despite the name, the cookies don't seem to be connected with the Texas Rangers or Texas, or with any particular part of the country, for that matter.

These cookies have a rich, satisfying taste and toothsomeness that gives them great staying power and appeal. They are particularly good with a glass of milk.

2 cups all-purpose white flour	²/₃ cup sugar
³/₄ teaspoon baking powder	2 large eggs
³/₄ teaspoon baking soda	2¹/₂ teaspoons vanilla extract
Generous ¹/₂ teaspoon salt	2 cups old-fashioned rolled oats
²/₃ cup (1 stick plus 2²/₃ tablespoons) unsalted butter, slightly softened	2 cups corn flakes, crushed
¹/₂ cup white vegetable shortening	1¹/₄ cups (5 ounces) chopped pecans
1¹/₃ cups packed light brown sugar	1¹/₄ cups (about 3¹/₂ ounces) shredded or flaked sweetened coconut

Preheat the oven to 375 degrees F. Grease several baking sheets or coat with nonstick spray.

In a medium bowl, thoroughly stir together the flour, baking powder, baking soda, and salt; set aside. In a large bowl, with an electric mixer on medium speed, beat together the butter and shortening until lightened. Add the brown sugar and sugar and beat until fluffy and smooth. Add the eggs and vanilla and beat until evenly incorporated. Beat or stir in the flour mixture until evenly incorporated. Stir in the oats, corn flakes, pecans, and coconut until evenly incorporated. Let the dough stand for 5 to 10 minutes, or until firmed up slightly.

Shape portions of the dough into generous golf-ball-sized balls with lightly greased hands. Place on the baking sheets, spacing about 3 inches apart. Using your hand, pat down the balls until about ⅓ inch thick.

Bake the cookies, one sheet at a time, in the upper third of the oven for 8 to 11 minutes, or until tinged with brown and just beginning to firm up in the centers; be careful not to overbake. Transfer the sheet to a wire rack and let stand until the cookies firm up slightly, about 3 minutes. Using a spatula, transfer the cookies to wire racks. Let stand until completely cooled.

Store in an airtight container for up to 1 week or freeze for up to 1 month.

oat, coconut, and sesame seed cookies

German Chocolate Coconut-Pecan Cookies

These well-flavored, crispy-chewy cookies were inspired by the decadent coconut-pecan-chocolate combination made famous in German chocolate cake. The cake became a hit in the United States in the late 1950s, after the recipe ran in a Dallas newspaper and was then circulated to other papers around the country. In 1958, it was modified slightly by General Foods and printed on all its packages of German's sweet chocolate, where it still appears.

There is nothing German about the cake (or my cookies); German's chocolate was named for Samuel German, a Baker's chocolate company employee who created the semisweet blend in 1852. This chocolate goes nicely with the pecans and coconut, producing cookies with a wonderfully nutty taste.

2¼ cups (about 6½ ounces) shredded or flaked sweetened coconut

1½ cups (about 6 ounces) chopped pecans

1¾ cups all-purpose white flour

1½ teaspoons baking powder

¼ teaspoon salt

1 cup packed light brown sugar

¾ cup (1½ sticks) unsalted butter, slightly softened

1 large egg

2 tablespoons light or dark corn syrup

2½ teaspoons vanilla extract

¼ teaspoon coconut extract *or* 3 drops almond extract

1 4-ounce bar German's sweet chocolate, finely chopped or coarsely grated

Preheat the oven to 350 degrees F. Grease several baking sheets or coat with nonstick spray.

Spread the coconut and pecans on a rimmed baking sheet and toast in the oven, stirring occasionally, for 7 to 9 minutes, or until lightly browned; be careful not to burn. Let stand until cool; set aside.

In a medium bowl, thoroughly stir together the flour, baking powder, and salt; set aside. In a large bowl, with an electric mixer on medium speed, beat together the brown sugar and butter until very well blended and light. Beat in the egg, corn syrup, vanilla, and coconut or almond extract until well blended. Beat or stir in the flour mixture, then the pecans, coconut, and chocolate, until evenly incorporated.

Drop the dough onto the baking sheets by heaping measuring table-spoonfuls, spacing about 3 inches apart. Using the tip of a table knife, spread out the cookies to about 1½ inches in diameter.

Bake the cookies, one sheet at a time, in the upper third of the oven for 6 to 9 minutes, or until lightly browned all over and slightly darker at the edges. Reverse the sheet from front to back halfway through baking to ensure even browning. Transfer the sheet to a wire rack and let stand until the cookies firm up slightly, 1 to 2 minutes. Using a spatula, transfer the cookies to wire racks. Let stand until completely cooled.

Store in an airtight container for up to 10 days or freeze for up to 2 months.

oat, coconut, and sesame seed cookies

chocolate-dipped coconut macaroons

makes about 24
(2¾-inch) macaroons.

These plump cookies were inspired by some big, begging-to-be-bought chocolate-topped macaroons I discovered at the famous Lancaster Central Market in the heart of Pennsylvania Dutch country. A hand-lettered sign at the Ric's Breads stall proclaimed the cookies "daintily dipped in dark chocolate," but in truth, both the dipping and the macaroons were too generous to be called "dainty." (This is not a criticism. Real Pennsylvania Dutch market fare is never dainty!)

The bustling Central Market has operated by the town square continuously since the 1730s, although the red-brick building now housing it dates from 1889. The cookies I sampled are based on a modern recipe, but macaroons—sometimes spelled "mackroons" in the eighteenth and nineteenth centuries—have long been popular in the region. The earliest versions were either plain or almond. Coconut macaroons began showing up in the early 1800s, though they were not topped with chocolate.

As written, this recipe produces large, loaded-with-coconut mounds. Feel free to make yours smaller, but remember, they won't be Pennsylvania Dutch market style! Also, remember that smaller cookies will bake more quickly, so reduce the baking time accordingly. Last, be sure not to omit the sweetened condensed milk from the recipe; it keeps the cookies moist and tender.

7½ cups (about 1 pound 5 ounces) shredded or flaked sweetened coconut
3 tablespoons sweetened condensed milk
⅔ cup egg whites (4–5 large egg whites), free of yolk and at room temperature
Generous ¼ teaspoon cream of tartar
⅔ cup sugar
1 teaspoon vanilla extract
⅛ teaspoon coconut or almond extract

DIPPING CHOCOLATE
6 ounces bittersweet (*not* unsweetened) or semisweet chocolate (divided), plus more if needed
2 ounces unsweetened chocolate
2½ tablespoons white vegetable shortening

Preheat the oven to 325 degrees F. Grease several baking sheets or coat with nonstick spray.

Spread the coconut on a large rimmed baking sheet and toast in the oven, stirring frequently, for 7 to 9 minutes, or until just beginning to color at the edges. In a large bowl, stir together the coconut and condensed milk until well blended; set aside.

In a large bowl, with an electric mixer on low speed (use a whisk-shaped beater, if available), beat together the egg whites and cream of tartar until frothy. Increase the speed to medium-high and beat just until opaque and soft peaks form. Add the sugar, 2 tablespoons at a time, beating after each addition. Add the vanilla and coconut or almond extract. Increase the speed to high. Beat until the mixture forms very stiff, glossy peaks, about 2 minutes. Fold in the coconut mixture until evenly incorporated.

Drop the mixture onto the baking sheets using a ¼-cup measure, spacing about 2½ inches apart.

Bake the macaroons, one sheet at a time, in the middle of the oven for 13 to 18 minutes, or until lightly tinged with brown on top and barely firm when lightly pressed. Transfer the sheet to a wire rack and let stand until the macaroons firm up slightly, 1 to 2 minutes. Using a spatula, transfer the macaroons to wire racks. Let stand until completely cooled. (They will sink slightly as they cool.) Place the macaroons on a baking sheet and refrigerate until chilled.

Line a large rimmed baking sheet with wax paper.

FOR THE DIPPING CHOCOLATE
In a small saucepan, melt 4 ounces of the bittersweet or semisweet chocolate, the unsweetened chocolate, and shortening over low heat, stirring frequently, until just melted. Transfer to a small bowl. Stir in the remaining 2 ounces bittersweet or semisweet chocolate until it partially melts and the mixture has cooled to barely warm. (If the entire 2 ounces melts, stir in 1 ounce more and continue cooling the mixture by stirring.) Immediately dip the tops of the chilled macaroons into the chocolate; gently shake off the excess. Place the macaroons slightly apart on the wax-paper-lined baking sheet. Stir the dipping chocolate after every 5 or 6 macaroons to keep it well blended. If the pool of chocolate is too shallow to easily dip the last few macaroons, spoon it over them instead. (Leftover chocolate can also be drizzled over all the macaroons, if desired, although it's best not to top them with a thick layer.) Immediately transfer the sheet of macaroons to the refrigerator for 15 to 20 minutes, or until the chocolate sets. Let the macaroons come to room temperature before serving.

Store in a single layer or layered with wax paper in an airtight container in a cool place, but not the refrigerator, for up to 3 days or freeze for up to 1 month.

TIP
It's important to follow the directions for melting and cooling the dipping chocolate and chilling the macaroons before and after dipping. This will ensure the chocolate sets up glossy and smooth.

chewy coconut wafers

From the variety and number of coconut jumbles, little "cakes," and macaroons in nine-teenth- and early-twentieth-century American cookbooks, I've concluded that coconut was once considerably more popular in cookies than it is today. It may simply be that American tastes have changed. Or perhaps it's because newer, higher-impact flavoring ingredients—like chocolate morsels, peanut butter, and macadamia nuts—have now stolen the cookie-baking show.

In any case, there are still rewards from baking good, plain, coconut drop cookies like these. They're chewy and crisp, with a fine fragrance and flavor. My recipe is roughly based on the "Cocoanut Wafers" in the 1915 *Textbook of Cooking* by Carlotta C. Greer, who headed the Foods and Household Management Department at Cleveland's East Technical High School.

1¹/₃ cups (3³/₄ ounces) shredded or flaked sweetened coconut, plus about ¹/₃ cup, for topping
¹/₄ cup old-fashioned rolled oats
¹/₄ cup all-purpose white flour
¹/₄ teaspoon baking soda
Generous ¹/₈ teaspoon salt

¹/₂ cup plus 1 tablespoon packed light brown sugar
3 tablespoons unsalted butter, melted
1 large egg
1¹/₂ teaspoons vanilla extract
¹/₈ teaspoon coconut extract (optional)

Preheat the oven to 350 degrees F. Line several baking sheets with aluminum foil. Grease the foil or coat with nonstick spray.

Spread 1⅓ cups of the coconut on a rimmed baking sheet and toast in the oven, stirring frequently, for 6 to 9 minutes, or until well browned; be careful not to burn. Immediately turn out into a small bowl and let stand until cooled; set aside.

In a small bowl, thoroughly stir together the oats, flour, baking soda, and salt; set aside. In a medium bowl, whisk together the brown sugar, butter, egg, vanilla, and coconut extract, if using, until the sugar dissolves. Whisk in the oat mixture and toasted coconut until well blended.

Drop the dough onto the baking sheets by generous measuring tea-spoonfuls, spacing about 2½ inches apart. Sprinkle a little of the remaining ⅓ cup untoasted coconut over each cookie.

Bake the cookies, one sheet at at time, in the upper third of the oven for 10 to 12 minutes, or until nicely browned but not burned. Reverse the sheet from front to back halfway through baking to ensure even browning. Slide the cookies, still attached to the foil, onto a wire rack. Let stand until completely cooled. Carefully peel the cookies from the foil. If the cooled cookies stick, they are underbaked. Return to the oven and bake for 3 to 4 minutes more.

Store in an airtight container for up to 4 days or freeze for up to 1 month.

coconut-banana chews

Coconut jumbles and macaroons have been around since at least the seventeenth century, but as far as I can tell, coconut-banana cookies are a new idea. I created these to go with a ginger-orange sorbet. The cookies have a seductive tropical flavor and are pleasantly moist and chewy. Since they are coated with coconut, they look and taste a bit like macaroons, but they're based on a conventional, easy-to-make cookie dough.

These are best eaten fresh. They are especially good with a summer fruit compote or, as I intended, with a tropical fruit sorbet.

2 cups all-purpose white flour
1 teaspoon baking powder
¼ teaspoon salt
1 cup sugar
¾ cup (1½ sticks) unsalted butter, slightly softened
1 large egg yolk
1½ teaspoons vanilla extract

½ teaspoon coconut extract *or* ⅛ teaspoon almond extract
⅛ teaspoon finely grated orange zest (colored part of the skin; optional)
⅓ cup mashed overripe banana (about 1 small)
2½ cups (about 7 ounces) shredded or flaked sweetened coconut (divided)

In a medium bowl, thoroughly stir together the flour, baking powder, and salt; set aside. In a large bowl, with an electric mixer on medium speed, beat together the sugar and butter until very well blended, about 2 minutes. Beat in the egg yolk, vanilla, coconut or almond extract, and orange zest, if using, until evenly incorporated. Beat in half of the flour mixture, then the banana and ½ cup of the coconut, until well blended. Beat or stir in the remaining flour mixture until evenly incorporated. Cover and refrigerate the dough for at least 1 hour and preferably 2 hours, or until firmed up.

Preheat the oven to 325 degrees F. Grease several baking sheets or coat with nonstick spray.

Shape the dough into 1¼-inch balls with lightly greased hands. Spread the remaining 2 cups coconut in a shallow bowl. Roll the balls in the coconut until heavily coated. Place on the baking sheets, spacing about 2½ inches apart.

Bake the cookies, one sheet at a time, in the upper third of the oven for 17 to 22 minutes, or until lightly browned all over and just firm when pressed in the centers. Reverse the sheet from front to back halfway through baking to ensure even browning. Transfer the sheet to a wire rack and let stand until the cookies firm up slightly, 3 to 4 minutes. Using a spatula, transfer the cookies to wire racks. Let stand until completely cooled.

Store in an airtight container for up to 3 days or freeze for up to 1 month.

Best Benne seed wafers

These wafers, roughly based on an old Charleston recipe, are so good that it's hard to eat just one. They're very thin, brittle, and almost candy-like, with a nutty, brown-sugar flavor. (People often think that they contain peanuts as well as sesame seeds.)

The name comes from the fact that sesame seeds are called benne seeds in coastal South Carolina, apparently reflecting the impact of slaves from West Africa. According to African culinary history scholar Jessica Harris, *benne* is the Wolof language word for sesame and likely came by way of Senegal.

Since culinary ideas have a habit of traveling, benne seed cookies occasionally turn up outside South Carolina, particularly in port cities like Wilmington, Savannah, and New Orleans. I've even seen a recipe much farther north in an 1873 Maryland cookbook, *Fifty Years in a Maryland Kitchen.*

³/₄ cup (scant 4 ounces) hulled sesame seeds

³/₄ cup all-purpose white flour

¼ teaspoon baking soda

¼ teaspoon salt

1½ cups packed dark brown sugar

³/₄ cup (1½ sticks) unsalted butter, melted

1 large egg

1½ teaspoons vanilla extract

Preheat the oven to 350 degrees F. Lightly grease several baking sheets or coat with nonstick spray. Line the baking sheets with aluminum foil. Grease the foil or coat with nonstick spray.

Place the sesame seeds in a small baking pan and toast in the oven, stirring frequently, for 6 to 8 minutes, or until lightly browned; be careful not to burn.

Reduce the oven temperature to 325 degrees F.

In a small bowl, thoroughly stir together the sesame seeds, flour, baking soda, and salt; set aside. In a medium bowl, whisk together the brown sugar, butter, egg, and vanilla until the sugar dissolves. Whisk in the sesame-seed mixture until well blended. Let stand for 10 minutes, or until cooled.

Shape portions of the dough into ¾-inch balls with lightly greased hands; the dough will be soft. Place on the baking sheets, spacing about 2¾ inches apart.

Tip

Because the recipe calls for a relatively large quantity of sesame seeds, it's most economical to buy them in bulk. Look in bakery-supply shops or health food stores for hulled seeds. (Unhulled sesame seeds have a dull, brownish appearance.)

Bake the cookies, one sheet at a time, in the upper third of the oven for 10 to 12 minutes, or until nicely browned; be careful not to burn. Reverse the sheet from front to back halfway through baking to ensure even browning. Slide the cookies, still attached to the foil, onto a wire rack and let stand until they firm up slightly, about 5 minutes. Carefully peel the cookies from the foil and transfer to wire racks. Let stand until completely cooled. If the cookies don't become brittle-crisp as they cool, they are underbaked. Return to a foil-lined baking sheet and bake for 3 to 4 minutes more.

Store in an airtight container for up to 10 days or freeze for up to 1 month.

9

Ginger, Spice, and Molasses Cookies

old-fashioned
gingerbread cookies

makes about 70
(2½-to-3-inch) cookies.

This is a deliciously crisp and spicy gingerbread cookie, although the cook's original entry identified it only as "Mrs. Sheifley's Ginger Cookies" and offered no praise. The dough has just the right balance of spices, sugar, and molasses. It also rolls out easily (not always the case with molasses doughs) and can be used for gingerbread people, plain rounds, or assorted cutout cookies.

The recipe is from Laura Henrietta Hensel Weaver's handwritten notebook, now in the Landis Valley Farm Museum collection, near Lancaster, Pennsylvania. Born in 1861, Mrs. Weaver began jotting down brief receipts from about the 1880s onward. Her almost cryptic two-line ginger cookie entry—which worked precisely as written—included only the exact quantities of sugar, butter, molasses, and spices, along with terse instructions to dissolve the baking soda in water, a common technique in her day. As was also fairly typical of the time, the recipe simply called for enough flour to stiffen the dough. (I've furnished the amount needed in the updated version.)

1 cup (2 sticks) unsalted butter, slightly softened

1 cup sugar

1 tablespoon ground ginger

1 tablespoon ground cinnamon

Scant 1½ teaspoons ground cloves

¼ teaspoon salt

2 teaspoons baking soda, dissolved in 2 tablespoons water

1 cup light molasses

5 cups all-purpose white flour (divided), plus more if needed

In a large bowl, with an electric mixer on medium speed, beat together the butter, sugar, ginger, cinnamon, cloves, and salt until smooth and fluffy. Beat in the baking soda mixture and molasses until well blended. Beat in 2 cups of the flour. Beat or vigorously stir in the remaining 3 cups flour. If necessary, add a few tablespoons more flour to make a slightly stiff, but not at all dry, dough. Stir or knead the dough for several minutes, or until very well blended. Let the dough stand at room temperature for 1 hour, or until its stickiness is reduced.

Divide the dough into thirds. Place each portion between large sheets of wax paper. Roll out each portion a scant ¼ inch thick; check the underside of the dough and smooth out any wrinkles that form. Stack the rolled portions (paper still attached) on a baking sheet. Refrigerate for at least 45 minutes or up to 8 hours, or freeze for 20 minutes to speed chilling.

Preheat the oven to 350 degrees F. Grease several baking sheets or coat with nonstick spray.

Working with one portion at a time and leaving the remaining dough chilled, gently peel away, then pat one sheet of wax paper back into place. Flip the dough over, then peel off and discard the second sheet. Using a 2½-inch fluted or plain round cutter or assorted cutters, cut out the cookies. (If at any point the dough softens too much to handle easily, transfer the paper and cookies to a baking sheet and refrigerate or freeze until firm again.) Using a spatula, carefully transfer the cookies to the baking sheets, spacing about 1¼ inches apart. Reroll any dough scraps. Continue cutting out the cookies until all the dough is used.

Bake the cookies, one sheet at a time, in the upper third of the oven for 5 to 7 minutes, or until firm in the centers, lightly colored on top, and just slightly darker at the edges. (For softer cookies, underbake slightly; for very crisp ones, overbake slightly.) Reverse the sheet from front to back halfway through baking to ensure even browning. Transfer the sheet to a wire rack and let stand until the cookies firm up slightly, 1 to 2 minutes. Using a spatula, transfer the cookies to wire racks and let stand until completely cooled.

Store in an airtight container for up to 3 weeks or freeze for up to 2 months.

ginger-spice crinkles

A wonderful blend of spices, orange zest, and just a touch of molasses makes these aromatic cookies special. They have slightly crinkled tops and are reminiscent of gingersnaps, but are a little mellower and are crispy-soft rather than crunchy. Also, the smaller amount of molasses used means this ingredient enhances rather than dominates, allowing the distinctive spice combination to star. The recipe is adapted from one shared by a junior high school friend's mother, Tulsa resident Grace Setterholm.

2 cups all-purpose white flour

1 teaspoon baking powder

½ teaspoon baking soda

¼ teaspoon salt

1½ teaspoons ground ginger

1 teaspoon ground cloves

1 teaspoon ground nutmeg

¾ teaspoon ground cinnamon

½ cup (1 stick) unsalted butter, slightly softened

½ cup white vegetable shortening

¾ cup plus 2 tablespoons packed light brown sugar

2½ tablespoons light or dark molasses

1 large egg

¼ teaspoon finely grated orange zest (colored part of the skin)

¼ cup sugar, for topping

Preheat the oven to 375 degrees F. Grease several baking sheets or coat with nonstick spray.

In a medium bowl, thoroughly stir together the flour, baking powder, baking soda, salt, ginger, cloves, nutmeg, and cinnamon; set aside. In a large bowl, with an electric mixer on medium speed, beat together the butter, shortening, brown sugar, and molasses until well blended and fluffy. Beat in the egg and orange zest until very well blended and smooth. Beat in half of the flour mixture until evenly incorporated. Beat or stir in the remaining flour mixture until evenly incorporated. Let the dough stand for 5 minutes, or until firmed up slightly.

Shape portions of the dough into generous 1-inch balls with lightly greased hands. Put the ¼ cup sugar in a shallow bowl. Roll each ball in the sugar until lightly coated. Place on the baking sheets, spacing about 2½ inches apart. Using your hand, pat down the cookie tops just slightly.

Bake the cookies, one sheet at a time, in the upper third of the oven for 8 to 11 minutes, or until barely firm in the centers and faintly browned at the edges. Reverse the sheet from front to back halfway through baking to ensure even browning. Transfer the sheet to a wire rack and let stand until the cookies firm up slightly, 1 to 2 minutes. Using a spatula, transfer the cookies to wire racks. Let stand until completely cooled.

Store in an airtight container for up to 10 days or freeze for up to 2 months.

moravian MoLasses cookies

Dark, spicy, and whisper-thin, these cookies are a tradition in communities settled by Moravians, members of an early Protestant religious group who began arriving in America from central Europe in the 1700s. This particular recipe is from the vicinity of Old Salem, a charmingly preserved eighteenth-century Moravian historical district that's now part of Winston-Salem, North Carolina. Families bake these brittle-crisp cookies year-round, but particularly at Christmas, perhaps because of their welcoming fragrance.

Old recipes often call for huge quantities of ingredients and yield hundreds of cookies. I've cut down this one to less than half its original size, and—depending on how thin you're able to roll the dough—it still makes around a hundred cookies! I always assumed that the large batches were to accommodate a full day of family baking, but this is not necessarily the reason. Since the dough keeps very well, some households make up a batch, refrigerate it, and bake a few sheets of cookies fresh each day.

2⅓ cups all-purpose white flour, plus more if needed

2 teaspoons ground cinnamon

2 teaspoons ground ginger

1 teaspoon ground cloves

½ teaspoon ground allspice

½ teaspoon salt

⅔ cup light molasses

Generous ½ cup packed light brown sugar

½ cup good-quality lard or white vegetable shortening

¼ teaspoon baking soda, dissolved in 1 tablespoon water

In a medium bowl, thoroughly stir together the flour, cinnamon, ginger, cloves, allspice, and salt; set aside. In a large bowl, with an electric mixer on medium speed, beat together the molasses, brown sugar, and lard or shortening until well blended and smooth. Beat in the baking soda mixture. Beat in half of the flour mixture until evenly incorporated. Gradually stir in the remaining flour mixture until evenly incorporated. Working in the bowl, knead the dough by hand for 30 to 40 seconds; if the dough seems at all soft, sprinkle on 1 to 2 tablespoons more flour and knead it in.

Wrap the dough in heavy-duty plastic wrap or place in an airtight plastic bag. Set aside in a cool place, but not the refrigerator, for at least 1 hour and preferably several; then refrigerate if not using right away. (The dough can be refrigerated for up to 5 days; let warm up slightly and knead briefly before using.)

Preheat the oven to 350 degrees F. Set out several baking sheets.

Divide the dough into thirds. Place one portion on a large sheet of parchment paper. Top with a large sheet of wax paper. Roll out the dough as thinly as possible (no thicker than ⅛ inch). Gently peel off and discard the wax paper. Slide the parchment onto a baking sheet. Using 2¼-to-2½-inch assorted cutters or a fluted or plain round cutter, cut out the cookies, leaving about ½ inch between them. Pull away the dough scraps from around the cookies; if the dough seems too soft to handle, transfer the sheet to the freezer or refrigerator and chill the dough briefly. Reroll any dough scraps. Continue cutting out the cookies until all the dough is used. Repeat with the remaining dough portions.

Bake the cookies, one sheet at a time, in the middle of the oven for 5 to 9 minutes, or until just barely firm when pressed in the centers and just beginning to darken at the edges; be careful not to overbake. Reverse the sheet from front to back halfway through baking to ensure even browning. Transfer the sheet to a wire rack and let stand until the cookies firm up slightly, 1 to 2 minutes. Using a thin-bladed spatula, transfer the cookies to wire racks. Let stand until completely cooled.

Store in an airtight container for up to 1 month or freeze for up to 2 months.

TIP

The dough becomes much more manageable and easier to roll if allowed to rest for an hour or so at room temperature. However, since it still takes a lot of practice to roll the cookies really thin and transfer them to the baking sheets, I call for rolling out the dough on parchment paper.

Joe Froggers

Joe Froggers are crisp, large molasses-and-rum-flavored cookies said to have originated in Marblehead, Massachusetts. The present-day cookies may have derived from early molasses cookies in that area, but nobody really knows. The big, attractive, thinnish rounds have a unique fragrance and flavor due to the combination of spices and rum. (Water can be substituted for the rum, if you wish.)

3¼ cups all-purpose white flour, plus more if needed
2 teaspoons ground ginger
¾ teaspoon ground cloves
¾ teaspoon ground nutmeg
½ teaspoon ground allspice
1 teaspoon baking soda
Generous ¼ teaspoon salt

1 cup light or dark molasses
3 tablespoons light or dark rum
¾ cup plus 2 tablespoons white vegetable shortening
¾ cup packed light brown sugar

About ¼ cup sugar, for topping

In a large bowl, thoroughly stir together the flour, ginger, cloves, nutmeg, allspice, baking soda, and salt; set aside. In another large bowl, with an electric mixer on medium speed, beat together the molasses, rum, shortening, and brown sugar until very well blended and smooth, about 2 minutes. Beat in half of the flour mixture until evenly incorporated. Vigorously stir or beat in the remaining flour mixture until evenly incorporated. If necessary, add 1 to 2 tablespoons more flour to make a slightly stiff, but not at all dry, dough.

Divide the dough into thirds. Place each portion between large sheets of wax paper. Roll out each portion a scant ¼ inch thick; check the underside of the dough and smooth out any wrinkles that form. Stack the rolled portions (paper still attached) on a baking sheet. Refrigerate for 1½ hours or up to 8 hours, or freeze for 45 minutes to speed chilling.

Preheat the oven to 350 degrees F. Grease several baking sheets or coat with nonstick spray.

Working with one portion at a time and leaving the remaining dough chilled, gently peel away, then pat one sheet of wax paper back into place. Flip the dough over, then peel off and discard the second sheet. Using a 3-to-3¼-inch fluted or plain round cutter, cut out the cookies. (If at any point the dough softens too much to handle easily, transfer the paper and cookies to a baking sheet and refrigerate or freeze until firm again.) Using a spatula, carefully transfer the cookies to the baking sheets, spacing about 1½ inches apart. Very generously sprinkle the cookies with sugar. Reroll any dough scraps. Continue cutting out the cookies until all the dough is used.

Bake the cookies, one sheet at a time, in the upper third of the oven for 9 to 12 minutes, or until almost firm in the centers and just barely darker at the edges. (For crunchy-crisp cookies, overbake slightly; for less crisp cookies, underbake slightly.) Reverse the sheet from front to back halfway through baking to ensure even browning. Transfer the sheet to a wire rack and let stand until the cookies firm up slightly, 1 to 2 minutes. Using a spatula, transfer the cookies to wire racks. Let stand until completely cooled.

Store in an airtight container for up to 3 weeks or freeze for up to 2 months.

"smother, duff, and jo-floggers"

How did Joe Froggers get their name? The story I've heard most often is that the cookies were named for a man called Uncle Joe, who lived by a frog pond and made molasses cookies as large as lily pads. A slightly different explanation is that Uncle Joe was a local cookie baker, whose molasses cookies fishermen often paid for with rum and carried on their voyages. A third story is that the cookies were created by a black tavern proprietor called Black Joe. Many of his customers were fishermen and sailors who took his cookies along to sea.

Sandra Oliver, a New England culinary historian and the editor of *Food History News*, says that these explanations are all more fiction than fact, though the details she's uncovered are equally colorful. Uncle Joe, or Black Joe, may have existed around the Revolutionary War, but his name was Joe Flogger, not Frogger. He may have been black, or possibly Native American. Although he didn't cook or bake, his wife did, perhaps professionally. Perhaps most important, Oliver, the author of a fine book on coastal New England culinary traditions called *Saltwater Foodways*, has also verified that at one time coastal New England fishermen ate something—but not cookies—called jo floggers. Her book cites an 1853 eastern maritime industry report that mentioned "smother, duff, and jo-floggers," and described them as "Potpie of seabird, pudding, and pancakes—the fisherman's three Ps."

So there you have it: A few facts along with examples of what can happen when bits of truth are embellished and scrambled by active imaginations or failing memories over a long stretch of time!

Pennsylvania Dutch Molasses softies

These thick, chewy sweets were among the most popular Pennsylvania Dutch cookies and are still a favorite of traditional home cooks. Big, unabashedly homespun, and boldly flavored, they taste similar to the best-known Pennsylvania Dutch dessert, shoofly pie. In fact, as is true of some shoofly pie recipes, these cookies contain no spices, so molasses and brown sugar come through clearly.

Locally, these are usually called "cakes," because of their large size and slightly cake-like (though still moist and chewy) texture. Before baking, they are often brushed with an egg-yolk wash, which gives them a slightly shiny look.

3²/₃ cups all-purpose white flour

½ teaspoon salt

¾ cup (1½ sticks) unsalted butter, slightly softened

½ cup white vegetable shortening or good-quality lard

1¹/₃ cups packed light brown sugar

1 cup light or dark molasses

½ teaspoon finely grated orange zest (colored part of the skin; optional)

1 cup sour cream

2 teaspoons baking soda

2 large egg yolks, thoroughly beaten with 2 teaspoons water

In a large bowl, thoroughly stir together the flour and salt; set aside. In another large bowl, with an electric mixer on medium speed, beat together the butter, shortening, and brown sugar until light and fluffy. Beat the molasses and orange zest, if using, into the butter mixture until evenly incorporated. In a small bowl, stir together the sour cream and baking soda until well blended. Beat the sour-cream mixture into the molasses mixture. Gradually beat in the flour mixture until smooth and well blended. Cover and refrigerate the dough until firm enough to handle, at least 4 hours or up to overnight.

Preheat the oven to 375 degrees F. Grease several baking sheets or coat with nonstick spray.

Divide the dough in half. Working with one portion at a time and leaving the remaining dough chilled, shape portions of the mixture into generous golf-ball-sized balls with lightly greased hands. Place on the baking sheets, spacing about 3½ inches apart. Using your hand, press down the balls until about ½ inch thick. Evenly brush the cookies with the egg-yolk mixture; try not to drip, as the egg will burn on the baking sheet.

Bake the cookies, one sheet at a time, in the middle of the oven for 7 to 10 minutes, or until browned on top and just beginning to firm up when tapped in the centers; be careful not to overbake. Reverse the sheet from front to back halfway through baking to ensure even browning. Transfer the sheet to a wire rack and let stand until the cookies firm up slightly, 3 to 4 minutes. Using a spatula, carefully transfer the cookies to wire racks. Let stand until completely cooled.

Store in an airtight container for up to 1 week or freeze for up to 1½ months.

molasses applesaucers

Applesauce cookies turn up frequently in twentieth-century American cookbooks, and I tested a number before devising this one. Most of the recipes sounded appealing, but the resulting cookies just didn't measure up. Then I noticed molasses-applesauce cookies in several Midwestern community cookbooks and decided to see if the combination worked better than applesauce alone. It does!

In fact, the pairing of molasses and applesauce is wonderful in cookies—mellow, fruity, and spicy all at the same time. Together, these ingredients lend a succulence and old-fashioned flavor that make these cookies hard to resist. They are big, plump, and soft. I designed them to be mixed by hand in a large saucepan, so they are also easy to make.

3¾ cups all-purpose white flour

2¾ teaspoons ground cinnamon

1 teaspoon baking soda

Generous ½ teaspoon salt

1½ cups sweetened applesauce

1½ cups (7½ ounces) raisins

1½ teaspoons finely grated lemon zest (colored part of the skin)

1 cup (2 sticks) cold unsalted butter, cut into chunks

1½ cups packed light brown sugar

¾ cup plus 2 tablespoons light molasses

1 large egg, plus 1 large egg yolk

2 teaspoons vanilla extract

3 tablespoons sugar, for shaping

In a medium bowl, thoroughly stir together the flour, cinnamon, baking soda, and salt; set aside.

In a large saucepan, stir together the applesauce, raisins, and lemon zest. Bring to a simmer over medium-high heat. Cook, stirring frequently, until the applesauce is very thick and the raisins are rehydrated, about 10 minutes; be careful not to burn. Let stand until cooled slightly. Stir in the butter, brown sugar, and molasses until the butter melts and the ingredients are well blended. Stir in the egg and egg yolk and vanilla until evenly incorporated. Stir in the flour mixture until evenly incorporated. Cover and refrigerate the dough until firm enough to handle, at least 2 hours or up to 24 hours.

ginger, spice, and molasses cookies

Preheat the oven to 350 degrees F. Grease several baking sheets or coat with nonstick spray.

Shape scant ¼-cup portions of dough into balls with lightly greased hands. Place on the baking sheets, spacing about 3 inches apart. Spread the 3 tablespoons sugar in a shallow bowl. Grease the bottom of a large, flat-bottomed drinking glass. Dipping the bottom of the glass into the sugar before each cookie, press down until the rounds are about 2½ inches in diameter. (If necessary, wipe the bottom of the glass, regrease, and continue.)

Bake the cookies, one sheet at a time, in the upper third of the oven for 11 to 14 minutes, or until slightly darker at the edges and just barely firm in the centers. Reverse the sheet from front to back halfway through baking to ensure even browning. Transfer the sheet to a wire rack and let stand until the cookies firm up slightly, 2 to 3 minutes. Using a spatula, transfer the cookies to wire racks. Let stand until completely cooled.

Store in an airtight container for up to 1 week or freeze for up to 2 months.

words of kitchen wisdom

"Many test their ovens in this way: if the hand can be held in [the oven] from twenty to thirty-five seconds (while counting twenty or thirty-five), it is a 'quick' oven, from thirty-five to forty-five seconds is 'moderate,' and from forty-five to sixty seconds is 'slow.'"

– Estelle Woods Wilcox (ed.), *Buckeye Cookery and Practical Housekeeping*, 1880

Farmers' Favorite Molasses Cookies

I'm grateful to Ardyce Habeger Samp of Flandreau, South Dakota, for sharing this attractive, lightly spiced molasses cookie with me. Mrs. Samp is a former newspaper food columnist, the author of several books of reminiscences of rural midwestern life, and a well-known local historian and South Dakota civic leader.

Mrs. Samp says that at one time, almost everybody in her part of the country baked molasses cookies, often with molasses purchased from a traveling medicinals and grocery distributor known as "the Watkins man." Now, she laments, many households just settle for store-bought cookies.

This particular recipe was a favorite of Mrs. Samp's late husband and was originally baked by his mother. She adds that one of her own early batches wasn't met with the hoped-for enthusiasm: "I sent some of these to my husband during the war when he was on a ship in the South Pacific. It took three weeks for the mail to arrive. When he opened the box, they did not look like the ones his mother used to make."

Assuming that these don't go on a long journey to the South Pacific, they should get an excellent reception. They are evenly shaped and, before being iced, look like gingersnaps, though they're milder, sweeter, and a little fancier, and have a pleasing chewy, rather than crunchy, texture.

2 cups all-purpose white flour
1 teaspoon baking soda
½ teaspoon salt
1 teaspoon ground cinnamon
1 teaspoon ground ginger
½ teaspoon ground cloves
¾ cup plus 2 tablespoons sugar
½ cup white vegetable shortening
¼ cup (½ stick) unsalted butter, slightly softened

¼ cup light or dark molasses
1 large egg

ICING (OPTIONAL)

2 cups powdered sugar, sifted after measuring, if lumpy, plus more if needed
1 tablespoon unsalted butter, melted
Scant 2½ tablespoons light cream or milk, plus more if needed
1 teaspoon vanilla extract

In a medium bowl, thoroughly stir together the flour, baking soda, salt, cinnamon, ginger, and cloves; set aside. In a large bowl, with an electric mixer on medium speed, beat together the sugar, shortening, butter, and molasses until well blended and fluffy. Beat in the egg until very well blended and smooth. Beat in half of the flour mixture until evenly incorporated. Beat or stir in the remaining flour mixture until evenly incorporated. Cover and refrigerate the dough for at least 1½ hours or up to overnight.

Preheat the oven to 350 degrees F. Grease several baking sheets or coat with nonstick spray.

Shape portions of the dough into 1-inch balls with lightly greased hands. Place on the baking sheets, spacing about 2½ inches apart. Using your hand, pat down the cookie tops just slightly.

Bake the cookies, one sheet at a time, in the upper third of the oven for 10 to 14 minutes, or until barely firm in the centers and faintly browned at the edges. Reverse the sheet from front to back halfway through baking to ensure even browning. Transfer the sheet to a wire rack and let stand until the cookies firm up slightly, 1 to 2 minutes. Using a spatula, transfer the cookies to wire racks. Let stand until completely cooled.

FOR THE ICING, IF USING
In a medium bowl, stir together the powdered sugar, butter, cream or milk, and vanilla until very well blended and smooth. If the icing is too thick to spread, thin it with a bit more cream or milk; if too thin, stir in a bit more powdered sugar.

Using a table knife, spread a small amount of icing over the center of each cookie.

Store in an airtight container for up to 10 days or freeze for up to 2 months.

TIP
Mrs. Samp considers the icing optional, but I think it's a nice touch. If you omit the icing, dress up the cookies by rolling the balls of dough in sugar before baking.

ginger, spice, and molasses cookies

old-Fashioned Glazed Molasses cookies

Not too spicy or heavy on the molasses, but not namby-pamby either, these were inspired by a favorite cookie from childhood. A small country grocery store that my family patronized used to sell cookies similar to these—though, frankly, they weren't as tasty. What really impressed me about them was the baked-on royal icing, which had a porcelain-like sheen and a slight crunchiness.

Here, I've recreated the royal-icing glaze and improved the cookies. The result is a winning combination of crispy-chewy texture, handsome appearance, and fine flavor. They are still among my favorite cookies.

3 cups all-purpose white flour, plus more if needed

1 teaspoon baking soda

½ teaspoon ground cinnamon

½ teaspoon ground ginger

Scant ½ teaspoon salt

½ cup (1 stick) unsalted butter, slightly softened

½ cup white vegetable shortening

⅔ cup packed light brown sugar

1 large egg yolk (reserve the white for the glaze)

½ cup light or dark molasses

GLAZE

1 cup powdered sugar

1 large egg white

1 tablespoon fresh lemon juice

In a medium bowl, thoroughly stir together the 3 cups flour, baking soda, cinnamon, ginger, and salt; set aside. In a large bowl, with an electric mixer on medium speed, beat together the butter, shortening, and brown sugar until light and well blended. Beat in the egg yolk until evenly incorporated and fluffy. Beat in the molasses. Stir or beat in the flour mixture until evenly incorporated. If the dough seems very soft, stir in up to 3 tablespoons more flour.

Divide the dough in half. Place each portion between large sheets of wax paper. Roll out each portion ¼ inch thick; check the underside of the dough and smooth out any wrinkles that form. Stack the rolled portions (paper still attached) on a baking sheet. Refrigerate for 1½ hours, or until chilled and firm, or freeze for 45 minutes to speed chilling. (The dough may be held for up to 8 hours.)

Preheat the oven to 325 degrees F. Grease several baking sheets or coat with nonstick spray.

In a medium bowl, with an electric mixer on low speed (use a whisk-shaped beater, if available), beat the powdered sugar and egg white until blended. Increase the speed to high and beat until glossy and stiffened. Beat in the lemon juice. If necessary, thin the mixture with water to produce a smooth, spreadable glaze. Cover the bowl with a damp kitchen towel to keep the glaze from drying out; set aside.

Working with one portion at a time and leaving the remaining dough chilled, gently peel away, then pat one sheet of wax paper back into place. Flip the dough over, then peel off and discard the second sheet. Using a 2½-to-3-inch round or fluted cutter, cut out enough cookies to fill one baking sheet. (If at any point the dough softens too much to handle easily, transfer the paper and cookies to a baking sheet and refrigerate or freeze until firm again.) Using a spatula, carefully transfer the cookies to a baking sheet, spacing about 2 inches apart.

Check the consistency of the glaze and thin it with a few drops of water, if necessary. Using a table knife, spread a smooth, even layer of glaze over the top of each cookie all the way to the edges. Bake the cookies as soon as all on the sheet are glazed. Reroll any dough scraps. Continue cutting out and glazing the cookies until all the dough is used.

Bake the cookies, one sheet at a time, in the middle of the oven for 11 to 13 minutes, or until the glaze is just tinged with brown. Reverse the sheet from front to back halfway through baking to ensure even browning. Transfer the sheet to a wire rack and let stand until the cookies firm up slightly, 1 to 2 minutes. Using a spatula, transfer the cookies to wire racks and let stand until completely cooled.

Store in a single layer or layered with wax paper in an airtight container for up to 2 weeks or freeze for up to 1 month.

ozarksorghum (or molasses) crisps

Ozark cooks have long, hard-earned experience in preparing tasty food with meager larders. So I probably shouldn't have been surprised that these seemingly plain, unprepossessing cookies turned out to be so good. At first glance, the recipe didn't look promising—no butter, chocolate chips, spices, citrus, vanilla, or nuts. The key ingredients were lard, brown sugar, sorghum, and apple cider vinegar—typical hardscrabble Ozark Mountain staples, but not the stuff dreams are usually made of.

Tasting the cookies and closely examining the recipe quickly changed my mind. Here was a great example of just how much can be achieved with little. Lard (good, fresh lard, that is) lends these cookies a lovely crisp texture with no greasy taste. (Use white vegetable shortening if good lard is unavailable.)

Sorghum, a popular regional syrup made from the pressed stems of sorghum grass, adds sweetness, plus a slightly toasty taste reminiscent of very mild molasses. The vinegar serves the same purpose lemon juice would in a more amply stocked kitchen; it contributes zip, as well as the acid needed to activate the baking soda and make the cookies rise.

3 cups all-purpose white flour, plus more if needed	1 cup packed light brown sugar
1 teaspoon baking soda	1 large egg
¾ teaspoon salt	1 tablespoon apple cider vinegar
1 cup good-quality lard or white vegetable shortening	½ cup sorghum or light molasses

In a medium bowl, thoroughly stir together the flour, baking soda, and salt; set aside. In a large bowl, with an electric mixer on medium speed, beat together the lard or shortening and brown sugar until light and well blended. Beat in the egg and vinegar until evenly incorporated and fluffy. Beat in the sorghum or molasses. Stir or beat in the 3 cups flour mixture until evenly incorporated. If the dough seems too soft to handle, stir in up to 4 tablespoons more flour. Let stand for about 10 minutes, or until firmed up slightly.

Divide the dough in half. Place each portion between large sheets of wax paper. Roll out each portion a scant ¼ inch thick; check the underside of the dough and smooth out any wrinkles that form. Stack the rolled portions (paper still attached) on a baking sheet. Refrigerate the dough for

Tips
• Sorghum is often sold in health food stores, particularly in the autumn. However, molasses labeled as "light" may be substituted with excellent results.

• Obtaining good-quality lard is problematic in areas of the country where it isn't widely used. It should be nearly odorless and completely free of rancid or animal tastes. If in doubt, use vegetable shortening.

at least 3 hours or up to 24 hours, or freeze for 1½ hours to speed chilling.

Preheat the oven to 375 degrees F. Grease several baking sheets or coat with nonstick spray.

Working with one portion at a time and leaving the remaining dough chilled, gently peel away, then pat one sheet of wax paper back into place. Flip the dough over, then peel off and discard the second sheet. Using a 2½-to-3-inch round cutter or assorted cutters, cut out enough cookies to fill one baking sheet. (If at any point the dough softens too much to handle easily, transfer the paper and cookies to a baking sheet and refrigerate or freeze until firm again.) Using a spatula, carefully transfer the cookies to a baking sheet, spacing about 2 inches apart. (Bake the cookies while still cold, as they will spread too much if allowed to warm.) Reroll any dough scraps. Continue cutting out the cookies until all the dough is used.

Bake the cookies, one sheet at a time, in the upper third of the oven for 5 to 9 minutes, or until faintly tinged with brown, slightly darker at the edges, and almost firm when pressed in the centers. Reverse the sheet from front to back halfway through baking to ensure even browning. Transfer the sheet to a wire rack and let stand until the cookies firm up slightly, 1 to 2 minutes. Using a spatula, transfer the cookies to wire racks. Let stand until completely cooled.

Store in an airtight container for up to 2 weeks or freeze for up to 2 months.

Granny's spice Thins

Makes 100 to 120
(2½-to-3-inch)
cookies.

I got this superb old spice cookie recipe from Marie Kahn of Wilmington, North Carolina. The original, straightforwardly titled "Granny's Brown Cakes," has been handed down through Marie's family for at least four generations and probably more. Whatever her era, this recipe's creator had a brilliant sense of spices. Her blending of cinnamon, cloves, allspice, and cardamom, heightened with lemon zest, provides a beautiful balance of fragrance, sweetness, and intriguing flavor. The cookies, which should be rolled out very thin, also have an appealing brittleness.

My guess is that the recipe probably originated in the mid- to late 1800s. The fact that it contains baking soda, which was not widely known or available before the 1820s, suggests the cookie was devised after that. The name "brown cakes" is also significant; cookies were often referred to as cakes in the nineteenth century.

I've fleshed out and updated the cook's skimpy measuring, mixing, and baking instructions and cut the recipe down to about a quarter of the original. It was obviously scaled for a full day of baking and yielded about 500 "cakes."

2½ cups all-purpose white flour

2½ teaspoons ground cinnamon

1¼ teaspoons ground cloves

1½ teaspoons ground allspice

1 teaspoon ground cardamom

¾ teaspoon baking soda

¼ teaspoon salt

¼ cup (½ stick) unsalted butter, slightly softened

¼ cup white vegetable shortening

¾ cup dark corn syrup

¾ cup sugar

¾ teaspoon finely grated lemon zest (colored part of the skin)

In a medium bowl, thoroughly stir together the flour, cinnamon, cloves, allspice, cardamom, baking soda, and salt; set aside. In a large bowl, with an electric mixer on medium speed, beat together the butter, shortening, corn syrup, sugar, and lemon zest until lightened and smooth. Beat in about half of the flour mixture. Stir in the remaining flour mixture until evenly incorporated; the dough will be fairly stiff.

Divide the dough into thirds. Place each portion between large sheets of wax paper. Roll out each portion a scant ⅛ inch thick; check the underside of the dough and smooth out any wrinkles that form. Stack the rolled portions (paper still attached) on a baking sheet. Refrigerate the dough for 30 minutes, or until chilled and slightly firm but not stiff, or freeze for 15 minutes to speed chilling.

Tip

Don't try to substitute margarine for the butter, as the recipe will not work. The dough will not firm up enough during chilling to readily transfer to baking sheets.

Preheat the oven to 325 degrees F. Grease several baking sheets or coat with nonstick spray.

Working on the chilled baking sheet and with one portion at a time (leave the remaining dough chilled), gently peel away, then pat one sheet of wax paper back into place. Flip the dough over, then peel off the second sheet. Using assorted 2-to-3-inch cutters, cut out the cookies. (If at any point the dough softens too much to handle easily, transfer the baking sheet with the paper and cookies to the refrigerator or freezer until firm again.) Using a spatula, carefully transfer the cookies to the baking sheets, spacing about 1 inch apart. Reroll any dough scraps. Continue cutting out the cookies until all the dough is used.

Bake the cookies, one sheet at a time, in the center of the oven for 5 to 8 minutes, or until just slightly darker around the edges (the longer the baking time, the more brittle-crisp the cookies). Reverse the sheet from front to back halfway through baking to ensure even browning. Transfer the sheet to a wire rack and let stand until the cookies firm up slightly, 1 to 2 minutes. Using a spatula, transfer the cookies to wire racks. Let stand until completely cooled.

Store in an airtight container for up to 3 weeks or freeze for up to 2 months.

nutmeggins

Years ago, the mother of one of my son's nursery school playmates shared this recipe with me. She was originally from Arkansas and said that the cookies had been a family favorite for several generations. Recently, I found a similar recipe called "Tea Cakes" in *What to Cook and How to Cook It,* an 1899 cookbook compiled by a Kentucky woman named Mrs. W. A. Johnson, indicating that the cookie has been popular in the region for a very long time.

Essentially, these are simple, rolled spice cookies, but the combination of buttermilk and nutmeg gives them a distinctive flavor and texture. Since the cookies are formed by cutting the rolled-out dough into rectangles with a knife, preparation goes quickly. The technique yields oblong cookies with a homespun look.

3½ cups all-purpose white flour

1½ teaspoons freshly grated nutmeg
    or 1¼ teaspoons ground nutmeg

1 teaspoon baking powder

½ teaspoon baking soda
    Generous ¼ teaspoon salt

1½ cups sugar

½ cup (1 stick) cold unsalted butter, cut into chunks

½ cup white vegetable shortening

1 large egg

½ cup buttermilk, plus a little more for topping

2½ teaspoons vanilla extract

3½ tablespoons sugar, combined with 1 teaspoon freshly grated nutmeg or ¾ teaspoon ground nutmeg, for topping

In a medium bowl, thoroughly stir together the flour, nutmeg, baking powder, baking soda, and salt; set aside. In a large bowl, with an electric mixer on medium speed, beat together the sugar, butter, shortening, and egg until very fluffy and well blended. Gradually beat in the buttermilk and vanilla until evenly incorporated. Beat or stir in the flour mixture until well blended and smooth; the dough will be slightly soft. Let stand for 5 to 10 minutes, or until firmed up slightly.

Divide the dough into thirds. Place each portion between large sheets of wax paper. Roll out each portion into a ¼-inch-thick rectangle; check the underside of the dough and smooth out any wrinkles that form. Stack the rolled portions (paper still attached) on a baking sheet. Refrigerate the dough for 30 to 40 minutes, or until chilled and firm, or freeze for 5 minutes to speed chilling.

Preheat the oven to 375 degrees F. Grease several baking sheets or coat with nonstick spray.

Tip

If possible, use freshly grated nutmeg for best flavor. Note that preground nutmeg is more compact due to settling, so the recipe calls for a little less of it.

Working with one portion at a time and leaving the remaining dough chilled, gently peel away, then pat one sheet of wax paper back into place. Flip the dough over, then peel off and discard the second sheet. Using a sharp paring knife, cut the dough into 1¼-by-2½-inch rectangles. (If at any point the dough softens too much to handle easily, transfer the paper and cookies to a baking sheet and refrigerate or freeze until firm again.) Using a spatula, carefully transfer the cookies to the baking sheets, spacing about 1¼ inches apart. Reroll any dough scraps. Continue cutting the cookies until all the dough is used. Using a pastry brush or a paper towel, brush the cookie tops evenly with buttermilk. Sprinkle some of the nutmeg-sugar mixture over them.

Bake the cookies, one sheet at a time, in the upper third of the oven for 6 to 9 minutes, or until browned at the edges. Reverse the sheet from front to back halfway through baking to ensure even browning. Using a spatula, immediately transfer the cookies to wire racks. Let stand until completely cooled.

Store in an airtight container for up to 2 weeks or freeze for up to 2 months.

sour cream Hermits

My usual preference is for crisp cookies, but these soft, fragrant Sour Cream Hermits are one of my favorites. They are the kind of cookies I picture grandmothers making, even though neither of mine actually did. Besides being good, these are very easy to make.

Hermit recipes invariably contain spices and dried fruit, usually raisins. Many hermits also call for molasses, or perhaps honey, and still others include a quantity of milk, buttermilk, or sour cream. (The latter are sometimes referred to as "soft hermits," because of their moist, slightly cake-like texture.)

My recipe is roughly based on one contributed by a Mrs. Allen to a 1912 Warren, Pennsylvania, Presbyterian fund-raiser cookbook.

1¼ cups (6¼ ounces) coarsely chopped raisins	2 cups packed light or dark brown sugar
2¾ cups all-purpose white flour	1 cup (2 sticks) unsalted butter, slightly softened
1¼ teaspoons ground cinnamon	2 large eggs
1 teaspoon ground nutmeg	2 teaspoons vanilla extract
1 teaspoon baking soda	¾ cup sour cream
Generous ¼ teaspoon salt	1 cup (4 ounces) chopped walnuts or pecans (optional)
⅛ teaspoon ground cloves	

Preheat the oven to 350 degrees F. Grease several baking sheets or coat with nonstick spray.

In a small bowl, combine the raisins and enough hot water to cover; set aside. In a medium bowl, thoroughly stir together the flour, cinnamon, nutmeg, baking soda, salt, and cloves; set aside. In a large bowl, with an electric mixer on medium speed, beat together the brown sugar and butter until very well blended. Beat in the eggs and vanilla until fluffy and evenly incorporated. Beat in the sour cream until evenly incorporated. Reduce the speed to medium and beat in the flour mixture just until evenly incorporated. Thoroughly drain the raisins. Stir the raisins and walnuts or pecans into the dough.

Drop the dough onto the baking sheets in golf-ball-sized mounds, spacing about 2½ inches apart.

Bake the cookies, one sheet at a time, in the middle of the oven for 8 to 11 minutes, or until tinged with brown and barely firm to the touch. Reverse the sheet from front to back halfway through baking to ensure even browning. Transfer the sheet to a wire rack and let stand until the cookies firm up slightly, 1 to 2 minutes. Using a spatula, transfer the cookies to wire racks. Let stand until completely cooled.

Store in a single layer or layered with wax paper in an airtight container for up to 1 week or freeze for up to 1 month.

The Popular Hermit

Hermits had their heyday in the late nineteenth and early twentieth centuries, when just about every cookbook or recipe file contained at least one such recipe, and usually several. Some hermits were rolled thick and some thin; others were dropped or hand-shaped; still others were baked in a pan and cut into bars. Since old recipes and cookbooks almost never include introductory notes, I've not found any solid information on where the name came from. One charming explanation suggested in Sharon Tyler Herbst's *Food Lover's Companion* has to do with hermits' keeping qualities: they are better after being hidden away for a day or so.

MOM'SLebkuchen

My husband's mother, Miriam Baggett, has been making these spicy molasses drop cookies for him every Christmas as long as he can remember, and they are a family favorite. Fragrant and full-bodied, with dabs of royal icing on top, they look like little snowcapped mountains.

The recipe has been in my mother-in-law's family for at least four generations and, as the name suggests, was brought to the United States from Germany. However, family cooks have gradually adapted the recipe to take advantage of American ingredients and to suit changing tastes, and today it is rather different from the lebkuchen Germans make. As is true of many Americanized lebkuchen recipes, this one substitutes molasses and brown sugar for the original honey and granulated sugar. And it calls for pecans and bourbon, North American products that are still little known in Germany.

1²/₃ cups (about 8 ounces) chopped pitted dates

1 cup (about 5½ ounces) diced candied pineapple

1 cup (about 6 ounces) chopped mixed red and green candied cherries

³/₄ cup (about 4 ounces) mixed diced candied fruit

1 cup (4 ounces) chopped pecans

1 cup (4 ounces) chopped walnuts

½ cup (about 2 ounces) chopped slivered almonds

⅓ cup good-quality brandy, plus more if needed

¼ cup good-quality bourbon

3 cups all-purpose white flour, plus more if needed

1½ teaspoons ground cinnamon

1½ teaspoons ground ginger

1½ teaspoons ground allspice

1½ teaspoons ground cloves

½ teaspoon baking soda

½ teaspoon baking powder

1 cup light molasses

¼ cup corn oil or other flavorless vegetable oil

²/₃ cup packed light brown sugar

2 large eggs, plus 1 large egg yolk (reserve the white for the icing)

ICING

1 large egg white

1 tablespoon fresh lemon juice

½ teaspoon cream of tartar

1³/₄ cups powdered sugar, sifted after measuring, if lumpy (divided)

¼ teaspoon lemon extract

In a large, nonreactive bowl, thoroughly stir together the dates, pineapple, cherries, mixed fruit, nuts, brandy, and bourbon. Cover and let stand for at least 8 hours or up to several days, stirring several times; if the mixture absorbs all the liquid, stir in several tablespoons water (or additional brandy, if preferred).

Preheat the oven to 350 degrees F. Grease several large baking sheets or coat with nonstick spray.

In a medium bowl, thoroughly stir together the flour, cinnamon, ginger, allspice, cloves, baking soda, and baking powder; set aside. In a large bowl, with an electric mixer on medium speed, beat together the molasses, oil, and brown sugar until well blended. Beat in the eggs and egg yolk until well blended; it is all right if the mixture looks curdled. Stir in the flour mixture and fruit mixture until evenly incorporated. If the dough is too soft to drop by spoonfuls, stir in up to 3 tablespoons more flour.

Drop the dough onto the baking sheets by generous measuring tablespoonfuls, spacing about 1½ inches apart.

Bake the cookies, one sheet at a time, in the upper third of the oven for 11 to 15 minutes, or until just firm when pressed in the centers and slightly darker at the edges. Reverse the sheet from front to back halfway through baking to ensure even browning. Transfer the sheet to a wire rack and let stand until the cookies firm up slightly, 1 to 2 minutes. Using a spatula, transfer the cookies to wire racks. Let stand until completely cooled.

FOR THE ICING

In a large bowl, with an electric mixer on medium speed (use a whisk-shaped beater, if available), beat together the egg white, lemon juice, and cream of tartar until frothy and opaque. Gradually beat in 1 cup of the powdered sugar. Beat in 1 tablespoon water and the lemon extract. Gradually beat in the remaining ¾ cup powdered sugar. Beat on high speed until the icing is stiff and glossy. If the icing is too stiff to spread, thin with additional water until spreadable.

Using a table knife, swirl a small amount of icing over the top of each cookie. Let stand for several hours, or until the icing completely sets. For best flavor, let the cookies mellow for 24 hours before serving.

Store in a single layer or layered with wax paper in an airtight container for up to 3 weeks (the white icing begins to discolor after a week or so) or freeze for up to 2 months. If freezing, leave the cookies uniced, then ice after they thaw.

words of kitchen wisdom
"It is best to begin by weighing out the ingredients, sifting the flour, pounding and sifting the sugar and spice, washing the butter, and preparing the fruit."

– A Lady of Philadelphia (Eliza Leslie), *Seventy-Five Receipts for Pastry, Cakes and Sweetmeats*, 1828

10

Cookie Decorating and Crafts

ALL-PurPose
sugar cookie
dough

This basic sugar cookie dough is easy to roll out and handle, making it a good choice for cookie projects, such as Painted Cookie Jigsaw Puzzles (page 343), Cookie Pizzas with the Works (page 349), and Stained Glass and Light Catcher Cookies (page 357). The finished cookies are fairly sturdy and not overly sweet, so they are perfect for decorating with Royal Icing (page 370), Easy Powdered-Sugar Icing (page 373), or Chocolate Luster Glaze (page 374). The dough has a mild flavor (which you can adjust to suit your own taste by adding lemon or almond extract, if desired), and the cookies are pleasantly crisp.

The following directions are for making the dough and preparing traditional cut-out cookies. Turn to individual recipes for instructions on how to handle the dough once it is mixed.

3 cups all-purpose white flour, plus more if needed

¾ teaspoon baking powder

½ teaspoon salt

1 cup (2 sticks) unsalted butter, *or* ½ cup unsalted butter and ½ cup regular stick margarine, slightly softened

Scant 1 cup sugar

1 large egg

1 tablespoon milk

2½ teaspoons vanilla extract

¼ teaspoon lemon or almond extract (optional)

Assorted jimmies, colored sugar, or sprinkles, for topping (optional)

In a large bowl, thoroughly stir together the flour, baking powder, and salt; set aside. In a large bowl, with an electric mixer on medium speed, beat together the butter or butter and margarine and sugar until very light and fluffy. Beat in the egg, milk, vanilla, and lemon or almond extract, if using, until very well blended and smooth. Gradually beat or stir in the flour mixture to form a smooth, slightly stiff dough. If it seems soft, stir in up to 3 tablespoons more flour. Let the dough stand for about 5 minutes, or until firmed up slightly.

Divide the dough in half. Place each portion between large sheets of wax paper. Roll out the portions a scant ¼ inch thick; check the underside of the dough and smooth out any wrinkles that form. Stack the rolled portions (paper still attached) on a baking sheet. Refrigerate the dough for 45 minutes, or until chilled and firm, or freeze for 25 minutes to speed chilling.

TiP
Note that for economy, you can use half butter and half stick margarine in the recipe. However, be sure to use only regular stick margarine; diet or light margarine contains too much water and insufficient fat and will not work.

Preheat the oven to 375 degrees F. Grease several baking sheets or coat with nonstick spray.

Working with one portion at a time and leaving the remaining dough chilled, gently peel away, then pat one sheet of wax paper back into place. Flip the dough over, then peel off and discard the second sheet. Using assorted 2½-to-3-inch cutters, cut out the cookies. (If at any point the dough softens too much to handle easily, transfer the paper and cookies to a baking sheet and refrigerate or freeze until firm again.) Using a spatula, carefully transfer the cookies to the baking sheets, spacing about 2 inches apart. Reroll any dough scraps. Continue cutting out the cookies until all the dough is used. If planning to hang up the cookies, form holes with a toothpick or the point of a small knife, then place short lengths of toothpicks or spaghetti in the holes to keep them from closing during baking. Sprinkle the cookies with jimmies, colored sugar, or sprinkles, if desired, patting down lightly. Or add dry stenciling, faux etching, or other decorations, if desired. (See pages 379-382 for decorating techniques.)

Bake the cookies, one sheet at a time, in the upper third of the oven for 8 to 11 minutes, or until lightly colored on top and slightly darker at the edges. Reverse the sheet from front to back halfway through baking to ensure even browning. Transfer the sheet to a wire rack and let stand until the cookies firm up slightly, 1 to 2 minutes. If toothpick or spaghetti pieces were inserted to form hanging holes, carefully remove them now. Using a spatula, transfer the cookies to wire racks. Let stand until completely cooled.

Decorate previously undecorated cookies with icing, glaze, or wet stenciling, if desired. (See pages 379-382.)

Store in an airtight container for up to 2 weeks or freeze for up to 2 months.

TIP
If you have a heavy-duty stand mixer with a large bowl, the recipe can be easily doubled.

Big Batch
Gingerbread
Dough

makes about 24 (5-inch-tall)
gingerbread people or
35 to 45 assorted cookies.

This recipe is used for making the Gingerbread House (page 361), a big batch of 5-inch-tall gingerbread people, or an extra-large batch of assorted gingerbread cutout cookies. The dough is also called for in Chocolate Gingerbread Bears (page 355).

Besides being tasty, this dough is easy to make, economical, and holds up and handles well during rolling and cutting. If you don't have a heavy-duty stand mixer with a large bowl, halve the following recipe and make it twice.

Follow the rolling, cutting, and baking instructions below for making gingerbread people or cutout cookies.

6½ cups all-purpose flour, plus more if needed
2 tablespoons ground cinnamon
1 tablespoon plus 2 teaspoons ground ginger
1 teaspoon ground cloves
1 teaspoon salt
½ teaspoon baking powder

1½ cups packed light brown sugar
1 cup (2 sticks) unsalted butter or regular stick margarine, slightly softened
2 tablespoons corn oil or other flavorless vegetable oil
1½ cups light molasses

Thoroughly stir together the flour, cinnamon, ginger, cloves, salt, and baking powder in a large bowl; set aside. In another large bowl, with an electric mixer on medium speed, beat together the brown sugar, butter or margarine, and oil until smooth and fluffy. Beat in the molasses and 2½ tablespoons water until well blended. Beat in half of the flour mixture until evenly incorporated. Stir in the remaining flour mixture until blended. Working in the bowl, knead the dough until very well blended and smooth and shiny. If the dough is stiff and dry, beat in up to 3 tablespoons more water; if too soft, stir in more flour until firmer and more manageable, but not dry.

Divide the dough into thirds. Place the portions in airtight plastic bags. Set aside in a cool place or refrigerate for at least 4 hours to reduce stickiness before rolling; if refrigerating, let the dough warm up slightly before using. (The dough may be refrigerated for up to 4 days; let stand at room temperature for 15 minutes before using.)

Working with one portion at a time, knead the dough briefly until softened just slightly. Place each portion between large sheets of wax paper. Roll out a scant ¼ inch thick; check the underside of the dough and

Tip

If you use margarine in the recipe, be sure to use regular stick margarine, not diet or light margarine, which has more water and less fat and can drastically alter the consistency of the dough.

smooth out any wrinkles that form. Stack the rolled portions (paper still attached) on a baking sheet. Refrigerate the dough for 30 minutes, or until firm but not hard, or freeze for 15 minutes to speed chilling.

Preheat the oven to 350 degrees F. Grease several baking sheets or coat with nonstick spray.

Working with one portion at a time and leaving the remaining dough chilled, gently peel away, then pat one sheet of wax paper back into place. Flip the dough over, then peel off the second sheet. Using a 5-inch gingerbread person cutter or assorted cutters, cut out the cookies. Using a spatula, immediately transfer them to the baking sheets, spacing about 2 inches apart. (If at any point the dough softens too much to handle easily, transfer the paper and cookies to a baking sheet and refrigerate or freeze until firm again.) Reroll any dough scraps. Continue cutting out the cookies until all the dough is used. If planning to hang the cookies, form holes with a toothpick or the point of a small knife, then place short lengths of toothpicks or spaghetti in the holes to keep them from closing during baking. Add colored sprinkles, dry stenciling, faux etching, or other decorating techniques, as desired. (See pages 379-382 for decorating techniques.)

Bake the cookies, one sheet at a time, in the middle of the oven for 6 to 12 minutes, or until just darker at the edges and barely firm when pressed in the centers. (For softer cookies, underbake slightly; for crisper cookies, overbake slightly.) Reverse the sheet from front to back halfway through baking to ensure even browning. Transfer the sheet to a wire rack and let stand until the cookies firm up slightly, 3 to 4 minutes. Using a spatula, transfer the cookies to wire racks. Let stand until completely cooled.

Decorate previously undecorated cookies with icing, piping, or wet stenciling, if desired. (See pages 379-382.)

piped Lemon Butter cookies
with Lemon Buttercream Frosting

Both the dough and the buttercream for these handsome cookies contain lemon zest and lemon juice, which give them a slight tang and balance the sweetness of the frosting. They make a perfect addition to a tea tray.

Note that this recipe requires a food processor. It also calls for a pastry bag and a ½-inch open star tip for piping the dough and topping the finished cookies with rosettes of buttercream. This inexpensive decorating equipment makes it easy to produce professional-looking cookies with just a little practice.

2¼ cups all-purpose white flour

¼ teaspoon baking soda

¼ teaspoon salt

1 cup (2 sticks) unsalted butter, slightly softened

¾ cup powdered sugar

⅓ cup sugar

4 large egg yolks

1 tablespoon finely grated lemon zest (colored part of the skin)

3 tablespoons fresh lemon juice

2 teaspoons vanilla extract

¼ teaspoon lemon extract

LEMON BUTTERCREAM FROSTING

2⅓ cups powdered sugar, plus more if needed

1½ teaspoons finely grated lemon zest (colored part of the skin)

7 tablespoons (1 stick minus 1 tablespoon) unsalted butter, slightly softened

1½ teaspoons fresh lemon juice, plus more if needed

1–2 drops yellow liquid food coloring (optional)

Preheat the oven to 350 degrees F. Grease several baking sheets or coat with nonstick spray.

In a medium bowl, thoroughly stir together the flour, baking soda, and salt; set aside. In a food processor, process the butter and sugars in on/off pulses, then continuously until well blended and smooth. Add the egg yolks, lemon zest, lemon juice, vanilla, and lemon extract and process until evenly incorporated. Add the flour mixture and process just until thoroughly incorporated; do not overprocess. The dough should be fairly soft to facilitate piping; if it seems too stiff, add up to 4 tablespoons water, pulsing to incorporate.

Spoon the dough into a pastry bag fitted with a ½-inch open star tip. Pipe 1½-inch-wide swirls onto the baking sheet, spacing about 2 inches apart.

Bake the cookies, one sheet at a time, in the upper third of the oven for 7 to 10 minutes, or until just tinged with brown at the edges. Reverse the sheet from front to back halfway through baking to ensure even browning. Transfer the sheet to a wire rack and let stand until the cookies firm up slightly, 1 to 2 minutes. Using a spatula, transfer the cookies to wire racks. Let stand until completely cooled.

FOR THE FROSTING

In a food processor, process the powdered sugar and lemon zest until the zest is evenly incorporated, about 2 minutes. Add the butter and process until very well blended and smooth. Add 1½ teaspoons lemon juice and food coloring, if using, and process until smooth and well blended. If necessary, add a bit more powdered sugar to stiffen the frosting or a bit more lemon juice to thin it so that it is of piping consistency.

Spoon the frosting into a pastry bag fitted with a ½-inch open star tip. Pipe 1-to-1½-inch frosting swirls onto the cookies. Let stand until the frosting completely sets, at least 1 hour.

Store in a single layer or layered with wax paper in an airtight container in a cool place for up to 2 days, refrigerate for up to 1 week, or freeze for up to 2 months.

TIP

If you're new to using a pastry bag, lay out a sheet of wax paper to practice on. After firmly inserting the piping tip into the bottom of the bag, fold the bag top back into a cuff several inches deep; this will keep the top clean and make spooning the dough into the bag easier. Stand the bag in a large, heavy tumbler. Fill the piping bag no more than half full, then unfold the cuff and very tightly twist the bag top closed. Pipe by holding the pastry tip just slightly above the surface and squeezing out the contents while rotating the bag just slightly. (Most right-handed cooks prefer to hold and squeeze the bag with their right hand and lightly prop up the tip of the bag with the fingers of their left hand.) Stop and quickly lift the tip up and away when the swirl or rosette is formed. You can scrape up the practice cookies and return the dough to the pastry bag as many times as necessary to get the knack of piping.

New Year's cookies

One of the most charming but little-known American cookie customs flourished throughout the nineteenth century in the Dutch settlements in New York and the Hudson River valley. On New Year's Day, families gave large cutout and imprinted cookies (known as "cakes") as gifts to their youngsters and the traditional horde of holiday callers who dropped by.

The cookies were made both at home and by commercial bakers, who, as New York culinary historian Peter G. Rose puts it, often showed off by offering extremely large, elaborately stamped cakes made from fancy molds and "cake boards" that local woodcarvers created to order for them. Some bakers offered their New Year's cakes in standard half-pound and one-pound sizes. Homemade versions were usually smaller— 7 inches or less—and imprinted with much simpler designs.

Bakers used the carved "boards" in the same way Pennsylvania German cooks used what they called springerle molds—by pressing them down on a rolled layer of dough. This embedded the design elements, such as animals, birds, human figures, and floral motifs, into the surface. The cookies were usually cut out by tracing around the outside of the mold with a knife or a pastry wheel called a jagger. Then the mold was carefully lifted off and the cookies baked.

The cookies were usually studded with caraway seeds, which, though uncommon in sweet baked goods nowadays, were a very popular flavoring in early America. Aniseed can easily replace the caraway and is more likely to appeal to modern tastes, though as Rose points out, this substitution is not authentic.

Eventually, the custom of giving out New Year's cakes spread. This recipe is slightly adapted from the "New Year's Cake" recipe in *Miss Leslie's New Cookery Book,* written by Philadelphia cookbook author Eliza Leslie and published in 1857. These are pleasant cookies—faintly sweet, crunchy-crisp, and, if made with aniseed, a little reminiscent of anise biscotti.

3 cups all-purpose white flour

1/2 teaspoon salt

1/4 teaspoon baking soda

1/4 teaspoon cream of tartar

Generous 1 cup sugar

2/3 cup (1 stick plus 2²/₃ tablespoons) unsalted butter, slightly softened

1 tablespoon caraway seed or aniseed *or* 1/2 tablespoon of each, coarsely ground or crushed with a mortar and pestle or spice grinder

3–4 tablespoons milk, plus more if needed

In a medium bowl, thoroughly stir together the flour, salt, baking soda, and cream of tartar; set aside. In a large bowl, with an electric mixer on medium speed, beat together the sugar, butter, and caraway seed and/or aniseed until well blended and fluffy. Reduce the speed to low and gradually beat in the milk until evenly incorporated. Beat in half of the flour mixture until evenly incorporated. Stir in the remaining flour mixture. If the dough is too dry to hold together, gradually stir in a bit more milk. Let the dough stand in a cool place for at least 20 to 30 minutes or up to 2 hours.

Preheat the oven to 325 degrees F. Grease several baking sheets or coat with nonstick spray. Prepare the mold(s) by very lightly brushing the surface with vegetable oil; be sure to reach all the design crevices. Using a paper towel, blot off all the excess oil.

Divide the dough in half. Place each portion between large sheets of wax paper. Roll out the portions ¼ to ⅓ inch thick; check the underside of the dough and smooth out any wrinkles that form. Gently peel away and discard the top sheet of wax paper. Place a mold on the dough. Press down firmly to imprint the design. Using a sharp knife, pastry wheel, or cookie cutter the same shape but slightly larger than the mold being used, cut around the mold. Carefully peel the dough (mold still attached) from the paper and turn so the dough is facing up. Gently press the dough down all over to further embed the design in it. (This is especially important if the design in the mold or stamp is deeply set.) Carefully peel the dough from the mold and transfer to the baking sheet. Continue to stamp more cookies, spacing about 1½ inches apart. (If at any point the dough is too soft to handle easily, refrigerate or freeze until firm again.) Lightly re-oil the mold(s) only if the dough begins to stick. Reroll any dough scraps. Continue forming the cookies until all the dough is used.

Bake the cookies, one sheet at a time, in the middle of the oven until slightly darker at the edges; the time will depend on the cookie size, with 3-inch or similar cookies needing 10 to 20 minutes and larger cookies needing 20 to 30 minutes. (Fully baked cookies will be crunchy and slightly hard; for softer cookies, underbake slightly.) Reverse the sheet from front to back halfway through baking to ensure even browning. Transfer the sheet to a wire rack and let stand until the cookies firm up slightly, 3 to 4 minutes. Using a spatula, transfer the cookies to wire racks. Let stand until completely cooled.

Store in an airtight container for up to 3 weeks or freeze for up to 2 months.

TIP

If a springerle mold is unavailable, you can make small New Year's cakes using modern cookie stamps. Another possibility is to follow the lead of some ingenious cooks of the past and use the design of a cut-glass bowl or crystal tumbler pressed into the dough surface. (I've had particularly good results using the starburst pattern etched in the bottom of a small cut-glass bowl.) It's also possible to produce nice-looking cookies by using several small molds together, as in the photograph on page 340.

A Master Printer

The tradition of New Year's cookies has disappeared into history, but some of the carved molds and cake boards used to decorate them have survived. Linda Campbell Franklin's encyclopedic *300 Years of Kitchen Collectibles* includes photographs and descriptions of a number of these "cake prints," as they were often called, including several quite extraordinary ones. The most beautiful and elaborate were carved (and signed) by John Conger, a master "printcutter" who Franklin has confirmed lived and worked on New York's Lower East Side from the 1830s through the late 1860s. Conger's carving was exquisitely detailed and fine, and his works featured large, wonderfully pleasing designs. Today, they sell for several thousand dollars apiece; one has been valued at $8,000 to $10,000.

painted cookie jigsaw puzzles

makes 4 (5-by-7-inch) rectangular puzzles.

This is an easy children's cookie craft project in which rectangles of dough are painted and decorated, then cut into puzzle pieces and baked. The rectangles can be painted with simple seasonal scenes or messages to fit any holiday theme; for example, a grinning jack-o'-lantern for Halloween, a heart and "love you" message for Valentine's Day, balloons for a birthday, or an ornamented tree for Christmas. (The most attractive paintings often result from simple shapes such as stars, hearts, flowers, pumpkins, and borders featuring lines and dots.) Completed puzzles make great homemade family gifts.

Another possibility for a small party or group is to have children make puzzles printed with their own names or decorated as desired. Part of the fun comes just from decorating their personal masterpieces, and part comes from resisting temptation long enough to fit the pieces together and enjoy the look of their creations. (Uneaten pieces of each child's puzzle should be packed up so they can be taken home.)

The paint recipe yields enough paint to add abundant decorative accents to four puzzles. Double the recipe to make enough paint to thickly cover large areas or to provide a larger selection of colors. The paint can be prepared a day or so in advance; refrigerate, tightly covered, until needed.

For convenience, you can also prepare the rectangles of dough in advance, then wrap and freeze them until needed.

1 recipe All-Purpose Sugar Cookie Dough (page 332)

1 recipe Edible Tempera Paints (page 378)

Divide the dough in half. Place each portion between large sheets of wax paper. Roll out each portion into a ¼-inch-thick rectangle; check the underside of the dough and smooth out any wrinkles that form. Stack the rolled portions (paper still attached) on a baking sheet. Refrigerate the dough for 30 minutes, or until chilled and firm but not hard, or freeze for 15 minutes to speed chilling.

Meanwhile, prepare the paints as directed in the recipe.

Working with one portion at a time and leaving the remaining dough chilled, gently peel away, then pat one sheet of wax paper back into place. Flip the dough over, then peel off and discard the second sheet. Cut the dough into two puzzle-size rectangles; if perfect rectangles are

desired, measure and mark them with a ruler first. Peel away the excess dough from the rectangles, reserving it in a plastic bag for making cutout cookies, if desired. Cut the wax paper under the rectangles so they can be moved separately. With the paper still attached, lift up a rectangle and place it, dough side down, on a sheet of parchment paper. Peel off and discard the wax paper. Repeat the process with the second rectangle. Repeat the entire process with the remaining dough.

Preheat the oven to 350 degrees F.

Paint and decorate each puzzle rectangle as desired. Carefully slide the parchment pieces holding the puzzles onto baking sheets. Using a pizza wheel or small knife, cut each rectangle into 2-to-2½-inch jigsaw-style puzzle pieces; it's best to keep the shapes simple and use straight lines. (If at any point the dough softens too much to handle easily, transfer the parchment and puzzles to a baking sheet and refrigerate or freeze until firm again.)

Bake the puzzles, one sheet at a time, in the center of the oven for 12 to 18 minutes, or until tinged with brown at the edges and just firm when pressed in the centers. Reverse the sheet from front to back halfway through baking to ensure even browning. Transfer the sheet to a wire rack and let stand until the puzzles firm up slightly, 1 to 2 minutes. Carefully retrace the puzzle cuts so the pieces will come apart when cooled. Slide the parchment with the puzzles onto wire racks. Let stand until completely cooled.

Store each puzzle flat and intact in its own airtight container for up to 2 weeks or freeze for up to 2 months. Or disassemble the puzzle and store all the pieces in an airtight container.

TIPS

- Be sure to place each rectangle of dough on a sheet of parchment paper; this serves as a convenient work surface to catch drips and spills as the puzzles are painted, and then is easily lifted so the puzzle can be transferred to a baking sheet.

- It's best not to make puzzles larger than about 5 by 8 inches or smaller than 5 by 5 inches. If possible, use a pizza wheel to cut the pieces, and don't cut them into very small or highly irregular pieces; the pieces will be less likely to break.

cookie mold cookies

This recipe is designed to use with the typical decorative American ceramic cookie molds sold in kitchenware shops, and it will also work with the carved wooden molds traditionally used for European *speculaas* cookies. Most brands of these molds are not made to be used in the oven, so cookies are formed by pushing the dough into a mold, then rapping the mold to release the cookie onto a baking sheet.

For best results with these molds, follow the manufacturer's directions on using and caring for them. (If none are provided, follow the directions provided here; they have been proven to work with several different brands.) Also, use only dough specifically designed for cookie molds; regular doughs may not readily release from molds, and the imprinted decorative elements may blur during baking because the dough puffs too much.

This basic dough can be varied to produce vanilla cookies, brown-sugar cookies, or—using the variation at the end—darker spiced cookies. They are all crunchy when first baked but gradually become slightly chewy.

$3^3/_4$ cups all-purpose white flour, plus more for the molds

$^1/_3$ cup cornstarch

$^3/_4$ teaspoon salt

$1^2/_3$ cups sugar or packed light brown sugar

$^1/_2$ cup (1 stick) unsalted butter, slightly softened

1 tablespoon corn oil or other flavorless vegetable oil

$^1/_3$ cup light or dark corn syrup

1 large egg yolk

$2^1/_2$ teaspoons vanilla extract

$^1/_2$ teaspoon almond or lemon extract

$^1/_4$ cup milk

In a large bowl, thoroughly stir together the flour, cornstarch, and salt; set aside. In a large bowl, with an electric mixer on medium speed, beat together the sugar or brown sugar, butter, and oil until well blended and lightened. Beat in the corn syrup, egg yolk, vanilla, and almond or lemon extract until evenly incorporated. Beat in half of the flour mixture until evenly incorporated. Gradually beat in the milk. Stir in the remaining flour mixture until evenly incorporated. The dough should be fairly stiff but not dry; if it seems dry and crumbly, knead in up to 2 tablespoons water until evenly moistened and smooth. Place the dough in a plastic bag and refrigerate for at least 2 hours or up to 2 days.

Line several baking sheets with parchment paper. Prepare the molds by very lightly brushing the surface with vegetable oil; be sure to reach all the design crevices. Using a paper towel, blot off all the excess oil. Lightly sift flour over the molds; tip them back and forth until all the crevices are coated. Tap out all the excess flour. The molds must be dusted after each cookie but need to be re-oiled only occasionally.

If the dough seems very stiff or dry after being stored, knead lightly, adding a few drops of water as necessary; however, be very careful not to overwork the dough. Working with half of the dough at a time and keeping the remaining dough chilled, pull off portions large enough to fill the mold being used. Press the dough into the mold. When the interior of the mold is completely filled with dough, press down all over to remove air pockets. Push any dough protruding over the edges back inside the mold. Using a large, sharp, preferably serrated knife, cut away any excess dough so the back of the cookie will lie flat on the baking sheet. Then press the dough back into the mold once again.

To remove a cookie from a ceramic mold, hold the mold perpendicular to a wooden cutting board and rap the edge sharply against the board several times; rotate the mold and rap the edge sharply several more times. The dough should loosen; if necessary, start the loosening process by lifting up one edge with the point of a small knife. (If using a wooden mold, hold it perpendicular to a hard surface and rap its edge sharply against the surface several times. Rotate the mold and repeat until the cookie loosens.) When the cookie is loosened, tap it out onto the baking sheet. If you are planning to hang the cookies, form a hole near the top of each with a toothpick or the point of a sharp knife, then place short lengths of toothpicks or spaghetti in the holes to keep them from closing during baking. Lightly cover the cookies with wax paper and refrigerate for 40 to 50 minutes to help set the designs.

Preheat the oven to 300 degrees F.

Tips

- Use only a dough designed for cookie molds.
- Don't make any changes in the recipe or ingredients.
- Prepare the mold for use exactly as directed; if the dough doesn't release readily, the mold may have been oiled too heavily. Remove the flour with a brush and paper towels; then re-flour and try again.
- Bake the cookies only at the temperature indicated.
- Never put the molds in the oven unless the manufacturer's directions suggest this use.
- If bits of dough or flour stick in a mold's design, wash it thoroughly, removing any buildup with a scrub brush, if necessary. Then dry it well and start over as directed in the recipe.
- Before storing molds, always wash and dry them thoroughly.

Bake the cookies, one sheet at a time, in the middle of the oven until just tinged with brown at the edges; the time will depend on the cookie size, with 3-to-4-inch cookies needing 15 to 20 minutes and 5-to-6-inch cookies needing a few minutes longer. Transfer the sheet to a wire rack and let stand until the cookies firm up slightly, at least 5 minutes. Carefully remove any toothpick or spaghetti pieces from the hanging holes. Using a spatula, transfer the cookies to wire racks. Let stand until completely cooled.

Store in an airtight container for up to 10 days or freeze for up to 1½ months.

VARIATION   Spiced Cookie Mold Cookies

1 tablespoon ground cinnamon
1 teaspoon ground ginger
½ teaspoon ground nutmeg
¼ teaspoon ground cloves

Add to the flour mixture. Proceed as directed.

cookie pizzas with the works

The idea of forming—and eating!—large, pizza-shaped cookies is irresistible to children. They love covering the dough with the "pizza sauce" (cherry preserves), piling on their favorite toppings, such as chopped nuts and chocolate morsels, and then finishing by sprinkling on the "cheese" (finely chopped or shredded white chocolate), "tomatoes" (dried cranberries), and even chopped "peppers" (pistachios). Like real pizzas, these sweet pizzas are cut with a pizza wheel and served in wedges. They look surprisingly like the real thing!

This recipe is designed to make two 12-inch cookie pizzas. Bake them at once, or freeze half the dough and bake the second pizza at a later date. If making both pizzas, divide the toppings listed between the two; if making one pizza, use only half the total amount of the toppings called for and save the second half for the second baking.

1 recipe All-Purpose Sugar Cookie Dough (page 332)

1 1/3 cups sour cherry preserves

2/3 cup (about 2 3/4 ounces) coarsely chopped dried sweetened cranberries

2/3 cup (about 2 3/4 ounces) chopped pecans or walnuts (optional)

2/3 cup (about 1 3/4 ounces) shredded or flaked sweetened coconut (optional)

1 cup (6 ounces) semisweet chocolate morsels

2/3 cup (about 3 ounces) finely chopped or grated top-quality white chocolate or coarsely chopped top-quality white chocolate morsels

1/4 cup (1 ounce) dried sweetened cranberries

1/4 cup (about 1 ounce) chopped pistachios (optional)

Preheat the oven to 350 degrees F. For each pizza, grease a 12-inch pizza pan or coat with nonstick spray.

Divide the dough in half. For each pizza, shape one portion into a disk in the center of a pizza pan. With lightly greased hands, pat and press the dough out until it covers the entire pan bottom in an evenly thick layer. Push any uneven dough edges back inside the pan, shaping so the crust edge is smooth and about 2/3 inch thick all the way around; the thicker edge keeps the dough from overbaking while the interior gets done.

In a small bowl, stir together the cherry preserves and chopped cranberries. For each pizza, spread half of the "sauce" evenly over the dough to within 1/4 inch of the edge.

Bake one pizza at a time in the middle of the oven for 16 to 19 minutes, or until the dough is tinged with brown all over and just slightly darker at the edges. Remove from the oven. For each pizza, evenly sprinkle with half the pecans or walnuts (if using), coconut (if using), and semisweet chocolate morsels. Top each with half the white chocolate, followed by half the cranberries and pistachios, if using. Return to the oven and bake for 4 to 5 minutes, or until the white chocolate begins to melt and brown on top. Transfer the sheet to a wire rack and let stand until cooled to warm. Using a pizza cutter or a large, sharp knife, cut the pizza into quarters, eighths, and then sixteenths; wipe the knife clean between cuts. Let stand until completely cooled.

Store in the pizza pan, covered with foil, or in an airtight container for up to 1 week or freeze for up to 1 month.

yuLe DOLLies

Holiday cookie decorating isn't new in America, though most eighteenth- and nine-teenth-century families settled for simple presentations like brushing on an egg wash or sprinkling on sugar, seeds, or nuts. Commercial bakers led the way in the current trend toward fancy decorating. One particularly colorful example of this phenomenon was the "Yule Dollie"—an elaborately ornamented doll-shaped sugar cookie sold by bakeries in several eastern cities during the late nineteenth and early twentieth centuries.

Featuring the highly stylized forms of full-skirted, wasp-waisted maidens, the cookies were prepared and promoted to capture the Christmas trade. Frequently, bakers decorated their cookies with several different-colored icings, then added piping or painted on garment elements such as collars, cuffs, buttons, trims, and overskirts, in enough detail to create a paper-doll look. Sometimes, they also glued proportionally sized color pictures of smiling young faces (called scrap pictures) atop the dollies' torsos, often with a startlingly realistic effect. (In his well-researched *The Christmas Cook,* William Woys Weaver notes that some religious leaders objected to the dollies' secular nature and encouraged the making of "Yule Angels" instead.)

While I haven't come upon any modern cookie cutters that duplicate the shape of the nineteenth-century dollies, today's readily available gingerbread-girl cutters can stand in quite well. In fact, when prettily decorated, modern Yule Dollies are every bit as charming as their Victorian-era counterparts. I've found that a 5-inch girl cutter (sometimes sold with a matching boy cutter) is particularly convenient, providing ample surface area for piping or painting on aprons, ruffles, cummerbunds, and various other fashion accents, as well as facial details. I usually skip the scrap-picture faces so the cookies will be entirely edible, but if you wish to use them, search through doll or toy catalogs, magazines, wrapping papers, and greeting cards for suitable pictures to cut out. Glue them in place with a dab of icing *after the cookies are baked,* and be sure they are scraped off before the cookies are eaten.

You can make Yule Dollies using All-Purpose Sugar Cookie Dough (page 332), or, to stay in period, use this slightly blander dough, Mrs. D. A. Lincoln's "Plain Cookies" recipe, which I've adapted a bit from her 1884 *Boston Cooking-School Cook Book.* Also, you can either paint on details using homemade tempera paints prior to baking (a simple method pleasing to young children) or decorate elaborately by piping and brushing on details using royal icing after the cookies have baked and cooled. (Painting requires small pastry brushes or clean artists' brushes; icing requires piping equipment and small brushes.) Both the painted and iced details can be enhanced with edible glitter

and silver or gold dragées, colored sugar, and assorted nonpareils. Piping, floodwork, and flocking decorating techniques are all appropriate for decorating the dollies after baking (see pages 381–382).

3 cups all-purpose white flour

1 teaspoon baking powder

²/₃ cup (1 stick plus 2²/₃ tablespoons) unsalted butter, slightly softened

1 cup sugar

¹/₂ teaspoon salt

¹/₄ cup milk

1 large egg

2 teaspoons vanilla extract

1 recipe Royal Icing (page 370) or 2 recipes Edible Tempera Paints (page 378)

Assorted decorations, such as edible glitter, colored sugar, and nonpareils, for topping (optional)

Preheat the oven to 350 degrees F. If you are planning to decorate the cookies with royal icing after baking, grease several baking sheets or coat with nonstick spray; if you are planning to paint the cookies before baking, line several baking sheets with parchment paper.

In a large bowl, thoroughly stir together the flour and baking powder; set aside. In a large bowl, with an electric mixer on medium speed, beat the butter until very light and fluffy. Beat in the sugar, salt, milk, egg, and vanilla until very well blended and smooth. Gradually beat in half of the flour mixture. Beat or stir in the remaining flour mixture to form a smooth dough. If the dough seems dry, beat in just enough water to make it manageable and smooth.

Divide the dough in half. Place each portion between large sheets of wax paper. Roll out the portions a generous ¹/₈ inch thick; check the under-side of the dough and smooth out any wrinkles that form. Stack the rolled portions (paper still attached) on a baking sheet. Refrigerate the dough for 30 minutes, or until chilled and firm, or freeze for 15 minutes to speed chilling.

Working with one portion at a time and leaving the remaining dough chilled, gently peel away, then pat one sheet of wax paper back into place. Flip the dough over, then peel off and discard the second sheet. Using a 5-inch gingerbread-girl cutter or other girl cutter, cut out the cookies. (If at any point the dough softens too much to handle easily, transfer the paper and cookies to a baking sheet and refrigerate or freeze until firm again.) Using a spatula, carefully transfer the cookies to the baking sheets, spacing about 2 inches apart. Reroll any dough scraps. Continue cutting out the cookies until all the dough is used. If decorating with tempera paints, apply these to the cookies before baking. Add all desired painted clothing and facial details; use a light coat of paint for a "wash" effect and a slightly heavier application for a brighter effect. Also add any edible glitter, colored sugar, or nonpareils, if using, before the paints dry.

Bake the cookies, one sheet at a time, in the upper third of the oven for 7 to 10 minutes, or until barely colored on top and just brown at the edges. Reverse the sheet from front to back halfway through baking to ensure even browning. Transfer the sheet to a wire rack and let stand until the cookies firm up slightly, 1 to 2 minutes. Using a spatula, transfer the cookies to wire racks. Let stand until completely cooled.

Cooled undecorated cookies can be decorated with piped- and/or brushed-on royal icing and sprinkles or nonpareils, as shown in the photograph on page 352, or as desired.

Store in an airtight container for up to 2 weeks or freeze for up to 1 month.

chocolate
gingerbread bears

Brightly decorated chocolate gingerbread-bear cookies make great homemade gifts or holiday ornaments, or an enjoyable edible craft activity for middle schoolers or older children. To cut out the cookies, you'll need one or more large teddy-bear cutters or a family of bear cutters—preferably in the 3-to-6-inch range.

While the piped powdered-sugar icing is optional, it adds a great deal to the cookies. The icing will require several paper cones or a pastry bag fitted with a fine writing tip.

1 recipe Big Batch Gingerbread Dough (page 334)

1 recipe Chocolate Luster Glaze (page 374)

Multicolored cookie "decors" about the size of Red Hots

1 recipe Easy Powdered-Sugar Icing (page 373; optional)

Liquid food coloring, for tinting the icing (optional)

Cut out and bake the cookies as directed in the Big Batch Gingerbread Dough recipe; remember to make hanging holes before baking if the cookies will be used as tree ornaments. When the cookies are completely cooled, using a table knife, completely cover each bear with a smooth, even layer of chocolate glaze; it should cover nicely but not be too thick. Let the cookies stand on wire racks until the glaze sets, about 45 minutes.

Prepare the bears' eyes by picking out enough white or other light-colored decors to create a pair of eyeballs for each cookie. Add a dot of chocolate glaze where each eye is to be positioned. Place the eyes on the faces. Dip a toothpick or the point of a paring knife into the chocolate glaze. Put a dot of glaze in the center of each decor for the pupils. If desired, also add buttons, using colored decors.

Let the cookies stand for at least 1½ hours, or until the glaze completely sets. If adding decorative piping, prepare the powdered-sugar icing and tint it in the desired accent colors. Using a paper cone or a pastry bag fitted with a fine writing tip, pipe a nose, a mouth, and decorative details such as boots, mittens, belts, and neck scarves on the bears. (If desired, pipe so that areas are readied for accenting floodwork; see page 382 for details on this technique.)

Let the cookies stand until all the icing accents are completely set, at least 1½ hours and preferably longer.

Store in a single layer or layered with wax paper in an airtight container or individually packaged for up to 3 weeks or freeze for up to 2 months. If frozen, thaw the cookies on wire racks before serving.

stained glass
and Light catcher
cookies

By taking advantage of a very simple cookie-craft technique, it's easy to create strikingly pretty cookies with translucent areas that look like colored glass. The "glass" is created by melting coarsely crushed hard candy. Depending on the shape of the cookies and the size and shape of the cutaway areas that are filled, it's possible to make simple light catcher or multipaned stained-glass-window cookies. The cookies are nice for homemade gifts or decorations and can be made by even young children if they are supervised.

Note that this recipe works with either All-Purpose Sugar Cookie Dough or Big Batch Gingerbread Dough, although the latter produces a more dramatic effect.

1 recipe Big Batch Gingerbread Dough (page 334)
      or All-Purpose Sugar Cookie Dough (page 332)
1 12-to-16-ounce bag assorted lollipops (thin, disk-
      shaped ones are the easiest to crush) or other
      clear, hard, brightly colored candy

Make the dough, roll out, and chill.

Prepare the unwrapped lollipops or candy by placing each color in a separate plastic bag (or a double layer of regular plastic bags). Tightly close the bags. Using a kitchen mallet or the back of a large, metal spoon, pound until crushed moderately fine. Remove and discard the lollipop sticks, if using lollipops.

Preheat the oven to 350 degrees F. Line several baking sheets with aluminum foil. Coat the foil with nonstick spray.

Using 2½-to-3-inch cutters, cut out the cookies. Using a spatula, carefully transfer the cookies to the baking sheets, spacing 2½ inches apart. To make simple light catchers, cut away a "window" from each cookie using a slightly smaller cutter of the same or a complementary shape; choose one that leaves at least a ¼-inch margin of dough all around. For a stained-glass-window look, cut away several different smaller areas using a thimble, the larger end of a pastry tip, or mini cutters; the cutaways should form an attractive pattern, just as cathedral windowpanes do. Add hanging holes, if desired.

TIP
Don't omit the aluminum foil; it's essential for this recipe.

Bake the cookies, one sheet at a time, in the center of the oven for 7 to 11 minutes, or until just barely tinged with brown at the edges; be careful not to overbake. Transfer the sheet to a wire rack and let stand until the cookies are cool enough to handle.

Using small spoons or your fingertips, add enough crushed candy to fill the cutaways; each cutaway can be filled with a different color, or you can experiment, using complementary colors in different areas of the same cutaway for a rainbow or multicolored-pane effect. Using a small pastry brush or a clean artists' brush, brush off any stray bits of candy from the dough. Return the cookies to the oven and bake just until the candy melts and looks glasslike, 2 to 5 minutes, depending on the brand of candy used and the amount you've used.

Transfer the sheets to wire racks. Let stand without moving the cookies until the "glass" cools down and hardens, 7 to 10 minutes. Don't touch the cookies during cooling, as the "glass" is extremely hot. When the cookies are cooled to barely warm, carefully peel them from the foil. Let stand on wire racks until completely cooled.

Store the cookies in an airtight container or individually wrapped for up to 2 weeks or freeze for up to 2 months. To display light catcher cookies, center them on large squares of good-quality plastic wrap, pull the excess wrap together into a bunch, and tie it tightly shut with a colorful hanging ribbon. (The unwrapped cookies can't be displayed for long, as the "glass" areas become sticky.)

gingerbread House

A gingerbread house makes a festive centerpiece or decoration, as well as a fun family project. Although the gingerbread house is most closely associated with Christmas, it can be decorated as a Halloween witch's cottage, an Easter bunny hutch, a housewarming gift, or to suit any other theme desired.

This gingerbread house is about 11 inches tall (including the chimney top) and has a simple front portico. However, for an even easier project, you may omit the portico, if desired. It's best to do the house in stages—the pattern pieces can be cut out and the dough made and baked well before the house is put together and decorated. Once the house is assembled, it must stand so the icing can set before decorating begins. At each step, allow enough time for the project to be enjoyable, rather than feeling pressured to finish in a hurry.

1   recipe Big Batch Gingerbread Dough (page 334)
1   recipe Royal Icing (page 370), or more if needed
     Decorations as desired

German Inspiration

The now widely popular American custom of creating holiday gingerbread houses is borrowed from Germany. The idea was promoted there in the early nineteenth century through the Grimm brothers' publishing of the Hansel and Gretel folktale. In this story, two children find a witch's house made of gingerbread while wandering in the forest. By the end of the century, the gingerbread house idea was even more widely circulated when composer Engelbert Humperdinck based his *Hansel and Gretel* opera on the theme. Making gingerbread houses at home didn't catch on in America, however, until the latter half of the twentieth century.

making the pattern

Cut the pattern pieces from two manila folders. These are not only sturdy and smooth but also provide a convenient fold for forming the house front and back and the portico front. As long as the pattern pieces are carefully labeled, they can be made in advance and set aside until needed.

Using the illustration (opposite page) as a guide, cut out and label the following *pattern pieces*:

A   HOUSE ROOF: 6½-inch-square piece

B   HOUSE SIDES: 5-by-6-inch piece

C   HOUSE FRONT AND BACK: Mark *but don't cut* a 3-by-9½-inch piece *placed on a fold* as shown in the illustration.

Mark a point 6 inches up from the bottom on the side opposite the fold as shown. Connect the lines between the side and the point of the roof peak using a ruler, then cut away the excess paper following the line drawn. Cut away the front and backs of the upstairs window openings from the pattern, using the illustration as a guide. Unfold the paper for the finished pattern piece.

D   CHIMNEY FRONT: 1-by-3½-inch piece

E   CHIMNEY BACK: 1-by-2¼-inch piece

F   CHIMNEY SIDES: 1-by-3½-inch piece placed along the roof line as shown in the illustration and cut to form the angled chimney base.

G   PORTICO FRONT: Mark *but don't cut* a 1½-by-5½-inch piece *placed on a fold* as shown. With the folder still folded, mark a point 4 inches up from the bottom on the side opposite the fold, as shown in the illustration. Connect the lines between the side and the point of the roof peak using a ruler. Then cut away the excess paper following the line drawn. Finally, cut away the arched portico entryway opening, using the illustration as a guide. Unfold the paper for the finished pattern piece.

H   PORTICO ROOF: 1½-by-3¼-inch piece

I   PORTICO SIDES: 1-by-4-inch piece

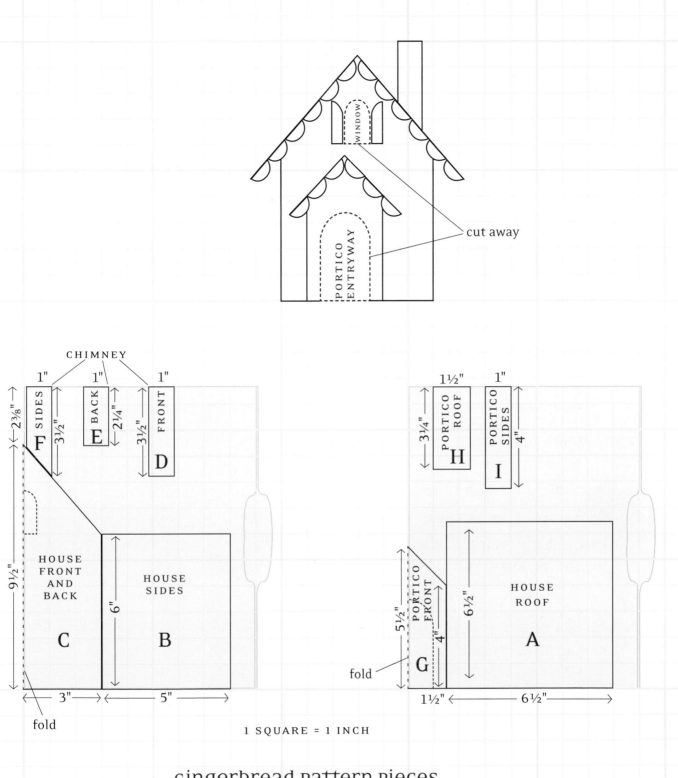

cut away

CHIMNEY

1"   1"   1"

2⅜"

SIDES
F
3½"

BACK
E
2¼"

FRONT
3½"
D

WINDOW

PORTICO
ENTRYWAY

1½"   1"

3¼"
PORTICO
ROOF
H

PORTICO
SIDES
4"
I

9½"

HOUSE
FRONT
AND
BACK

C

HOUSE
SIDES

6"

B

3"   5"

fold

5½"

PORTICO
FRONT

G

4"

fold

1½"

HOUSE
ROOF

6½"

A

6½"

1 SQUARE = 1 INCH

Gingerbread Pattern Pieces

363

making and baking the house pieces

Have ready a batch of gingerbread dough. The dough needs to be made ahead and allowed to stand at room temperature for at least 1 hour and then refrigerated for another hour. It can also be made up to 4 days ahead and refrigerated; let warm up slightly before using.

Be sure to have plenty of parchment paper on hand, since it will be used to roll out all the dough.

When cutting out the dough pieces, work neatly and keep all the dough pieces as straight and true to their patterns as possible. Just as in real home construction, uneven, crooked boards will result in a wobbly structure.

Using the previously prepared patterns, you will cut out the following dough pieces:

A   HOUSE ROOF *(cut 2)*

B   HOUSE SIDES *(cut 2)*

C   HOUSE FRONT/HOUSE BACK *(cut 2)* Also cut away the upstairs window openings following the pattern; cut the cutaway pieces in half lengthwise and save to use as shutters.

D   CHIMNEY FRONT *(cut 1)*

E   CHIMNEY BACK *(cut 1)*

F   CHIMNEY SIDES *(cut 1,* then turn over the pattern and *cut 1 more* for the second side)

G   PORTICO PEAKED FRONT *(cut 1)* Also cut away the arched entryway opening following the pattern; save the cutaway piece to use as the front door.

H   PORTICO ROOF *(cut 2)*

I   PORTICO SIDES *(cut 2)*

Preheat the oven to 350 degrees F.

Divide the dough in half. Briefly knead one dough portion to make it more pliable. Shape it into a rough rectangle. Place the dough on a 24-inch-long sheet of parchment paper. Top with a large sheet of wax paper. Roll out the dough a scant ¼ inch thick, keeping the layer as uniformly thick as possible. (To keep the parchment from sliding around, tape it firmly to the countertop, or drape an end over the counter edge and lean your body against it.) Peel off and discard the wax paper. Slide the rolled portion (parchment still attached) onto a large cutting board.

Very lightly lay the pattern pieces on the dough, working with the largest pieces first; don't press down. (If the pattern pieces stick, the dough is too warm. Transfer it to the refrigerator for 20 minutes, then proceed.) Using a sharp knife, carefully cut around the pattern pieces; wipe the knife clean between cuts. As you cut out each piece, immediately lift the pattern from the dough and set aside.

Lift the excess dough scraps from the parchment, reserving them in a plastic bag to keep them from drying out. Using a sharp knife or scissors, cut through the parchment to separate the various dough pieces. Place the large house pieces together on one baking sheet and the smaller pieces together on a separate sheet, spacing about 1 inch apart.

Repeat the kneading, rolling, and cutting with the second dough portion until all the pattern pieces listed are prepared. If a scalloped front eaves trim (as shown in the photograph on page 360) is desired, combine the scraps and reroll to ⅛ inch thick. Using a 1-inch round cutter or the larger end of a medium-sized metal pastry piping tip, cut out about 12 rounds. Cut the rounds in half and transfer to a baking sheet coated with nonstick spray.

If desired, cut away a small window opening in the front door as shown in the photograph.

Also before baking, you may add a curved roof-tile design to the roof pieces by pressing the curve of a flatware spoon into the dough surface to produce indentations at regular intervals (see the photograph). If desired, add clapboard texture to the house sides, front, and back by dragging the back of a lightly oiled dinner fork horizontally across the surface of the dough.

Bake the dough pieces, one sheet at a time, in the upper third of the oven until tinged with brown at the edges and barely firm when pressed in the centers; if in doubt, it is better to overbake slightly rather than underbake. Large pieces will take 10 to 18 minutes, medium ones 8 to 15 minutes, and very small pieces 5 to 9 minutes. The house sides must be straight. If they spread during baking, transfer them to a cutting board and trim the 6-inch sides until straight, using a large, serrated knife. Transfer the sheet to a wire rack and let stand until the pieces are firmed up, about 10 minutes. Using a spatula, carefully transfer the pieces to wire racks. Let stand until completely cooled.

The house can be constructed immediately, or the pieces can be stored flat in an airtight container for up to 3 weeks or frozen for up to 3 months. Let come to room temperature before using.

constructing the house

Royal icing is the glue for constructing your gingerbread house. The recipe yields enough for gluing, decorative piping, and "snow." (For elaborate piping and a lot of snow or to cover the cardboard base with frosting, a second batch of royal icing may be needed.) If desired, the icing can be prepared up to 3 days ahead and stored in an airtight container in the refrigerator.

If you plan to add any decorative piping to the front, back, or sides of the house or to the roof, chimney, or portico front, lay these pieces right side up on a work surface and add the decorations *now* before assembling the house. (It is much easier to pipe onto a flat surface than onto the upright constructed house.) Let the decorations dry before proceeding with the house assembly.

Once the icing is prepared, you have the option of using some of it to make Gingerbread-Colored Icing "Glue" (page 372), which blends into the seams and minimizes the glue lines so the construction looks tidier. (If you plan to cover all the seams with decorative piping as shown in the photograph, this is unnecessary.)

As you work, keep plastic wrap over the icing bowl to prevent it from drying out during the house assembly and decoration.

It's best to apply the icing "glue" with a pastry bag with a large writing tip in a generous ⅛-inch-thick line. Otherwise, using a spoon, apply it as neatly as possible.

TO CONSTRUCT THE HOUSE FRAME

Working on a large wax-paper-lined tray, begin by putting a line of icing along the edges of the house front on both sides. Add a line of icing along the vertical edge of one of the house side pieces. Using tins of canned goods to prop up all the pieces, stand the pieces up and attach the side to the house front; be sure to bring the icing-coated edges in contact with one another. Add a line of icing to the edge of the second side piece and attach it to the house front; the pieces should stand up as a unit. Add lines of glue to the remaining side edges and to the house back edges. Place the back between the remaining sides to form the frame. If necessary, slightly adjust the positioning of the pieces (and the cans you used as props) so the house stands square. Working from the inside of the frame, reinforce the seams with additional thick lines of icing. Let the frame stand for at least 30 minutes and preferably several hours so the icing can set.

When the house feels set, *carefully* center it on a very sturdy 10-by-12-inch cardboard base. Pipe or spoon heavy lines of frosting on the interior and exterior everywhere the frame and base make contact. If desired, finish the cardboard by brushing on a thin layer of frosting to cover the base with "snow." Prepare the house frame for receiving the roof by piping icing along all the edges that will come in contact with the roof. Check for the proper placement of the icing lines on the underside of the roof by briefly holding the roof in place on the house frame; this will leave an icing mark where the roof will come in contact with the frame. Lay a roof piece underside up on the paper. Following the icing lines left on the surface, add a thick line of icing where it will make contact under the peak edges and a thick horizontal icing line where the roof will rest on the house sides. Holding the roof piece in the middle, immediately center it, icing side down, and press lightly so it makes contact with both the front and back edges of the frame. Repeat the process with the second roof piece, adding a line of icing where the two roof pieces will peak and butt together. Put the second piece in place, adjusting it so it sits straight and butts against the first roof piece to form a peak. Put a line of icing in the roof-peak seam; wipe off any excess with a fingertip. Check the position of the roof and, if necessary, gently adjust so it sits straight and overhangs about the same amount all around. Prop with tin cans.

TO PREPARE THE CHIMNEY
When the roof is set, glue the four chimney pieces together using the same technique followed for the house. Immediately put the angled end of the chimney in place on the house roof to check for pitch. If the chimney does not stand straight up, carefully whittle around the chimney bottom with a sharp knife until the bottom angles align properly with the roof. Then put a generous line of icing all around the chimney bottom and set the chimney in place on the roof, using the illustration as a guide for placement, or place as desired.

cookie decorating and crafts

TO PREPARE THE PORTICO

Turn the peaked portico front piece underside up on the paper. Add a line of icing up and down on both side edges where the sides will join it. Put a line of icing along the vertical edges of the portico side pieces. Join the sides to the portico front; the portico frame should stand up. Using the illustration as a guide, press the portico frame into place on the house front or place as desired. Add additional frosting along the interior seams.

Prepare the portico frame for receiving the roof pieces by piping along all the edges that will come in contact with the roof. Check for proper placement of the icing lines on the underside of the roof by briefly holding the portico roof pieces in place on the portico frame; this will leave an icing mark where the pieces will touch the frame. Add thick lines of icing along the areas where the roof will rest on the portico sides and also where it will butt against the house front. Set the roof pieces into place, adjusting their position as necessary. Put some icing in the seam created by the portico peak.

Decorate the portico door as desired. Position it, open or closed as desired, at the portico opening. Decorate the shutters as desired. Put them in place on either side of the front and back windows, using the illustration as a guide.

Let the house stand, uncovered, for at least 8 hours and preferably 24 hours before decorating.

Decorating the House

To finish the house as shown in the photograph, pipe scroll-like decorations onto the small half-rounds to be used for the scalloped eaves. Let dry. Then add a fine line of frosting to the tops of the scallops and arrange them along the house and the portico as shown. Pipe all the seams decoratively; use a medium shell tip for the center roof top seam and the portico center top seam and a small shell tip for the other seams. Finish by adding patches of snow sprinkled with coarse crystal sugar and small silver dragées.

Other decorating touches and color schemes depend on the season or your whim. For Christmas, you may want royal icing snow and icicles, candy canes, and pinwheels, but a nontraditional color scheme, such as the one in the photograph, can look just as festive. For an Easter bunny hutch, snow would be replaced by pastel-tinted icing to cover the seams and to decorate the roof lines. Candies could include miniature eggs, jelly beans, Jordan almonds, and tiny chocolate bunnies. A Halloween cottage might feature harvest colors, a shredded-wheat "thatched" roof, and seasonal goodies like tiny pumpkin-shaped candies, licorice sticks, shelled nuts, and candy corn. A little house to serve as a housewarming gift could feature any fanciful detailing and cheerful color scheme desired.

Whatever the theme, when used generously, icing can go far in camouflaging smudges and crooked seams. It looks best when piped using a pastry bag with a writing tip or a small open star tip, but children will be perfectly happy spooning it into place and covering any messy spots with candies and nonpareils.

Royal icing

Royal icing has long been used by both professional and home bakers to decorate fancy cakes and cookies. If allowed to air-dry, royal icing becomes hard and smooth and lasts nearly indefinitely, so it is the perfect choice for decorating gingerbread houses and ornamental cookies that will be hung on a tree or displayed in some other fashion. It is also versatile and easy to work with, since it can be tinted with any color desired and quickly thinned for spreading to a smooth, matte finish, or thickened for piping decorative details. This icing is extremely sweet and becomes crusty and cement-like with time, so use it when looks and durability count more than palatability.

The following recipe makes enough icing to elaborately decorate a large batch of cutout cookies.

⅓ cup egg whites (about 3 large whites), free
   of yolk and at room temperature

2 teaspoons fresh lemon juice (divided)
   Pinch of salt

1 16-ounce box powdered sugar, plus more
   if needed

   Liquid or paste food coloring (optional)

In a large bowl, with an electric mixer on low speed (use a whisk-shaped beater, if available), beat together the egg whites, ½ teaspoon of the lemon juice, and the salt until frothy and opaque. Increase the speed to medium and beat for 30 seconds. Gradually beat in the powdered sugar, about ½ cup at a time, until evenly incorporated and smooth. Increase the speed to high, and beat in the remaining 1½ teaspoons lemon juice until the mixture stands in stiff peaks, 3 to 5 minutes. If the icing is too stiff to pipe or spread easily, beat in water, 1 teaspoon at a time; if too runny, beat in a little more powdered sugar. If the icing stiffens upon standing, thin it with a few more drops water. Keep plastic wrap or a damp kitchen towel over the bowl to prevent the icing from drying out as you work.

FOR TINTING THE ICING, IF DESIRED

Divide the icing among as many small bowls as needed, then stir in drops or dabs of food coloring until the desired color is obtained. For very intense shades, paste colors work best. Food coloring can be mixed together for virtually any custom color desired.

Store in an airtight container in the refrigerator for up to 4 days. Let come almost to room temperature and stir well before using.

TIP
For icing that is safe for those with compromised immune systems, be sure buy pasteurized eggs specifically designed to be safe when used raw.

Gingerbread-colored Royal Icing "Glue"

makes about
½ cup icing.

A gingerbread house is assembled with white royal icing, but if you prefer a "glue" that matches the color of the house and doesn't show along the seams, make this gingerbread-colored royal icing, using some of a batch already prepared. Then brush the dark icing over the places where the white icing shows.

½ cup Royal Icing (page 370)
1 tablespoon unsweetened Dutch-process cocoa powder, plus more if needed

1¼ teaspoons instant coffee powder or granules, dissolved in 1 teaspoon warm water
1–2 tablespoons powdered sugar (optional)

In a large bowl, with an electric mixer on low speed, beat together the royal icing, cocoa powder, and coffee mixture until well blended and smooth. Check the color against the color of the baked gingerbread; if a slightly darker color is desired, add a little more cocoa powder. If the icing is too stiff, add a little water; if it is too runny, stiffen it to the desired consistency with the powdered sugar.

Easy powdered-sugar icing

Makes enough icing
to completely cover,
then add piping to,
about 50 (3-inch) cookies.

This icing is simple to make and nice for adding a sweet touch or decorative accent to sugar cookies, gingerbreads, or chocolate cookies. The icing is easy to work with and forms a smooth, firm, slightly lustrous finish when it dries, though it is not as durable as royal icing.

The recipe may be halved or doubled, if desired.

1 16-ounce box powdered sugar, sifted, if lumpy, plus more if needed

2 teaspoons light corn syrup

$1/8$ teaspoon vanilla, almond, or lemon extract (optional)

Liquid food coloring (optional)

In a large bowl, with an electric mixer on low speed, beat together the powdered sugar, 3 tablespoons warm water, the corn syrup, and the vanilla, almond, or lemon extract, if using. Increase the speed to medium and beat until well blended and smooth. (Alternatively, in a medium bowl, stir together the powdered sugar, water, corn syrup, and extract until well blended and smooth.)

Adjust the icing consistency as needed by adding a bit more water to thin it or more powdered sugar to stiffen it. A fairly fluid consistency is needed to spread the icing easily and form a perfectly smooth, glossy surface; a stiff consistency is needed to pipe and form lines that hold their shape. If desired, divide the icing among separate small bowls and tint each a different color by stirring in 1 or 2 drops food coloring. The icing gradually dries out as it stands; thoroughly stir in 1 or 2 drops water to thin it as necessary, and cover with plastic wrap when not in use.

Using a table knife, apply the icing to the cookies. Or, to apply piped icing outlines or trims to cookies, spoon into paper cones or pastry bags fitted with fine writing tips.

To prevent piping from running or blurring on cookies decorated with powdered-sugar icing, be sure that it is completely set, at least 6 hours and preferably longer, before storing. (See specific piping tips on pages 381-382.)

Store in an airtight container in the refrigerator for up to 4 days. Let warm up slightly and stir before using.

chocolate Luster Glaze

It took a good deal of experimentation to come up with a chocolate glaze that spreads smoothly and easily, dries to a firm, lustrous finish, and is chocolatey enough to suit my taste. I like to use it to dress up vanilla-flavored cutout cookies and also for decorating Chocolate Gingerbread Bears (page 355).

1 ounce unsweetened chocolate, broken up or coarsely chopped	2½ tablespoons unsweetened Dutch-process cocoa powder
3¼ cups powdered sugar	2 teaspoons light or dark corn syrup
	1 teaspoon vanilla extract

In a small, microwave-safe bowl, microwave the chocolate on 50-percent power for 1 minute. Stir well. If necessary, continue microwaving on 50-percent power, stirring at 30-second intervals. Stop microwaving before the chocolate completely melts and let the residual heat finish the job. (Alternatively, melt the chocolate in a double boiler over simmering water, stirring frequently. Immediately remove from the heat.)

Sift the powdered sugar and cocoa powder together into a medium bowl. Combine the corn syrup and ⅓ cup water in a small saucepan. Heat to just boiling; stir well. Stir the syrup mixture into the powdered-sugar mixture until well blended and completely smooth. Stir in the melted chocolate and vanilla until completely smooth. Thin the glaze to a spreadable consistency with hot water, a few drops at a time, until completely blended and smooth. Set the bowl of glaze in a larger bowl half full of hot tap water to help keep the glaze warm while you work. (Reheat it to warm in a saucepan or in a microwave oven if it cools completely.) If the glaze thickens upon standing, stir in a few more drops of hot water until thoroughly blended; be sure to blend in very thoroughly, so the glaze maintains its luster.

Using a table knife, spreader, or small palette knife, cover the top of each cookie with a smooth, even layer of glaze. Let the cookies stand on wire racks until the glaze completely sets, at least 1½ hours and preferably several hours. Store in a single layer or layered with wax paper in an airtight container.

colored
decorating sugars

These days, many colored sanding sugars and crystal sugars are stocked in supermarkets with the baking supplies and in cake-decorating shops. But if you want a custom color or don't happen to have any sugar sprinkles on hand, it's easy and economical to make colored sugar at home. Homemade colored sugars tend to have more subtle and softer shades and a finer grain than commercial sugars, making them particularly nice for creating flocked or stenciled looks (see pages 382 and 379 for details). Homemade colors are also an attractive topping for plain or iced sugar cookies.

| Red, yellow, blue, and green liquid food coloring or diluted paste food coloring | 2–3 tablespoons sugar for each color, or more if needed |

FOR RED, YELLOW, BLUE, AND GREEN COLORED SUGAR

In a small plastic bag, combine 2 tablespoons sugar and 1 or 2 drops food coloring. Squeeze the bag until the coloring and sugar are well blended. If the shade is too intense, tone it down by mixing in more sugar; for a brighter shade, add more drops of food coloring and mix until evenly incorporated. When mixing, keep in mind that, like paints, the colors will lighten and fade slightly as the sugar dries out.

FOR CUSTOM-COLORED SUGAR

Mix two of the basic colors together thoroughly, then add them to the sugar. Experiment with your own combinations or use the mixing chart; the results may vary considerably depending on the brand of food coloring used. Start by combining the food coloring amounts specified with 2 tablespoons sugar. If desired, make the shades lighter by adding more sugar.

Liquid Food Coloring + 2 Tablespoons Sugar = Color

2 drops blue	+ 1 drop red	= powder blue		5 drops blue	+ 1 drop green	= turquoise
1 drop blue	+ 1 small drop red	= pale lavender		2 drops blue	+ 2 drops green	= sea foam
1 drop blue	+ 1 large drop red	= lilac		3 drops yellow	+ 1 drop blue	= lime green
1 small drop blue	+ 2 drops red	= dusty rose		6 drops yellow	+ 1 small drop red	= apricot
6 drops red	+ 1 drop blue	= pale raspberry		2 drops yellow	+ 1 small drop red	= peach
8 drops blue	+ 4 drops green	= evergreen		4 drops yellow	+ 1 small drop red	= orange sherbet
4 drop blue	+ 3 drops green	= mint		4 drops yellow	+ 3 drops red	= pumpkin

Some colored sugars can be used immediately, but shades containing larger quantities of coloring may clump together and are best dried out before use. (Any colors you plan to store should be dried so they won't clump during storage.)

To dry out the sugars, spread each color on a square of aluminum foil. Fold up the foil around the sugar to form a tray. Place the foil trays on a large baking sheet.

Preheat the oven to 200 degrees F for 5 minutes. Turn off the oven.

Dry the sugars in the oven for 20 to 30 minutes, stirring once or twice. Break up any lumps that formed during drying. If the sugars still seem moist, turn on the oven to 200 degrees F for 2 minutes, then turn off the oven and let the sugars dry for 10 to 15 minutes longer.

Sprinkle the colored sugars over cookies before baking, or use them for stenciled or flocked effects.

Store in small airtight bags indefinitely.

Edible
Tempera paints

Makes enough paint to
accent about 35 medium
cutout cookies.

Edible paints for decorating cookies can be made quickly with raw eggs, powdered sugar, and food coloring. These paints are always added to unbaked cookies; the eggs are safely cooked as the cookies bake.

The recipe yields enough paint to add decorative accents to about three dozen medium-sized cutout cookies. To make a larger quantity of paint for creating all-over designs, heavily painted pictures, or a larger selection of colors, double the amounts of eggs and powdered sugar called for.

For very bright, intense colors, use quite a few drops of liquid food coloring. Check the color by dabbing it on a bit of dough and adding more drops of coloring as needed. (Paste food colorings are more concentrated, but some are difficult to use because they don't readily dissolve in the egg mixture.) The colors will look smoother and brighter after they bake.

Note that some paint colors are prepared from an egg-and-yolk mixture and others use only an egg white. The egg-white mixture doesn't go on as smoothly but is better for blues, reds, and purples, which would be discolored by the yellow of the yolks.

2 large eggs (divided)

2 tablespoons powdered sugar (divided)
Liquid food coloring or paste food coloring, slightly diluted

Using a fork and working in a small bowl, beat together 1 egg, 1 egg yolk, and 1½ tablespoons of the powdered sugar until the sugar dissolves. Strain the mixture through a fine sieve into 3 or 4 custard cups. In a separate small bowl, beat together the remaining egg white and the remaining ½ tablespoon powdered sugar. Strain this mixture into 1 or 2 custard cups. Stir in the food coloring to obtain the shades as follows: For blue, red, or purple (a blue-red combination), add the food coloring to the egg-white mixture. For all other shades, add the food coloring to the egg-yolk mixture.

Using pastry brushes for larger areas and small artists' brushes for fine details, apply the paints to *unbaked* cookies. Apply a light coat of paint for a "wash" effect; apply a little more heavily for a smoother, more opaque, enameled effect.

Always bake painted cookies in a 325- to 350-degree-F oven—temperatures higher than 350 degrees F can discolor the paints. When cool, the paints become dry and smooth, so no special storage is required.

decorating techniques for rolled cutout cookies

Rolled cutout cookies, such as gingerbread and sugar cookies, can be quickly decorated with a few colored sprinkles or a zigzag of drizzled icing. But here are a few more techniques to add to your repertoire:

DRY STENCILING

Dry stenciling is done on unbaked cookies with a dry-stenciling material, such as fine crystal sugar, homemade colored sugar, or cocoa powder. The technique involves masking some portion of a smooth, flat, unbaked cookie by covering it with a section from a paper doily, handmade decorative cutouts (for example, snowflakes, hearts, or bells), or even plain strips of paper. (See the Easter egg cookies on page 376.) Then dust the exposed dough with the stenciling material, remove any stray bits with a small brush, and bake. Note that although cakes are usually dry-stenciled *after* baking, cookies are dry-stenciled before baking to ensure that the sugar or cocoa powder is securely affixed and that the cookies can be handled. As the cookies bake, the dusting material becomes embedded and stays in place.

WET STENCILING

Wet stenciling is done on baked and cooled cookies with paste food coloring. The technique involves masking some portion of a cookie by covering it with a plastic, light cardboard, heavy paper, or other waterproof stencil. Highlight the exposed cookie by dabbing on paste food coloring using a sponge or paper towel. For best results, place a small amount of the desired coloring on a sheet of wax paper. Dab the paste with a damp sponge until the paste is dissolved; then dab the exposed area to be stenciled. (Practice on a broken cookie if you want.) Stenciled cookies should be allowed to dry for at least 1 hour before being stored.

FAUX ETCHING

This technique gives rolled-out cookies an impressive etched or engraved look (see the photograph on page 380) but involves no real etching. All you need are several sizes of cookie cutters and an eye for putting together complementary shapes. For example, attractive patterns can be achieved by pressing down and imprinting the outline of almost any smaller shape—from geometric forms and alphabet letters to animals, birds, and flowers—onto a larger round, rectangular, or oval cookie. For more elaborate looks, use sets of nested cutters, such as

hearts, stars, or petals, to "etch" the cookies with a succession of progressively smaller hearts, stars, or petals. Or mix and match by etching with a succession of different but complementary shapes, such as a tiny heart inside a petal, inside a slightly larger heart on a scalloped cookie.

Keep in mind that etched designs look best on doughs that contain only small to moderate amounts of baking soda or baking powder and thus don't puff up excessively and blur the etched lines. Prepare unbaked cutout cookies for etching by placing them on baking sheets. Center the cookie cutter used for the etching on the larger cookie. Press down firmly enough to imprint the shape of the cutter into the dough but not so firmly that you cut completely through it. If imprinting with a series of cutters to create an elaborate design, simply repeat with successively smaller cutters until the surface area is filled.

COLOR WASH

The details on stamped, molded, or even etched shortbread and sugar cookies (and other light-colored cookies) can be easily enhanced by adding a muted food-coloring wash to whatever features are desired after the cookies are baked. For example, color leaves and flowers with green and yellow, hearts with pink, and birds with blue.

Prepare a wash by adding a drop or two of the desired color to a few teaspoons of water. Make as many different colored washes as desired. Using a small, clean artists' brush, test each color on a broken cookie to see how it looks before applying it. Tone down the color by diluting the wash with a bit more water, or intensify it by adding more food coloring. Lightly apply the wash over very fine details using small artists' brushes and over larger detail areas using a small pastry brush; it's best to add only a light wash and to keep the colors in the pastel range. Let the colored cookies stand for at least 1 to 2 hours, or until completely dry, before storing them.

PIPING

Most cookie piping requires either paper cones (which can be purchased or homemade) or small, thin, disposable plastic piping bags, or a sturdy pastry bag with a fine writing tip. If working with a number of different piping colors, it's best to use piping cones or disposable bags, as these are inexpensive and can be discarded when the piping is completed.

Unlike most other decorating techniques, attractive piping usually requires a little practice. This can be done on a sheet of wax paper. Always

cookie decorating and crafts

start by checking the consistency of the royal icing or powdered-sugar icing by piping a few practice lines before working on the cookies. The icing must be stiff enough to hold the piped line without running, but thin enough to pipe smoothly. Adjust the icing consistency with water or powdered sugar, if necessary, before continuing.

Don't fill a paper cone or piping bag more than half full and be sure to tightly fold down the cone top or very tightly twist the pastry bag top closed before beginning.

Pipe lines by holding the pastry tip just slightly above the surface and squeezing out the contents; most right-handed cooks prefer to hold and squeeze the cone or pastry bag with their right hand and lightly prop up the tip of the cone or bag with the fingers of their left hand. For a continuous line, it's important to keep the icing flowing evenly by gently and continuously squeezing. For dots, touch the tip to the surface, briefly start and stop pressure, then quickly lift the tip up and away from the surface.

FLOODWORK

Any cookies decorated with piped royal icing or powdered-sugar icing can also be decorated with floodwork. The technique involves piping a thin, continuous line of icing all the way around (or across) an area so that a barrier is formed around a space. (For example, an area that will make up a boot, apron, beard, or any other feature might be defined.) Once the icing line *completely sets*, the area inside the barrier is flooded with just enough additional icing (either piped or brushed on) so that the surface is smoothly covered but the icing doesn't run out over the piped edge. For best results, make the icing fairly stiff for piping, then thin it slightly for flooding. To ensure that the icing doesn't run over the lines, it's best to put the icing at the center of the area to be flooded, then gently work the icing out to the barrier using a fine paintbrush or knife.

FLOCKING

To suggest the textural effect of an elegant flocked fabric or trim, generously sprinkle a fairly fine-grained colored sugar over areas already decorated with royal icing or powdered-sugar icing *before* the icing has a chance to set; immediately shake off the excess sugar. For the best effect, the sugar used for flocking should be a color similar to the icing underneath. Depending on the look desired, you can flock a large, flat area or only the raised, piped details of a design.

Bibliography

Index

BiBLioqraphy

Anderson, Jean. *The American Century Cookbook.* New York: Clarkson Potter, 1997.

Anderson, Jean, and Elaine Hanna. *The Doubleday Cookbook.* Garden City, N.Y.: Doubleday & Company, 1975.

Barnum, Mrs. A. L., and Mrs. S. I. Delavan, eds. *1902 Cook Book.* Estherville, Iowa, 1902.

Benson Woman's Club. *Benson Woman's Club Cook Book.* Omaha, Nebr.: Douglas Printing Company, 1915.

Bolsterli, Margaret Jones, ed. *Vinegar Pie and Chicken Bread: A Woman's Diary of Life in the Rural South, 1890-1891.* Fayetteville: University of Arkansas Press, 1984.

Bryan, Lettice. *The Kentucky Housewife.* Cincinnati: Shepard & Stearns, 1839. (Facsimile edition, Paducah, Ky.: Image Graphics, no date.)

Clarke, Mrs. Anne. *Mrs. Clarke's Cookery Book.* Toronto, 1883.

Dabney, Joseph E. *Smokehouse Ham, Spoon Bread and Scuppernong Wine.* Nashville: Cumberland House, 1998.

DeGraf, Belle. *Mrs. DeGraf's Cook Book.* San Francisco: H. S. Crocker Company, 1922.

Dolby, Richard. *The Cook's Dictionary, and Housekeeper's Directory.* 2nd edition. London: Henry Colburn and Richard Bentley, 1832. (First edition, 1830.)

Earle, Alice Morse. *Home Life in Colonial Days.* New York: Grosset & Dunlap, 1898. (Reprint edition, Stockbridge, Mass.: Berkshire Traveller Press, 1974.)

Farmer, Fannie Merritt. *The Boston Cooking-School Cook Book.* Revised edition. Boston: Little, Brown & Company, 1921.

——. *The Boston Cooking-School Cook Book.* Revised edition. Boston: Little, Brown & Company, 1924.

——. *The Boston Cooking-School Cook Book* (also known as *The Fannie Farmer Cookbook*), revised by Wilma Lord Perkins. Boston: Little, Brown & Company, 1965.

——. *The 1896 Boston Cooking-School Cook Book.* (Facsimile edition, New York: Random House Value Publishing, 1997.)

Fisher, David Hackett. *Albion's Seed.* New York: Oxford University Press, 1989.

Fowler, Damon Lee. *Classical Southern Cooking.* New York: Crown Publishers, 1995.

Fussell, Betty. *I Hear America Cooking.* New York: Viking, 1986.

Gardiner, Anne Gibbons. *Mrs. Gardiner's Family Receipts from 1763.* Boston. (Reprint edition, Gail Weesner, ed., Boston: Rowan Tree Press, based on 1938 edition printed by the Gardiners.)

Gill, J. Thompson, ed. *The Complete Bread, Cake and Cracker Baker* in Two Parts. Chicago: Confectioner and Baker Publishing Company, 1881.

Hale, Sarah Josepha. *The Good Housekeeper.* Boston: Otis, Broaders, 1841. (First published, 1839; facsimile edition, *Early American Cookery,* Mineola, N.Y.: Dover Publications, 1996.)

Hawke, David Freeman. *Everyday Life in Early America.* New York: Harper & Row, 1988.

Hess, John L., and Karen Hess. *The Taste of America.* New York: Grossman/Viking, 1977.

Hess, Karen, ed. *Martha Washington's Booke of Cookery.* New York: Columbia University Press, 1981.

Heywood, Margaret Weimer, ed. *The International Cook Book.* Boston: Merchandisers, 1929.

Hill, Annabella P. *Mrs. Hill's Southern Practical Cookery and Receipt Book.* 1820. (Reprint edition, Columbia: University of South Carolina Press, 1955.)

Hooker, Richard J. *Food and Drink in America.* Indianapolis: The Bobbs-Merrill Company, 1981.

Howard, Mrs. B. C. *Fifty Years in a Maryland Kitchen.* 4th edition. Philadelphia: J. B. Lippincott Company, 1888. (First edition, 1873.)

Howard, Maria Willett. *Lowney's Cook Book.* Boston: Walter M. Lowney Company, 1908. (First published, 1907.)

Jones, Evan. *American Food: The Gastronomic Story.* New York: E. P. Dutton & Company, 1975.

Krondl, Michael. *Around the American Table.* Holbrook, Mass.: Adams Publishing, 1995.

Ladies Aid Society and Friends of First Methodist Episcopal Church, Deadwood, South Dakota. *Tried and True Cook Book.* 1891.

Ladies of the First Presbyterian Church, Dayton, Ohio. *Presbyterian Cook Book.* Dayton: John H. Thomas & Company, 1875. (First published, Ohio, 1873.)

Langdon, William Chauncy. *Everyday Things in American Life: 1607–1776.* New York: Charles Scribner's Sons, 1937.

Larkin, Jack. *The Reshaping of Everyday Life: 1790-1840.* New York: Harper & Row, 1988.

Lee, Mrs. N. K. M. (published under the name A Boston Housekeeper). *The Cook's Own Book.* Boston: Munroe & Francis, 1832. (Reprint edition, Edmund B. Stewart, ed., Merrifield, Va.: Rare Book Publishers, 1997.)

Leslie, Eliza. *Miss Leslie's New Cookery Book.* Philadelphia: T. B. Peterson & Brothers, 1857.

Leslie, Eliza (published under the name A Lady of Philadelphia). *Seventy-Five Receipts for Pastry, Cakes, and Sweetmeats.* Boston: Munroe & Francis, 1828. (Facsimile edition, Bedford, Mass.: Applewood Books, 1993.)

Lincoln, Mrs. D. A. *Mrs. Lincoln's Boston Cook Book.* Boston: Roberts Brothers, 1887. (First published, 1884; facsimile edition, *The Boston Cooking-School Cook Book,* Mineola, N.Y.: Dover Publications, 1996.)

Lundy, Ronni. *Shuck Beans, Stack Cakes and Honest Fried Chicken.* New York: Atlantic Monthly Press, 1991.

Lynn, Dr. Kristie, and Robert W. Pelton. *The Early American Cookbook.* Liberty.

Marsh, Dorothy B. *The New Good Housekeeping Cookbook.* New York: Harcourt, Brace & World, 1963.

Meyer, Arthur L. *Baking Across America.* Austin: University of Texas Press, 1998.

Modern Priscilla Cook Book: One Thousand Recipes Tested and Proved at the Priscilla Proving Plant. Boston: Priscilla Publishing Company, 1924.

Neal, Bill. *Biscuits, Spoonbread, and Sweet Potato Pie.* New York: Alfred A. Knopf, 1996. (First published, 1990.)

Oliver, Sandra L. *Saltwater Foodways.* Mystic, Conn.: Mystic Seaport Museum, 1995.

Parloa, Maria. *The Appledore Cook Book.* Boston: Graves, Locke & Company, 1878.

Porter, Mrs. M. E. *New Southern Cookery Book.* Philadelphia: John E. Potter & Company, 1871.

The Portland Woman's Exchange Cook Book. Portland, Oreg., 1913. (Facsimile edition, Portland, Oreg.: Glass-Dahlstrom Printers, 1973.)

Randolph, Mary. *The Virginia Housewife.* Philadelphia: E. H. Butler & Company, 1860. (Facsimile edition, New York: Avenel Books.)

Rhett, Blanche S., comp., and Lettie Gay, ed. *Two Hundred Years of Charleston Cooking.* Columbia: University of South Carolina Press, 1977. (First published, 1976.)

Rombauer, Irma S. *The Joy of Cooking.* St. Louis: A. C. Clayton Printing Company, 1931.

Root, Waverly, and Richard de Rachemon. *Eating in America: A History.* New York: Morrow, 1976.

Rorer, Sarah Tyson. *Mrs. Rorer's New Cook Book.* Philadelphia: Arnold & Company, 1898. (Reprint edition, New York: The Ladies' Home Journal Cook Book Club, 1970.)

——. *Mrs. Rorer's Philadelphia Cook Book.* Philadelphia: Arnold & Company, 1886.

Sax, Richard. *Classic Home Desserts.* Shelburne, Vt.: Chapters Publishing, 1994.

Second Auxiliary Missionary Society. *The Warren Cook Book.* 4th edition. Warren, Pa., 1912.

Seranne, Ann, ed. *America Cooks: The General Federation of Women's Clubs Cook Book.* New York: G. P. Putnam's Sons, 1967.

Simmons, Amelia. *American Cookery.* Hartford, Conn.: Hudson & Goodwin, 1796. (Facsimile edition, *The First American Cookbook,* New York: Dover Publications, 1958.)

Sokolov, Raymond. *Fading Feast.* Jaffrey, N.H.: David R. Godine, 1998. (First published, 1982.)

——. *Why We Eat What We Eat.* New York: Simon & Schuster, 1991. (Touchstone Edition, 1993.)

Tannahill, Reay. *Food in History.* New York: Stein & Day, 1973.

Trager, James. *The Food Chronology.* New York: Henry Holt & Company, 1995. (Owl Book Edition, 1997.)

Tyree, Marion Cabell, ed. *Housekeeping in Old Virginia.* Louisville, Ky.: John P. Morton & Company, 1879. (Facsimile edition, Louisville, Ky.: Favorite Recipes Press, 1965.)

Wakefield, Ruth. *Ruth Wakefield's Toll House Tried and True Recipes.* New York: M. Barrows & Company, 1936.

Wigginton, Eliot, ed. *The Foxfire Book.* Garden City, N.Y.: Anchor Books, 1972.

Wilcox, Estelle Woods, ed. *Buckeye Cookery and Practical Housekeeping.* Minneapolis: Buckeye Publishing Company, 1880. (Reprint edition, St. Paul: Minnesota Historical Society Press, 1988.)

Williams, Jacqueline B. *The Way We Ate.* Pullman: Washington State University Press, 1996.

Zimmer, Anne Carter. *The Robert E. Lee Family Cooking and Housekeeping Book.* Chapel Hill: University of North Carolina Press, 1997.

index